Environmental Law

Nancy K. Kubasek, J.D.

Department of Legal Studies
Bowling Green State University

Gary S. Silverman, D. Env.

Environmental Health Program
Bowling Green State University
Chapters 6 and 8

PRENTICE HALL
Upper Saddle River, New Jersey 07458

Editor-in-Chief: James Boyd
Sr. Acquisition Editor: Donald J. Hull
Marketing Director: Sandra Steiner
Managing Editor: Valerie Q. Lentz
Production Editor: David G. Cotugno
Cover Director: Jayne Conte
Manufacturing Buyer: Kenneth J. Clinton
Assistant Editor: John Larkin
Editorial Assistant: Jim Campbell

Cover Art: Raymond G. Barnes/Tony Stone Images
Cover Research: Karen Branson

©1997 by Prentice-Hall, Inc.
A Simon and Schuster Company
Upper Saddle River, NJ 07458

ISBN 0-13-541202-1

Library of Congress Cataloging-in-Publication Data

Kubasek, Nancy.
    Environmental law / Nancy K. Kubasek, Gary S. Silverman. — 2nd
ed.
        p.   cm.
    Includes index.
    ISBN 0-13-541202-1 (pbk.)
    1. Environmental law—United States.   2. Environmental protection—
United States.   I. Silverman, Gary S.
KF3775.Z9K83   1996
344.73'046—dc20
[347.30446]   96-27855
                                                                          CIP

Prentice-Hall International (UK) Limited, *London*
Prentice-Hall of Australia Pty. Limited, *Sydney*
Prentice-Hall Canada Inc., *Toronto*
Prentice-Hall Hispanoamericana, S. A., *Mexico*
Prentice-Hall of India Private Limited, *New Delhi*
Prentice-Hall of Japan, Inc., *Tokyo*
Simon & Schuster Asia Pte. Ltd., *Singapore*
Editora Prentice-Hall do Brazil, Ltda., *Rio de Janeiro*

Printed in the United States of America

10 9 8 7 6 5 4 3 2 1

Contents

Preface to the Second Edition

When I began teaching environmental law to undergraduates in 1982, there were very few such courses offered outside of law schools. There were even fewer resources available for teaching courses to anyone other than law students. Therefore, my first semester, I taught the course using one of the two available law school texts.

The next year I began putting together my own materials, materials that over the next few years evolved into an environmental law "text" designed especially for nonlaw students that I made available to my students through a copy service. To improve the quality of the materials before attempting to publish them, I asked my colleague, Dr. Gary Silverman, the director of our university's Environmental Health Program, to write the chapters on water quality control and management of waste and hazardous releases, areas in which he has special expertise.

The result was the first edition of *Environmental Law,* a book designed to introduce those without any legal or special scientific training to the system through which our nation attempts to preserve the environment. Although this book was written for college students, at either the undergraduate or master's level, it would be useful to anyone interested in learning about our system of environmental law. It also would be a helpful reference for anyone in business who is attempting to negotiate the morass of environmental regulations that affect businesses today.

Reflecting the fact that background knowledge is often important for understanding specific areas, this book provides two key types of background necessary for understanding environmental law. First, the initial chapters explain how our legal system functions in general. Second, the initial portions of the latter chapters provide the basic scientific knowledge necessary for understanding environmental law. Thus, the reader may gain a fundamental understanding of not only what the laws are but why they are needed.

Several people helped to make the first edition of this book, and consequently this second edition, a reality, and I would like to thank them for their contributions. Thorough and insightful reviews were provided by the following professors:

James Carp, Syracuse University

William Clements, Norwich University

Frank Cross, University of Texas

David Hoch, University of Southwestern Louisiana

Mary Kieffer, Ohio University

Richard Kunkle, The College of St. Thomas

Patricia Tulin, University of Hartford

Their reviews led to vast improvements of the final version of the first edition of this book. In fact, it is only because of a suggestion of one of these reviewers that a very important chapter of this book on energy policy and natural resource protection was written.

When changes in environmental law necessitated this revision of *Environmental Law,* helpful reviews were provided by Paula C. Murray, of the University of Texas, and Eric Oates, of the Wharton School. Numerous changes were made in response to their comments.

Additionally, the students and professors who used the first edition of this book and offered helpful criticisms cannot be omitted. While they are too numerous to list by name, their contributions were invaluable.

Several people at Prentice Hall deserve recognition for their efforts in bringing out this second edition. Donald Hull was once again the editor of this book, and, assisted by John Larkin, shepherded its transition into a second edition. Dave Cotugno was the production editor, and Jayne Conte was given the almost impossible task of providing a cover for the second edition that was as attractive and appropriate as the one designed by Maureen Eide for the first edition.

The widespread adoptions of the first edition of this book for a broad range of both undergraduate and graduate courses leads me to believe that the first edition went a long way toward satisfying the need for a basic introduction to environmental law. I realize, however, that there is always room for improvement, and so I tried to revise this text in a manner consistent with suggestions from users of the first edition. While the basic structure remains the same as that of the first edition, one important change I have incorporated reflects our increased use of technology for finding environmental information. At the end of every chapter, a list of useful World Wide Web sites can be found. So much environmental information is available on the Internet today that I would be remiss if I did not provide the reader with some of the more helpful sites. Obviously, some of the sites may change over time, but I tried to incorporate those sites that I felt would be of longer duration. If you know of any additional sites that would be useful to readers, I would appreciate your passing them on to me so that I can include them in future editions.

In finishing the second edition of this book, I realize that in spite of the conscientious review of all stages of the book's production by many people, it is almost inevitable that mistakes have crept in, for which I accept responsibility. I would therefore appreciate readers' corrections and comments as to how future editions may better achieve the goals this book is designed to attain. Please send your comments, criticisms, corrections, or suggestions to me at the Department of Legal Studies, Bowling Green State University, Bowling Green, Ohio 43403. Or e-mail me at (nkubase@cba.bgsu.edu).

Nancy K. Kubasek

PART I

An Introduction to the Law

A useful prelude to a functional understanding of environmental law is an appreciation of the U.S. legal system itself. The materials contained in chapters 1 through 3 will help you gain that appreciation. Having an understanding of how the legal system functions will also enable you to more easily have an impact on the future development of environmental law.

CHAPTER I

The American Legal System

SOURCES OF LAW

We react to environmental threats within a particular context. There-fore, our legal system must be understood before we can outline the possible reactions to environmental harm. The first step in the review is understanding the origin of our laws. Three articles of the U.S. Constitution create a federal government composed of three major branches. The legislative branch (under Article I) primarily creates laws, the executive branch (under Article II) primarily enforces laws, and the judicial branch (under Article III) primarily interprets laws. While performing their major functions as described in the relevant article, the executive and judicial branches also create law. Additionally, there is a fourth source of law, admin-istrative agencies. The following sections describe how each of these branches serves as a source of law. Table 1–1 shows where you can find the laws created by these branches of the federal government, as well as laws created by state and local governments. When you look for environmental laws, you will find that they may be created by all of these branches, and therefore may be found in all of these sources.

The Legislature as a Source of Statutory Law

Article I, Section 1, of the U.S. Constitution states, "All legislative Powers herein granted shall be vested in a Congress of the United States which shall consist of a House and Senate." It is important to understand the process by which Congress makes a law (called a statute), because Congress creates most environmental law. If we wish to change environmental laws, we must understand how to work through the legislative process. At every stage of the legislative process, groups that may be affected by a proposed law will seek to influence the proposal through lobbying. Some of these groups are highly organized forces that attempt to influence any proposed environmental legis-lation in Congress. Other groups are loosely knit, ad hoc organizations that emerged to influence a particular proposal.

The lobbying process with respect to environmental issues is somewhat complicated because it is not always a situation in which business lobbyists are working against environmental lobbyists. Within the environmentalist

TABLE 1–1 Where to Find Environmental Law

Level of Government	Legislative Law	Executive Orders	Common Law/ Judicial Interpretations	Administrative Regulations
Federal	*United States Code (USC)* *United States Code Annotated (USCA)* *United States Statutes at Large*	*Title 3 of the Code of Federal Regulations Codification of Presidential Proclamations and Executive Orders*	*United States Reports (U.S.)* *United States Supreme Court Reporter (S.Ct.)* *Federal Reporter (F., F2d)* *Federal Supplement (F. Supp.)* *Environmental Law Reporter (ELR)* *Federal agency reports* (titled by agency, e.g., *FCC Reports*)	*Code of Federal Regulations (CFR)* *Federal Registrar*
State	State code or state statutes (e.g., *Ohio Revised Code Baldwin's*)		Regional reporters State reporters	State administrative code or state administrative regulations
Local	Municipal ordinances		Varies; often difficult to find. Many municipalities do not publish case decisions, but keep them on microfilm. Interested parties usually must contact the clerk's office at the local courthouse.	Municipality administrative regulations

community itself, examples of divergent opinions concerning proposed legislation occur frequently. Some more established groups, such as the Defenders of Wildlife and the Environmental Defense Fund, tend to take more moderate positions and are more open to ideas for cutting the costs of environmental regulation. Such groups' moderate stances have prompted some former members to join organizations that take more extreme positions, including some such as Earth First!, that have essentially given up on the governmental process and take their case directly to the media by staging protest actions.

Those in the moderate group see themselves as practical and effective. They believe that, especially in recessionary climates, you will be ignored if you do not take economic arguments into account. Those in the more extreme group perceive the moderates as having sold out. Some of them also believe that the best way to get on television, and thus generate public support for one's position, is by taking an extreme stance. Still others from both camps see the proliferation of environmental lobbying groups, even when they hold diverse positions, as being positive, because it means more voices are sending the message to Congress that the public wants the environment to be protected.

In 1990, the major environmental groups spent approximately $217 million to support large Washington staffs of lobbyists, lawyers, fundraisers, and financial managers. This amount appears huge, but it is small in comparison to the amounts expended by various business interests to affect environmental legislation.[1] Nevertheless, from the amount spent by environmental lobbyists alone, you may infer that the lobbying effort is a significant aspect of the political process.

The emphasis for environmental lobbyists has traditionally been in Washington. But during the 1990s, as action at the state level becomes more important, we may see greater emphasis on lobbying below the federal level. Many national organizations already have local affiliates that lobby state legislatures when their interests are affected. And in 1990, the Sierra Club set up a formal program to train state-level lobbyists and distribute a $100,000 fund to help local chapters develop effective lobbying programs at the state level.[2]

Steps in the Legislative Process.   The federal legislative process is similar in many respects to the process followed by state legislatures, but each state constitution may require slightly different procedures. We focus on the federal process because it is the model on which state processes are based and because most environmental legislation is either federal or is modeled on federal law. The reason our environmental laws are primarily federal is that environmental problems do not recognize state borders, and therefore a uniform, nationwide approach is often necessary.

All laws originate from legislative proposals called bills. A bill is introduced into the House or Senate by a single member or by several members. The bill itself may well have been drafted by a lobbyist. As explained previ-

TABLE 1–2 Organizations Engaging in Environmental Lobbying

Business Interests	*Environmental Interests*
Business Roundtable	Environmental Defense Fund
Chemical Manufacturing Association	National Audubon Society
National Chamber of Commerce	Natural Resources Defense Council
National Environmental Development Council (a coalition of industries)	National Wildlife Federation
	Sierra Club
Utility Air Regulation Group (a coalition of utilities and trade associations)	Wilderness Society

ously, environmental groups often have their own lobbyists who attempt to persuade environmentally conscious legislators to introduce and support their bills. Various business interests also hire lobbyists. Table 1–2 lists some of the more active lobbying organizations that influence environmental legislation.

Once introduced, a bill is generally referred to the committee of the House or Senate that has jurisdiction over the subject matter of the bill. For example, a bill seeking to provide subsidies to firms willing to get half their energy from solar power will be referred to the House Committee on Energy and Commerce, which will, in turn, refer it to an appropriate subcommittee. Table 1–3 lists some of the committees and subcommittees to which environmental legislation may be referred. In most cases a bill is simultaneously introduced into both the Senate and the House and is referred to the appropriate committee and subcommittee in each. Once the bill is referred, the subcommittee holds hearings on the bill, listening to testimony from all concerned parties and establishing a hearing record. Lobbyists will be active during this time, sometimes through testimony at congressional hearings.

Following these hearings, the bill is marked up (drafted in precise form) and then referred to the subcommittee for a vote. When the vote is affirmative, the subcommittee forwards the bill to the full House or Senate committee, which may accept the subcommittee's recommendation, put a hold on the bill, or reject it. If the House or Senate committee has voted to accept the bill, the committee reports it to the full House or Senate membership for a vote. As a bill is going through this process, interested parties may follow its progress in the *Congressional Quarterly Weekly,* a publication that keeps track of what is happening to proposed legislation.

By the time the bill is passed by both the House and the Senate, a different version of the proposed law will usually have been adopted by each chamber. Therefore, the bill will need to go to a Senate-House Conference Committee, where, after compromise and reconciliation of the two bills, a single bill will be reported to the full House and Senate for voting. Very often you will hear discussions in the media about differences between House and

TABLE 1–3 Congressional Committees and Subcommittees Influencing Environmental Legislation

Senate	*House*

Agriculture Appropriations
  Energy and Water Development
  Interior and Related Agencies
Commerce, Science, and Transportation
  National Ocean Policy
Energy and Natural Resources
  Energy Regulation and Conservation
  Natural Resource Development and
    Production
  Water and Power
Environment and Public Works
  Nuclear Regulation
Finance
  Energy and Agricultural Taxation
Foreign Affairs
Labor and Human Resources
	Agriculture Appropriations
	  Energy and Water Development
	Education and Labor
	  Health and Safety
	Energy and Commerce
	  Energy Conservation and Power
	Foreign Affairs
	Government Operations
	  Environment, Energy, and Natural
	    Resources
	Interior and Insular Affairs
	  Energy and Environment
	  General Oversight, Northwest Power
	    and Forest Management
	  Mining and Natural Resources
	  Water and Power Resources
	Merchant Marine and Fisheries
	  Oceanography
	  Panama Shelf/Outer Continental Shelf
	Public Works and Transportation
	  Water Transportation
	Science and Technology
	  Energy Development and Applications
	  Energy Research and Production
	  Science, Research, and Technology
	Small Business
	  Energy, Environmental, and Safety Issues
	    Affecting Small Business
	Ways and Means

Senate versions of environmental laws that are making their way through this process. Often, one chamber's version will be supported by business interests and the other by environmental groups.

A final affirmative vote by both houses of Congress is required for a bill to become law. If passed, the bill is then forwarded to the president, who may either sign or veto it. When the president signs the bill into law, it becomes a statute. It then is written down and codified in the *United States Code* and the *United States Code Annotated.* If the president vetoes the bill, it may still become law if two-thirds of the Senate and House membership vote to override the veto. If the president takes no action within ten days of receiving the bill from Congress, the bill becomes law without his signature. One exception to this procedure is that if Congress adjourns before the ten-day period has elapsed, the bill does not become law. The bill will have been pocket vetoed by the president—that is, the president will have "stuck the bill in a pocket" and vetoed it by doing nothing. Supporters will then have to reintroduce the bill during the next session of Congress.

The Judicial Branch as a Source of Case Law

The federal courts and most state courts (discussed in chapter 2) constitute the judicial branch of government and are charged by their respective constitutions with interpreting the constitution and statutes on a case-by-case basis. Most cases interpreting these laws are reported in large volumes called *reporters,* compilations of federal or state *case law.* When two parties disagree about the meaning of a statute, they bring their case to the courts for interpretation. For example, if a bill to provide solar energy subsidies were signed by the president and became law, two parties might still disagree about its meaning and ask the federal courts to interpret it.

One disagreement that might arise under this bill could be the time limit within which the firm must obtain half its energy from solar power. Though you would think that something as important as a time for conversion would be clearly stated in the statute, such an omission is not unusual. Congress, especially in the environmental area, often makes very broad laws and leaves it to the courts to "fill in the gaps." As one senator said when Congress was about to pass the Superfund legislation, "All we know is the American people want these hazardous waste sites cleaned up. . . . [L]et the courts worry about the details."

Congress may have made the law intentionally vague because a more specific bill could not garner sufficient support for passage. The sponsors may have specifics in mind, but they know there will be strong opposition to those details. So they water down the language in the bill and hope that the courts will interpret the law so as to impose those specifics the drafters had in mind. While Congress never knows exactly how the courts will interpret a law, in the event that the judiciary interprets the law in a manner not intended by Congress, the legislative body can always amend the law, in effect overruling the judicial interpretation.

The judicial branch, when interpreting a law, sees itself as trying to ascertain congressional intent. The court first looks at the "plain language" of the statute, that is, words are given their ordinary meaning. The court then looks at the legislative history to determine the intent of the legislature. This history is found in the hearings held by the subcommittees and committees, as well as any debates on the Senate and House floors. Hearings are published in the *U.S. Congressional News and Administrative Reports* and may be ordered from the Government Printing Office or found in most university libraries in the government documents section. Debates about a bill are published in the daily *Congressional Record,* which may also be found in most libraries. When lawyers are arguing before the court on behalf of their interpretation of the law, many of their arguments will in fact be drawn from what is found in the *Congressional Record*. Thus, when trying to get a watered-down bill passed, its drafters will often try to insert language into the *Congressional Record* that would be supportive of their preferred interpretation of the law.

Not all judicially created law is based on a statutory or constitutional interpretation. Such laws for which there is no such basis are referred to as *common law*. Common law emerges from actual court cases. It develops when a problem arises for which there is no applicable statute or constitutional provision. We then have what is known as a *case of first impression*. Cases of first impression obviously provide judges with the greatest latitude to make law. The judge must create a law to resolve the problem. The rule laid down to resolve this case is called a *precedent*. If a similar case arises in the future, the courts have a tendency to follow the precedent. Very little environmental law, however, is created in this manner; most environmental law is based on statutes.

The rule that the court lays down when interpreting a statute or ascertaining the constitutionality of a statute is also known as a precedent. Such precedent will be relied on in the future when other judges are ruling on interpretations of statutes and the Constitution. This process of reliance on precedent is called *stare decisis,* which literally means "let the decision stand."

Not all precedents are equally important. The decisions of a court are binding precedent on only those courts on a lower level and in the same system. For example, precedents from the Ohio Supreme Court bind the Ohio appellate and Ohio trial courts. These precedents do not bind the Michigan courts. However, an Ohio precedent may be used in a Michigan case as a persuasive device. In other words, lawyers in a Michigan case may point out how Ohio resolved the law and argue that the Ohio court's reasoning was logical and therefore should be adopted. Likewise, in the federal system, a Fifth Circuit Court of Appeals decision would not have any precedential effect on another circuit court appeal. However, the precedent would be binding on the district courts within the Fifth Circuit.

Although the process of *stare decisis* seems straightforward, its application actually provides the judge with an opportunity to implant his or her values in the law. Judges have discretion in part because no two cases are ever exactly the same. The judge therefore will usually be able to *distinguish* (a legal term) the case at bar from the case that others are arguing should provide the precedent. When distinguishing a case, the judge finds a difference between the case before him and the precedent-setting case significant enough to allow him to rule differently in the second case. In many cases one lawyer will be arguing that the case before the court is similar to the potential precedent, and the opposing lawyer will be trying to point out significant differences between the two.

Another factor making reliance on precedent less predictable than one might assume is that there are frequently conflicting precedents, especially at the trial and initial appellate levels. Finally, a judge may always simply overrule the clearly applicable precedent. Whereas the judge will generally cite some reason for overruling the precedent, such as changes in technology or community values since the precedent was established, she need not do so. She may simply say that the prior ruling was erroneous and that overturning the precedent is simply a matter of "correcting" the law.

The U.S. Supreme Court and most state supreme courts have what is generally known as the power of judicial review, that is, the power to determine whether a statute is constitutional. Although not expressly provided for in the Constitution, the Supreme Court established this right in the landmark case of *Marbury v. Madison,* making the Supreme Court the final arbiter of the constitutionality of every law. This power gives the Court ultimate power to restrict legislative and executive branch activity.

Because most environmental law is federal statutory law, and because the U.S. Supreme Court is the final arbiter of the constitutionality of laws, most decisions you will read about in this book will be from the Court. As you will see, through its case-by-case interpretation of the Constitution and statutes, the Supreme Court has established a line of authoritative cases on various environmental matters.

The Executive Branch as a Source of Law

The executive branch includes the president, the president's staff, and the cabinet. The heads of all executive departments (e.g., the secretary of State, the secretary of Labor) make up the cabinet. The executive office is composed of various bodies, such as the Office of Management and Budget (OMB) and the Office of Personnel Management (OPM). The executive branch is influential in the rule-making processes of both the legislature and administrative agencies. The president influences Congress by proposing legislation, publicly supporting or opposing proposed laws, and using the veto. The OMB's role in influencing administrative regulations through cost-benefit analysis is detailed in chapter 3. The executive branch exercises direct rule making through its power to make treaties and issue executive orders.

Treaty Making.   The president has the power, subject to the advice and consent of the Senate, to make treaties. These treaties become the law of the land, based on the supremacy clause of the Constitution (Article XI), and supersede any state law. For instance, when President Reagan entered into the Montreal Protocol, a treaty mandating reductions in the production of chlorofluorocarbons and halons, that treaty became the law of the land, and its provisions superseded any existing federal or state laws inconsistent with the treaty. Thus, the Kentucky legislature could not subsequently pass a law that would allow the unlimited production of those chemicals within the state's borders. Treaty making is one of the few ways that the United States can influence the environmental policies of other nations.

Executive Orders.   Throughout history, the president has made laws by issuing executive orders. For example, in 1992, President Bush issued an executive order temporarily freezing the promulgation of new rules by administrative agencies, an act that had the potential to affect environmental law severely because agencies are constantly making rules implementing environmental laws.

The executive order as a source of law is also used by state governors to deal with emergencies and with budget functions. For example, a governor may order a freeze on hiring in the state university system or order an across-the-board cut in budgets in all state departments when quarterly tax revenues are lower than anticipated.

Administrative Agencies as a Source of Law

Less well known to the general public as a source of law are the federal regulatory agencies, among them the Environmental Protection Agency (EPA) and the Occupational Safety and Health Administration (OSHA). Congress has delegated to these agencies the authority to make rules governing the conduct of business and labor in certain areas. However, there was some concern about the delegation of so much power to bodies with no elected representatives, so their rule-making processes (described in chapter 3) are especially open to public participation. Proposed rules, as well as those rules finally implemented by an agency, must be published in the *Federal Register,* and the public must be given the opportunity to comment on these proposals.

Because of their substantial impact on the laws of this nation, administrative agencies sometimes represent what many observers have called a fourth branch of government. Most of the federal environmental laws mandate the creation of many administrative regulations; thus we describe this fourth branch of government in greater detail in chapter 3.

CLASSIFICATIONS OF LAW

Case and Statutory Law

As noted earlier, laws are classified as either case law or statutory law, depending on how they are made. Judges make case law; legislators make statutory law. We generally find statutory laws in codes and case law in case reporters. Even though this distinction is frequently made, it is important to remember that the two types of law are entwined through the process of statutory interpretation. We really do not know what a statute means until it is interpreted by the courts, whose judges attempt to construe congressional intent. Sometimes, as you know, the court may interpret the law in a manner not intended by Congress, and Congress may then respond by amending the statute to make its meaning clear.

Public and Private Law

Besides the statutory-case law distinction, another classification of law may be helpful in your study of environmental law: the distinction between public law and private law. *Public laws* are those set up to provide for the public welfare, and they are generally administered by administrative agencies. These laws usually regulate classes of people or organizations. Environmental law is considered public law. Other branches of public law include securities law, labor law, and antitrust law. *Private law,* on the other hand, generally regulates the conduct between two individual parties. Sometimes private law may be used in environmental matters. For example, if a company does not properly test a chemical and consequently sells a product that injures a consumer, that consumer may be able to bring a private action for compensation against the company. Such a private action would be called a tort, or personal injury case. Other private law actions include breach of contract and fraud.

Criminal Law and Civil Law

Perhaps an even more important distinction, however, is that between civil and criminal law. This distinction is important because the rules governing each are different, as are the outcomes sought in each case.

Criminal law is made up of those federal and state statutes that prohibit wrongs against the state or society in general, conduct such as arson, rape, murder, forgery, robbery, and illegal dumping of hazardous waste. The primary purposes of criminal law are to punish offenders and to deter them and others from committing similar acts, usually through imprisonment or fines. The prosecutor, the person initiating a criminal case, is the government, usually represented by a federal district attorney or a state prosecutor. The prosecutor is said to be representing society and the victim against the defendant, who is most likely to be an individual but may also be a corporation.

For purposes of both criminal and civil litigation, a corporation can sue and be sued, just like a person. Corporations, in the context of litigation, are sometimes referred to as artificial or juristic persons. If the corporation is a defendant, of course, it cannot be jailed. A fine will be imposed against the corporation in lieu of a jail term.

Crimes are generally divided into felonies and misdemeanors based on the severity of the harm the actions may cause. In most states, the more harmful *felonies* (e.g., rape, arson, criminal fraud) are commonly punishable by incarceration in a state penitentiary and by fines. The less harmful misdemeanors (e.g., shoplifting a magazine) are crimes usually punishable by shorter periods of imprisonment in a county or city jail, as well as by smaller fines. What may be a misdemeanor in one state could be a felony in another.

Civil law is usually defined as the body of laws regulating relations between individuals or between individuals and corporations. In a civil matter the party analogous to the prosecutor is the plaintiff. The plaintiff is usually seeking either compensation or equitable relief (an order for specific performance or an injunction). There are no divisions in civil law comparable to that between felonies and misdemeanors in the criminal system. In the civil system laws are divided by subject matter, with the most common civil matters being tort cases and contract cases. Other substantive areas of civil law include domestic relations (family law), bankruptcy, agency law, property, and business organizations.

Most people consider being convicted of a crime much more serious than being found guilty of violating a civil law. There is much greater "societal scorn" heaped on the criminal. Also, it is only criminal law that threatens the defendant with the loss of liberty. For those reasons the defendant in a criminal case is given greater procedural protections. First, although almost anyone can file a civil action against another person, before a criminal defendant can be tried for a serious federal crime, an indictment must be handed down against him or her. Most states also require an indictment by a grand jury when a defendant is charged with a felony. To get an indictment, the prosecutor must convince the grand jury, a body generally composed of fifteen to twenty-three citizens, that the prosecution has enough evidence to justify bringing the potential criminal defendant to trial.

When a defendant is charged with a misdemeanor, a local judge or magistrate will fulfill a role comparable to a grand jury. This initial step provides a safeguard against political prosecution. It is necessary because even when one is ultimately found not guilty, the act of being tried for a crime still tarnishes the defendant's reputation, so we want to make the trial of an innocent party as rare as possible.

Another difference lies in the burden of proof placed on the party bringing the action. In both cases the party filing the action must prove his or her case. However, a person filing a civil case must prove that the defendant violated the law by a *preponderance of evidence,* which can be thought of as proving that it is more likely than not that the defendant committed the act. If the defendant is charged with a crime, however, the prosecution must prove the defendant's guilt *beyond a reasonable doubt,* a much more stringent standard.

Environmental Criminal Prosecutions.   Our primary concern with criminal law lies in the fact that violations of many environmental statutes constitute criminal offenses. As we examine specific environmental statutes, note that the same act often gives rise to both criminal and civil penalties. Criminal penalties are often imposed for acts referred to as willful or knowing violations. The most publicized trend in criminal actions today is the increasing use of imprisonment of corporate violators, including those who violate criminal provisions of environmental laws. Since new federal sentencing guidelines took effect in 1987, incarceration has increased and plea bargains involving probation and community service have been less frequent. Further, when a company criminally violates an environmental law, that firm may have all its government contracts suspended.

One recent trend in environmental law has been an increasing use of criminal sanctions. The first major increase in the use of criminal sanctions to enforce environmental laws occurred in 1982, when the Department of Justice (DOJ) created a separate Environmental Crimes Unit in its Land and Natural Resources Division, and the EPA established an office for Criminal Investigations. In 1990, the EPA referred a record fifty-six cases to the Justice Department for criminal prosecution, surpassing the previous year's high of fifty. A record one hundred defendants were charged with crimes in 1990, and fifty-five were convicted and sentenced to a total of 75.3 years.

In 1994, a record number of 220 cases were referred to the Justice Department, with 250 defendants charged with environmental crimes. A total of ninety-nine years of prison and criminal fines of $36.8 million were imposed on the convicted defendants. The total amount of fines imposed in 1990 was $5.5 million.[3] (See figure 1–1 for a five-year statistical comparison of criminal prosecutions.) In one of the toughest criminal sentences handed down in an environmental case, a Pennsylvania waste-pit owner, William Fiore, was sentenced to serve six to twelve years in a state prison for deliberately piping 1.2 million gallons of toxic leachate into the Youghiogheny River near Pittsburgh. The largest criminal penalty ever assessed an individual for violating an environmental law was given in 1990 to a Wall Street trader. He was fined $2 million for filling wetlands without a permit.[4] The biggest criminal fine ever imposed on a corporation was the $22 million Exxon Valdez fine.[5]

Thus, since the early 1990s, the EPA has demonstrated a belief that criminal penalties have an important role to play in environmental enforcement. This view seems consistent with that of the public but not with that of corporate executives. A poll reported in the *Wall Street Journal* on March 11, 1992, revealed that 75 percent of the general public believed that executives should be held personally liable for their environmental crimes, but only 49 percent of five hundred executives of large corporations agreed. A majority of the public rated environmental crime as worse than price-fixing and insider trading, whereas 80 percent of corporate executives felt that the latter two were more serious.

A single act may lead to both criminal penalties and civil liability. For example, if a businessperson willfully violates the Resource Conservation and Recovery Act, both the person and the corporation may be subject to criminal penalties in the form of fines. Additionally, civil penalties may be assessed, and parties who were personally injured by the violations may also bring private civil damage suits.

The year 1990 was also a record year for the EPA in terms of civil enforcement, with the imposition of an all-time high of $38.5 million in civil judicial penalties and $22.8 million in administrative penalties. The largest

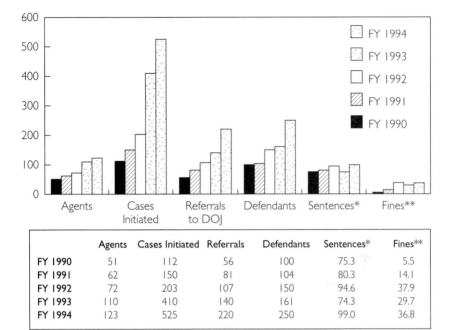

	Agents	Cases Initiated	Referrals	Defendants	Sentences*	Fines**
FY 1990	51	112	56	100	75.3	5.5
FY 1991	62	150	81	104	80.3	14.1
FY 1992	72	203	107	150	94.6	37.9
FY 1993	110	410	140	161	74.3	29.7
FY 1994	123	525	220	250	99.0	36.8

*Years of Incarceration
** Millions of Dollars

FIGURE I–I   Office of Criminal Enforcement Five-Year Statistical Comparison

Source: EPA, Office of Enforcement and Compliance Assurance, Enforcement and Compliance Assurance Accomplishments Report FY 1994 (May 1995), at 4-3.

settlement with a party charged with violating an environmental statute was reached when Texas Eastern Transmission Corporation paid a $15 million fine and agreed to perform $400 million in cleanup work at eighty-nine sites in fourteen states.[6]

The improved enforcement record of the early 1990s may be attributed to two factors. First, the administrator of the EPA, William Reilly, was determined to improve enforcement. Second, the EPA's enforcement budget was greatly increased. However, just because enforcement efforts have increased substantially, we do not necessarily prosecute most violators of environmental regulations. We must also recognize that the days of growing budgets for environmental enforcement probably ended in 1995. In January of 1996, President Clinton accepted a short-term budget bill that funded the EPA at 22 percent below the agency's 1995 funding.

An important criminal law case that has helped to make criminal sanctions more of a deterrent than they otherwise might have been is the 1975 U.S. Supreme Court case of *United States v. Park.*[7] That case laid down the rule that a corporate officer can be held criminally liable for failure to correct a regulatory violation, even when that officer directed a lower-level employee to take corrective action. The test for liability laid down in that case was that criminal liability would be imposed when a person, by virtue of his or her position in a corporation, had the responsibility and authority either to prevent the violation or promptly correct it and failed to do so.

In the 1986 case of *U.S. v. Hayes International Corporation,*[8] a defendant had arranged to have a private hauler dispose of waste the company had generated and was led to believe that the waste was being recycled. Only if the waste were being recycled did the hauler not need a permit under the act. The hauler in fact was not recycling the waste and did not have the appropriate permit. Despite the company's lack of actual knowledge that the hauler did not have a permit, both the company and its contracting officer were found guilty of violating the act. The Eleventh Circuit Court of Appeals upheld the convictions. The court created a presumption of knowledge on the part of those handling hazardous waste and said that such presumed knowledge could be used to prove circumstantially a knowing violation of the act.

In 1994, the EPA took another major step toward increasing its enforcement efforts by reorganizing enforcement and compliance programs and creating the Office of Enforcement and Compliance Assurance, with an emphasis on targeting serious violations.

Responding to Increased Enforcement. Firms are increasingly recognizing the potential for criminal liabilities being imposed on them. Because it is now clear that neither ignorance of the facts nor ignorance of the law is an excuse, corporations are beginning to encourage employees to take steps to protect themselves and their companies from liabilities.

First, employees in responsible positions are being encouraged to know the law. Second, when an official delegates a task mandated by an environmental regulation, he or she is advised to accompany that delegation with strict supervision to be sure of compliance. In prudent corporations, all environmental policies of the company are being put in writing, as are all communications with regulatory agencies, especially when an agency is waiving a regulatory requirement. Individuals who disagree with directives with respect to environmental policies are encouraged to make their objections known in writing to top corporate officials, who are encouraged to investigate such claims quickly. Prudent companies are also more carefully investigating those firms that they hire to do tasks that must be done in compliance with federal environmental regulations.

Finally, firms are increasingly making use of *environmental auditing.* The EPA defines an environmental audit as "a systematic, documented, periodic and objective review by regulated entities of facility operations and practices related to meeting environmental requirements." By its advocates, the environmental audit is seen as a means to verify environmental compliance, as well as an invaluable tool for assisting management in cutting costs, assessing risk, planning for growth, increasing environmental awareness in

TABLE 1–4 Elements of a Successful Environmental Auditing Program

- Explicit senior management support for environmental auditing and the willingness to follow up on the findings
- An environmental auditing function independent of audited activities
- Adequate auditor training and staffing
- Explicit audit program, objectives, scope, resources, and frequency
- A process that collects, analyzes, interprets, and documents information sufficient to achieve audit objectives
- A process that includes specific procedures to promptly prepare candid, clear, and appropriate written reports on audit findings, corrective actions, and schedules for implementation
- A process that includes quality assurance procedures to verify the accuracy and thoroughness of such audits

the firm, enhancing the firm's image with the public, and reducing fines and enforcement actions. Table 1–4 sets forth the elements the agency believes are necessary for a successful auditing program.

One of the stonger advocates of environmental audits is the EPA. To encourage the use of such audits and "self-policing" on the part of corporations, on December 19, 1995, the Administrator of the EPA signed the EPA's Final Policy on Penalty Reductions. Under this policy, if a firm can demonstrate that it discovers a violation and moves to correct it, the firm will not be subject to the gravity, or penalty, portion of any civil penalty. Under the EPA's Policy on Civil Penalties, the gravity portion is an amount of money added to the amount necessary to deprive the violator of any economic benefit from the violation that will "ensure that the violator is economically worse off than if it had obeyed the law."[9]

To qualify for this penalty reduction, the violator must meet certain conditions. First, the corporation must have discovered the violation either through a voluntary environmental audit or as a result of *due diligence,* which the EPA defines as systematic efforts to prevent, detect, and correct violations. Voluntary audits and due diligence do not include monitoring, sampling, or auditing required by a law, regulation, permit, judicial or administrative order, or consent agreement. Second, the corporation must voluntarily report the violation, fully and in writing, to federal, state, and local officials within ten days of its discovery, unless it is an unusually complex violation. Third, the corporation must have voluntarily corrected the violation. Fourth, the violation in question must not cause or threaten serious harm to human health or the environment. Fifth, either the same or similar violations must not have occurred at the facility at issue within the past three years, and there must not have been a pattern of repeated violations during the past five years. Finally, high-level corporate officials and managers must not have had any involvement in, or willful blindness to, the violation.

If a firm receives a reduction based on this policy, it may be required to publicly describe its due diligence practices. Also, if a company must enter into a written agreement, administrative consent order, or judicial consent order resulting from the violation, those documents must be made public.

The EPA plans to study the effects of the policy and make public its review after three years. Initial response to the final policy, which was actually a modification of an interim policy that had been issued in March of 1995, was generally favorable from the environmental community and more mixed from corporate counsel. Counsel for the Corporate Environment Enforcement Council commended the EPA for changes it had made from its interim policy that he thought would "offer responsible companies a reliable break in penalties without letting scofflaws off the hook,"[10] but he still had some major reservations. His main criticism, shared by many industry representatives, was that the policy did not provide an absolute privilege for environmental audits, a privilege that would have kept any agency or private party from being able to obtain the audit and use it against the corporation in a legal action.

In fact, a major issue debate during the 1990s has been whether these audits should be considered privileged information. Those in favor of an audit privilege argue that it is in everyone's best interest for firms to do environment audits. After all, if they do not know that they are in violation, how are they going to correct the violation? Yet if the management knows that violation information may be used against the firm, it would be reluctant to do the audit in the first place.

Initially, corporations turned to the courts to create an environmental audit privilege. Such efforts, however, have met with little success, and so corporations are now turning to both the state and federal legislatures. At the beginning of 1996, fourteen states had passed legislation establishing an environmental audit privilege, and several other states were considering similar laws. The bills all vary somewhat, but Virginia's is an example of the type of audit privilege legislation that is supported by corporate representatives.

The Virginia statute provides that information collected, generated, and developed during the course of an environmental audit is privileged from disclosure under ordinary circumstances.[11] The information is protected regardless of whether the audit is prepared by corporate employees or an independent contractor hired by the owner/operator of the firm, and no one who helps in the preparation of the audit document can be compelled to testify about its contents or preparation.[12]

There are four exceptional circumstances under which the privilege will not be upheld: (1) when information is uncovered that demonstrates a clear, imminent, and substantial danger to public health or the environment; (2) when information contained in the audit is already required by law to be disclosed; (3) when information contained in the audit was prepared independently of the voluntary environmental audit; and (4) when the audit docu-

ments, or portions thereof, were compiled in bad faith.[13] If none of the foregoing circumstances exist, to assert the privilege, the firm must only prove
that the audit (1) was conducted by or at the behest of the facility owner or
operator; (2) was voluntary; and (3) was designed to identify areas of environmental noncompliance with the law or identify opportunities for improved efficiency or pollution prevention.[14]

Of course, state audit privileges do not apply to federal enforcement action brought in federal court or citizens' suits under federal statutes but only
to state actions brought in state courts. Industry representatives are therefore
also lobbying to gain passage of a federal environmental audit privilege. A
typical audit protection law introduced, but not passed by Congress, was a
bill written in the House in 1995 to protect companies from any administrative, civil, or criminal penalties for a violation discovered during an audit if
the violation had been voluntarily disclosed to the EPA or another regulatory
body.[15] This privilege could only be used by firms that had not committed serious environmental violations during the three years before the audit.[16]

CONSTITUTIONAL PRINCIPLES UNDERLYING THE AMERICAN LEGAL SYSTEM

No discussion of the American legal system would be complete without a
discussion of the constitutional principles on which this system is based. The
Constitution, as originally drafted, was a conservative document. Most of
those who attended the Constitutional Convention were men of wealth, and
they understandably desired to protect their own interests. Because most of
the drafters owned property, protection of private property was a major objective. Protection of private property interests, in turn, means the protection
of business owners' interests.

The framers were also strongly influenced by the philosopher John
Locke. Locke saw government as a *social compact* by which people, living
in a state of nature, agreed to form a government that would make rules by
which all would abide. To prevent this government from being oppressive,
individuals, according to Locke, had to retain certain rights. These inalien-
able rights included the right to the pursuit of life, liberty, and property. The
U.S. Constitution was perceived as the embodiment of our social compact.

Although it is generally true that business and private property interests
have consequently been well served by many of the provisions of the Constitution, there have been exceptions. As the political makeup of justices on the
U.S. Supreme Court changes, interpretation of the Constitution also changes.
The concepts and constitutional provisions discussed briefly in the following
sections are those that have had the greatest impact on the scope of congressional authority to regulate private property interests and on laws designed to
protect the environment.

Federalism

Underlying the system of government established by the Constitution is the principle of *federalism,* which means that the authority to govern is divided between two sovereigns, or supreme lawmakers. In the United States these two sovereigns are the state and federal governments. One characteristic of federalism is its allocation of the power to control local matters to the local governments. Under the Constitution, all powers not given exclusively to the federal government or taken from the states are reserved to the states. The federal government has only those powers granted to it in the Constitution. Therefore, whenever federal legislation affecting the environment is passed, the question of the source of authority for that regulation always arises. As will be revealed shortly, the commerce clause is the predominant source of authority for the federal regulation of business and thus the source of authority for most environmental legislation.

In some areas the state and federal governments have concurrent authority; that is, both governments have the power to regulate the matter in question. This situation arises when authority to regulate in an area has been expressly, but not exclusively, given to the federal government by the Constitution. In such cases, the states may regulate in the area as long as the state regulation does not conflict with any federal regulation of the same subject matter. A conflict arises when a regulated party cannot comply with both the state and the federal laws at the same time. When the state law is more restrictive, and so compliance with the state law automatically constitutes compliance with the federal law, the state law may still be valid. However, states cannot pass less restrictive laws.

The outcome of direct conflicts between state and federal laws is dictated by the *supremacy clause.* This clause, found in Article VI of the Constitution, provides that the Constitution, laws, and treaties of the United States make up the supreme law of the land, "any Thing in the Constitution or Laws of any State to the Contrary notwithstanding." This principle is known as the principle of *federal supremacy:* Any state or local law that directly conflicts with the federal Constitution, laws, or treaties is void. Especially important for environmental law is the inclusion of rules established by federal administrative agencies as federal law.

Federal Preemption

The supremacy clause is also the basis for the doctrine of federal preemption. This doctrine is used to strike down a state law that does not directly conflict with a federal law but attempts to regulate an area in which federal legislation is so pervasive that it is evident that Congress wanted only federal regulation in that general area. It is often said in these cases that federal law "preempts the field."

Cases of federal preemption are especially likely to arise in matters pertaining to interstate commerce, where a local regulation imposes a substantial burden on the flow of interstate commerce through a particular state. This situation is discussed in greater detail in the next section. The law of federal preemption is one in which there really are no broad principles to be applied; the court simply looks at each individual case to try to determine whether Congress intended to preempt the subject matter in question from state regulation.

The Commerce Clause

The primary powers of Congress are listed in Article I of the Constitution. It is important to recognize, before proceeding any farther, that Congress has only limited legislative power. Congress possesses only that legislative power granted it by the Constitution. Thus, all acts of Congress not specifically authorized by the Constitution or necessary to accomplish an authorized end are invalid.

The commerce clause provides the authority for Congress to pass most of the federal environmental regulations. *Commerce* refers to trade or exchange of goods or services. This clause empowers the legislature to "regulate Commerce with foreign Nations, and among the several States, and with the Indian Tribes." Depending on the ideological makeup of the Supreme Court, of course, interpretations of the specific boundaries of this clause vary. Today, this clause is interpreted very broadly.

Whereas many would argue that a broad interpretation of the federal government's ability to regulate Congress is so well established as to be unassailable, others still challenge some federal regulations on the grounds that such regulation is an attempt to affect private matters rather than interstate commerce. An example of such a challenge in the environmental arena is provided by the case of *Hodel v. Virginia Surface Mining and Reclamation Association, Inc.*[17] The Hodel case arose after Congress passed a statute establishing a number of requirements for strip mining, the most controversial being a provision that any land used for strip mining be returned to approximately its original state. The mining association argued that the principal purpose of the act was to regulate the use of private land, a matter that falls within the state's police power; thus the act could not have been designed to be a regulation of interstate commerce.

In setting forth its rule, the Supreme Court reiterated its broad interpretation of the commerce clause with respect to environmental matters, saying, "the court must defer to a congressional finding that a regulated activity affects interstate commerce if there is any rational basis for such a finding. . . even activity that is purely intrastate in character may be regulated by Congress where the activity, combined with like conduct by others in similar situations, affects commerce among the States or within foreign nations." The Court in Hodel applied this test to the facts and found that Congress had a rational basis for determining that strip mining affects interstate commerce. Congress had relied heavily on the impact of mining on water pollution. The

Court also pointed out the need for national standards in light of the difficulties states had encountered when attempting to regulate the problem.

Most environmental regulation by the federal government, like the foregoing, is now presumed to be constitutional. In determining whether Congress has the authority to enact legislation under the commerce clause, the Supreme Court asks whether there is any rational basis for Congress to find that the activity to be regulated affects interstate commerce. If so, the Court asks whether there is any reasonable connection between the ends asserted and the regulatory scheme selected to achieve those ends. If both questions can be answered affirmatively, the legislation stands.

The Restrictive Effect of the Commerce Clause. In addition to being seen as a source of power for the federal government, the commerce clause is also interpreted as an implicit restriction on the states' authority to regulate matters affecting interstate commerce. After all, under the doctrine of federal preemption, if the federal government is supposed to regulate matters affecting interstate commerce, then the state should not regulate these matters. Thus states may not regulate interstate commerce.

This restriction has a history of changing interpretations so complex as to be beyond the scope of this book. Instead, we will focus on how the clause is interpreted today. In brief, it is a violation of the commerce clause for a state to pass a law that on its face discriminates against interstate commerce. If, however, the legislation involves the state's engaging in a proprietary action (an action whereby the state is not functioning as a government but is acting more in the role of a business), the legislation will be upheld. If a statute does not appear on its face to be discriminatory but has discriminatory effects on interstate commerce, a balancing test is applied, comparing the impact of the state's regulation on interstate commerce with the state's justification.

The issue of whether a state regulation is a violation of the commerce clause arises frequently in disputes surrounding the regulation of waste. States are searching for ways to restrict the importation of out-of-state waste without violating the commerce clause and are generally not succeeding. The earliest such case that went to the U.S. Supreme Court was *City of Philadelphia v. New York*.[18] In that 1978 case a New Jersey statute had prohibited the import of solid or liquid waste generated outside the state to be buried in a landfill in the state. The Court said that the state was attempting to slow or stop the flow of commerce for protectionist reasons, an action that is clearly in violation of the commerce clause, because (as explained earlier) interpretations of the clause prohibit states from passing legislation that inhibits interstate commerce.

Other states attempted to learn from New Jersey's experience. Ohio's legislature, recognizing that a statute discriminatory on its face could still be upheld if (1) the law has a legitimate purpose, (2) the statute serves that purpose, and (3) there is no nondiscriminatory alternative that would serve the same purpose, tried to pass a law that would meet that exception. The Ohio statute imposed higher taxes on out-of-state waste. Ohio had three justifications: (1) the sheer volume of waste flowing into the state, (2) the higher costs of out-of-state waste inspection, and (3) the increased threat of hazardous material entering Ohio and the consequent difficulty of policing its transportation. In striking down the law, the lower court said that protecting the environment was no justification unless something other than the source was the reason for the different treatment. The court found the latter two justifications to be unsupported. The case was appealed in 1991, and the decision upheld in 1992.

Michigan also tried to circumvent the restrictive impact of the commerce clause. Its law, however, fared much better than Ohio's in the lower court. Michigan's Solid Waste Management Act gave each Michigan county the right to accept or reject waste from any outside source. Because the law classified waste by county, and thus treated inter- and intrastate waste the same, there was no problem, according to the lower court. The U.S. Supreme Court, however, did not agree.

Michigan's law was struck down by the Supreme Court in the summer of 1992, with the court stating that states could not adopt "protectionist" measures to stop waste being generated in other states from being shipped to their dump sites. Even legitimate goals like protecting health and the environment could not be accomplished by economic protectionism.

While most states struggle with finding a way to draft a constitutional law allowing them to keep hazardous waste outside their state, Rhode Island is trying do just the opposite: Rhode Island wants to keep commercial trash inside the state. Rhode Island's Central Landfill cannot, by law, charge the state's municipalities more than $14 a ton to receive residential trash. Because that amount does not cover disposal costs, the landfill charges up to $59 per ton for commercial trash.

The high prices made Central Landfill noncompetitive with dumps in neighboring states, which was a boon to local trucking firms, because they were now hauling tons of waste to landfills in neighboring states. Consequently, the state's Solid Waste Management Corporation decreed that all the state's commercial trash had to go to a state-licensed disposal site, which meant Central Landfill. A trucking firm claiming the regulation was ruining its business sued the state on the ground that the regulation violated the commerce clause. The district court judge agreed and issued an injunction in the summer of 1991.

Because trash disposal is such a major problem, and cases seeming to support a position that state restrictions on out-of-state waste disposal violate the commerce clause, Congress is coming under increasing pressure to pass some form of legislation that would override at least part of the Supreme Court's ruling and allow states to restrict the importation of waste. Measures that would allow states to restrict interstate transport of nonhazardous waste have been introduced in both the House and Senate but thus far have not been passed.

The Fourth Amendment

The Fourth Amendment protects the right of individuals to be secure in their persons, homes, and personal property. It prohibits the government from conducting unreasonable searches of individuals and seizing their property to use as evidence against them. If such an unreasonable search and seizure occurs, the evidence obtained cannot be used in a trial.

An unreasonable search and seizure is basically one conducted without the government official's having first obtained a warrant from the court. The warrant must specify the items sought, as well as the persons and places to be searched. Government officials are able to obtain such a warrant only when they can show probable cause to believe that the search will turn up the specified evidence of criminal activity. Supreme Court decisions, however, have recently narrowed the protections of the Fourth Amendment by providing for circumstances in which no search warrant is needed. Improvements in technology have also caused problems in the application of the Fourth Amendment because it is now simpler to eavesdrop on people and to engage in other covert activities.

The Fourth Amendment applies to corporations as well as individuals. Fourth Amendment issues often arise when legislation authorizes warrantless searches by administrative agencies. For example, the EPA would prefer pollution-control regulations providing that when a firm is suspected of violating pollution limits, the EPA may conduct a surprise search to catch the violator. To the agency's dismay, the courts generally will not allow such warrantless searches. However, the standards for securing an administrative search warrant in such cases are much less stringent than in a criminal action. Generally, an administrative warrant requires a showing of a neutral enforcement plan that assures the court that selective enforcement will not occur.

The Fifth and Fourteenth Amendments

The Due Process Clause.   The Fifth and Fourteenth Amendments are often spoken of together because both contain what is known as the *due process clause,* the provision that no person shall be deprived of his or her right to life, liberty, or the pursuit of happiness without due process of law. The Fifth Amendment is a prohibition on the federal government, and the Fourteenth restricts states. There are two types of due process: *procedural* and *substantive.*

Originally, due process was interpreted only procedurally. It required that a person whose life, liberty, or property would be taken by a criminal conviction be given a fair trial—that is, he or she was entitled to notice of the alleged crime and the opportunity to confront his or her accusers before an impartial tribunal. The application of procedural due process soon spread beyond criminal matters, especially after passage of the Fourteenth Amendment.

What procedural safeguards does procedural due process require? That question is not easily answered. The procedures that the government must follow when there may be a taking of an individual's life, liberty, or property vary according to the nature of the taking. In general, as the magnitude of the potential deprivation increases, the extent of the procedures required also increases. For example, a student being suspended from the public school for three days would be entitled to fewer procedural guarantees than one being expelled for a year.

The concept of substantive due process refers to the basic fairness of laws that may deprive an individual of his or her liberty or property. In other words, when a law is passed that will restrict individuals' liberty or use of their property, the government must have a proper purpose for the restriction, or it violates substantive due process. What constitutes a proper governmental purpose is, of course, subject to interpretation by the courts.

In applying the concept of substantive due process, we usually say that the government cannot act arbitrarily and capriciously. When substantive due process analysis occurs, one asks whether the deprivation by the government involves the deprivation of a fundamental right. If so, the government cannot act unless it has a compelling reason to do so and there is not less-restrictive means for satisfying this compelling interest. If there is an alternate way to achieve the same end that causes less deprivation, then there has been a violation. If the deprivation is for other than a fundamental right, the government action must be rationally related to a legitimate state end. In other words, the state end was an exercise of the police power, and the means will logically lead to the specified state end.

The Takings Clause. The Fifth Amendment further provides that if the government takes private property for public use, it must pay the owner just compensation. The language of the Fifth Amendment states "nor shall private property be taken for public use without just compensation." Although the Fourteenth Amendment does not contain such a clause, the Supreme Court has interpreted the Fourteenth as incorporating this clause through its due process clause. Unlike the privilege against self-incrimination, which does not apply to corporations, both the due process clause and the provision for just compensation are applicable to corporations. The latter provision is of great importance in numerous environmental cases, in which representatives of the corporation frequently argue that the environmental regulations are so onerous as to constitute a taking of their land, for which compensation should be awarded.

In cases in which a party argues that regulations are so restrictive of private use as to constitute a taking of his or her private property for public use, the government will argue that the regulations are simply an exercise of its "police power," its power to protect the welfare of the citizens. In general, the courts seem to look at the diminution of the value of the property caused by the regulation and require compensation only when there has been a *drastic* reduction in the economic value of the property. In 1987, a five to four majority of the U.S. Supreme Court ruled that a state could impose restrictions on land use without having to compensate the owner for the land's reduced commercial value when the state "intends to prevent serious public harm."

This issue of when a regulation constitutes a taking has become increasingly debated during the 1990s as both the state and federal governments have passed more regulations protecting wetlands that were often held as private property. The most significant case on this issue was argued on March 2, 1992, before the U.S. Supreme Court. The case, *Lucas v. South Carolina Coastal Council,*[19] involved a dispute between a beachfront property owner and the state of South Carolina over a law prohibiting permanent construction on any eroding beach. Lucas had bought two beachfront lots for $975,000 in 1986, before the passage of the law in question. Lucas, who had not yet begun construction on his property when the law was passed, lost the right to use his property for condominiums, so he challenged the law as constituting a taking without just compensation. The state court agreed with Lucas that the regulation denied him full value of his property and thus constituted a taking, so it awarded him $1.2 million in damages. The South Carolina Supreme Court, citing U.S. Supreme Court precedents, disagreed and overturned the lower court decision.

Lucas appealed the decision to the U.S. Supreme Court, which handed down its opinion on June 29, 1992. This opinion reversed the state supreme court in a six to three decision. The Court held that a state regulation that deprives a private property owner of all economically beneficial uses of property, except those uses that would not have been permitted under background principles of state property and nuisance law, constitutes a taking of private property for which the Fifth Amendment's takings clause requires payment. The Court stated that the South Carolina court erred in applying the principle that the takings clause does not require compensation when the regulation at issue is designed to prevent "harmful or noxious uses" of property.

Obviously, this decision was met with concern on the part of environmentalists, who fear that this ruling may lead to significant restraint on the part of state governments, which may fear that passing laws to protect state coastlines may now cost them millions of dollars. Even before a decision was handed down, however, the debate triggered legislature activity. Republican Senator Steve Symms of Idaho is attempting to gain support for a law that would require agencies to "assess" and "minimize" the potential for taking private property whenever a regulation is issued. Another legislative proposal being considered in the House would require federal agencies to compensate owners of wetlands when use of their property was restricted. Many environmentalists are understandably concerned about these proposals.

From the perspective of the so-called "Property Firsters," or private property rights advocates, *Lucas* was a watershed case. *Lucas,* along with *Whitney v. U.S.,*[20] wherein a federal court found that the federal Surface Mining and Reclamation Act constituted a taking with respect to one mining company whose land had become completely useless as a result of the act, had restored to prominence the takings clause that had been relatively dormant for the previous fifty years. Strengthened by these victories, the property rights movement has been gaining momentum. A large number of property rights organizations are springing up all across the country, and many of the groups are forming informal alliances. Combining the old wings of the 1970s Sagebrush Rebellion in the West, miners, loggers, ranchers, and energy companies, with farmers and private property owners in the East and South, these groups are joining forces to attack what they see as government overreaching: wetlands preservation, endangered species protection, public park and greenway expansions, scenic river corridors, land use planning, and zoning laws and growth management plans.[21]

Table 1–5 lists some of these groups. One of the most influential organizations in the property rights movement is the Pacific Legal Foundation, the first nonprofit, public interest law firm devoted to litigating in defense of "individual and economic freedoms" on a national level. Since its founding in 1973, this firm has participated in more than one hundred cases. Perhaps their most significant victory was *Dolan v. Tigard,*[22] a victory for the property rights movement handed down in 1994.

The City of Tigard had conditioned granting Dolan a permit to expand her store and pave her parking lot on her dedicating a portion of her property for (1) a public greenway to minimize the flooding that would otherwise be likely to result from her construction, and (2) a pedestrian/bicycle pathway to decrease congestion in the business district where her store was expanding. While the Land Board of Appeals, State Court of Appeals, and State Supreme Court all affirmed the decision of the city, which had found that the land dedication requirements were reasonably related to her proposed con-

TABLE 1–5 Property Rights Advocacy Groups	
Alliance for America	A loose confederation of more than six hundred property rights organizations that communicate through a fax network and host an annual "Fly-in for Freedom" lobbying excursion to Washington, D.C.
Environmental Conservation Organization	A coalition of about five hundred that publishes a magazine, hosts conferences, and maintains a computer network for its membership.
Virginians for Property Rights	A clearinghouse for Virginians seeking information on property rights issues.
Oregonians in Action	An education center focusing on land use regulation and property rights that expanded to include a legal center.
Pacific Legal Foundation	A nonprofit public interest firm that works to protect private property rights and limit government.

struction and therefore not a taking, the U.S. Supreme Court disagreed. The Court said that in order for a requirement like the one at issue to be valid, the requirement must have some reasonable relationship or nexus to the use to which the property is being made, which was the standard used by the lower courts. However, in this case, what constituted sufficient evidence of that relationship for the lower courts was not sufficient for the Supreme Court.

Clearly, this case was a significant victory for property rights advocates because it sends a message that the courts will now look much more closely at zoning and land use decisions than they traditionally have. Equally clear is the intent of the property rights advocates to continue to try to make gains in the courts and also in the state and federal legislatures. And they are increasingly finding friends in the legislature, as evidenced by the large number of property rights bills proposed during recent congressional terms.

The Equal Protection Clause. The Fourteenth Amendment contains another clause that has been gaining importance in the environmental area since 1979: the Equal Protection Clause. This clause provides that no state "shall deny to any person within its jurisdiction the equal protection of its laws." These words provide the constitutional basis for concerns about environmental racism that are increasingly being raised by civil rights activists.

While many claim that the movement against environmental racism began to coalesce approximately ten years ago in South Carolina when church-led black residents organized to protest the siting of a toxic landfill in the neighborhood, the movement started to achieve prominence in 1992.[23] During February of that year, the public became aware of an increasing array of statistics that appear to show that minorities receive less protection from environmental laws than do whites.

A study of EPA records by the *National Law Journal* revealed that there was a 506 percent disparity in fines assessed under the Resource Conservation and Recovery Act (the law regulating hazardous dumps) in predominantly black versus predominantly white neighborhoods. The average fine in white neighborhoods was $335,556, whereas the average fine in black neighborhoods was $55,318.[24] A former EPA attorney said he believed that statistic was the most telling with respect to environmental racism.[25]

There were also much lower fines for cases alleging multiple environmental law violations in black neighborhoods. Average fines for such violations were 306 percent higher in white neighborhoods during the past seven years.[25] Moreover, penalties for violations of the Clean Water Act were 28 percent lower in minority communities, while fines for violating the Safe Drinking Water Act and the Clean Air Act were lower by 15 percent and 8 percent, respectively.[26]

Final evidence comes from the Superfund program, or cleaning up hazardous waste sites. It took an average of 20 percent more time for a dump site in a minority neighborhood to be placed on the list for cleanup than one in a white neighborhood. Actual cleanup efforts also took longer to complete in minority neighborhoods. And, finally, the cleanup of minority sites was more often what many perceived as less effective "containment" action, which consisted of walling off the site. In white neighborhoods the site was more likely to receive "permanent" treatment such as removing the hazardous waste or treating it to eliminate the toxins.[27]

Of course, some argue that the conclusions being drawn about environmental racism are unfair. For example, one of the factors the law says must be considered in assessing the size of a penalty is the financial condition of the violating facility. Often the facilities in minority neighborhoods are also in economically depressed areas, so their penalties would be lower.[28] Others claim there is no evidence for this rationale.

In December 1992, then Vice President–elect Gore's transition team met with members of environmental justice groups to discuss this issue. On February 11, 1994, President Clinton signed into law Executive Order 12898, titled "Federal Actions to Address Environmental Justice and Minority Populations in Low-Income Populations." The order required all federal agencies to develop individual strategies to prevent environmental hazards from having disproportionately negative effects on minority and low-income populations by making environmental justice a part of decision making in every aspect of agency operations.

A Constitutional Right to Environmental Protection?

Because as a nation we have a tendency to look to the Constitution to protect those rights most fundamental to us, it is only natural that when a concern for protecting the environment began to take the form of a national movement, people looked to the Constitution for a guarantee of a clean environment. Some legislators, in arguing for passage of the first major environmental statute, the National Environmental Policy Act, argued that a constitutional right to environmental quality in fact existed;[29] their claim, however, was not widely accepted. Some environmentalists had hoped to use the Ninth Amendment, broadly interpreted, to expand the right to privacy to include a right to a clean, unspoiled environment.

At least one case in which such a claim was made, *Tanner et al. v. Armco Steel et al.,*[30] a 1972 case, was unsuccessful. Still others have tried to argue that every time a governmental entity grants a permit to a polluting firm, that action constitutes state action, thereby subjecting the action to the possibility of subjection to claims of a violation of due process or an unconstitutional taking. The Supreme Court's reluctance to recognize such a right probably can be explained by two factors. First, there is nothing explicit in the Constitution or in its early interpretations to indicate that the drafters had any intention of protecting the environment. Second, from a practical perspective, it would be extraordinarily difficult for the courts to define the boundaries of such a right. Protecting the environment appears to be an area better left to legislators and administrative agencies.

The Public Trust Doctrine. The idea of the government as a trustee for environmental quality is not just an idea that environmentalists pulled from nowhere. The public trust doctrine is deeply imbedded in American law, forgotten for years but reborn in the 1970s. The concept traces its historical roots back to early Roman law where the doctrine of the public trust developed around the idea that certain common properties such as the air, seashores, and rivers were held in trusteeship by the government for the free and unimpeded use of the public.[31] This doctrine was subsequently applied in England to give ownership of public lands to the king but required that his subjects be given access to waterways for such purposes as fishing and trade.

This doctrine, on a limited scale, has been followed in the United States, primarily for rivers, shorelands, and natural areas, although its adoption has been on a somewhat piecemeal basis. The Northwest Ordinance of 1787, for example, stated that "the navigable waters leading into the Mississippi . . . shall be common highways and forever free . . . to the citizens of the United States." The leading case establishing this doctrine is the 1892 U.S. Supreme Court opinion in *Illinois Central Railroad Co. v. Illinois.* In 1869 the Illinois legislature passed a statute granting more than 1,000 acres of valuable land, including submerged lands under Lake Michigan and the shoreline along the city of Chicago's central city business district, to the Illinois Central Railroad Company. Four years later, the state passed another statute repealing this grant. It then filed an action to establish title to that property in the state's name.

The U.S. Supreme Court affirmed the state's title to the land, and in so doing explained the concept of holding title under the public trust doctrine:

> It is a title that is held in trust for the people of the state that they may enjoy the navigation of the waters, carry on commerce over them, and have the liberty of fishing therein, freed from the obstruction or interference of private parties. . . . The control of the state for purposes of the trust can never be lost, except as to such parcels as are used in promoting the interests of the public therein, or can be disposed of without any substantial impairment of the public interest in the lands and waters remaining.[32]

This precedent-setting case demonstrates the clearest application of the public trust doctrine: a situation in which title to public lands is about to be transferred to a private entity. More difficult cases arise when control of the land is being diverted to a different governmental entity that intends to put the land in public trust to a more questionable public use, or, perhaps in partnership with a private entity, to develop and exploit the land for its economic value.

One example arose in Illinois in 1970 when the Chicago Park District proposed, among other endeavors, the transfer of 3.839 acres of city parkland to the Chicago Public Building Commission for the construction of a new school. Area property owners sued, arguing that the public trust doctrine required the state to retain the land in its use as parkland. The Illinois Supreme Court, in *Paepke v. Building Commission,* disagreed, stating: "The mere dedication by the sovereign of lands to public park use does not give private property owners . . . the right to have the use continue unchanged."[33]

The Illinois court noted the conflict between those who wanted to preserve the parks in their pristine state and those administrators who, "under the pressures of the changing needs of an increasingly complex society, find it necessary, in good faith, and for the public good, to encroach to some extent upon lands heretofore inviolate to change," and held that the resolution of such conflicts is a matter properly given to the legislature and not the courts. And, in this case, the court found that the legislative authorization in question was sufficiently broad and comprehensive to allow the transfer.

In coming to its conclusion, the Illinois court cited with approval the approach developed by the Supreme Court of Wisconsin. That state approved proposed diversions in the use of public trust lands under conditions that demonstrated that

1. public bodies would control the use of the area in question;
2. the area would be devoted to public purposes and open to the public;
3. the diminution of the area of original use would be small compared with the entire area;
4. none of the public uses of the original area would be destroyed or greatly impaired; and
5. the disappointment of those wanting to use the area designated for a new use for former purposes was negligible when compared to the greater convenience afforded those members of the public using the new facility.

While noting that these standards were not controlling, the Wisconsin court found them to be a useful guide for situations similar to the immediate case.

A third type of case in which the public trust doctrine may come into play is where lands held in trust are threatened by proposed actions of the government. These cases often involve water pollution problems created by the government or developers. Most recently the doctrine has been applied in cases involving oil spills.

As you might infer from the foregoing discussion, the public trust doctrine is an important one, in terms of public rights and responsibilities with respect to natural resources, even though it does not rise to the level of a constitutional protection. Questions as to its scope, balancing the interests of the competing publics, and the extent to which the qualities of the trusted property are to be preserved against short-term use, however, still remain. We shall refer to this important doctrine later in the book.

CONCLUDING REMARKS

After reviewing how our legal system is structured, you can begin to realize how complex the task is to establish a comprehensive system of laws to regulate the environment. Because the United States is organized in accordance with the basic principles of federalism, we have, in essence, two parallel systems of government: a state and a federal system. Both are organized similarly, with legislative, judicial, and executive branches that are primarily responsible for, respectively, creating, interpreting, and enforcing the laws that govern our nation. A so-called fourth branch of government that combines all those governmental functions is now also fully functioning at both the state and local levels and is especially important in making and enforcing environmental regulations.

The laws these governments make are both civil and criminal. Both are important in preserving the environment. These two parallel governmental systems often have overlapping responsibilities as dictated by the U.S. Constitution. But because the Constitution is a broadly worded document, subject to interpretation by the U.S. Supreme Court, it is not always clear where the lines of authority between the state and federal governments are drawn. The commerce clause gives the U.S. Congress the authority to pass environmental regulations, whereas the states rely on the police power that they retain under the Constitution to pass such laws. Where there is potential for conflict, the courts must intervene and draw boundaries, relying on interpretations of the Supremacy Clause and applying the doctrine of federal preemption.

The Constitution also protects individual rights. Often, in environmental matters, individuals will argue that the government's attempts to regulate or protect the environment have gone too far and have infringed on constitutional freedoms. Cases in which such claims have arisen in the environmental area include those questioning the need for search warrants or whether a regulation is so onerous as to constitute a taking.

Whereas this chapter has focused on the structure and lawmaking function of the government, the judicial function of our system merits special consideration. Thus, chapter 2 takes an in-depth look at exactly how our legal system handles conflicts.

QUESTIONS FOR REVIEW AND DISCUSSION

1. Explain how statutory laws are created.
2. What does *stare decisis* mean?
3. Differentiate civil law from criminal law.
4. Explain the significance of the decisions in *U.S. v. Parks* and *U.S. v. Hayes International Corporation.*

5. What can corporate officials do to decrease their chances of being held criminally liable for violating environmental laws?
6. What is the relationship between the commerce clause and environmental law?
7. How does the Fourth Amendment affect enforcement of environmental regulations?
8. When does a regulation comprise an unconstitutional taking?

FOR FURTHER READING

Note, *Criminal Sanctions for Environmental Crimes and the Knowledge Requirements:* United States vs. International Harvester, 25 AM. CRIM. L. REV. 535 (1988).

RICHARD J. LEON, *Environmental Criminal Enforcement: A Mushrooming Cloud,* 63 ST. JOHN'S L. REV. 679 (1989).

ROBERT MCMURRY, & STEPHEN RAMSEY, *Environmental Crimes: The Use of Criminal Sanctions in Enforcing Environmental Laws,* 19 LOY. L.A. L. REV. 1133 (1986).

DONALD REBOVICH, DANGEROUS GROUND: THE WORLD OF HAZARDOUS WASTE CRIME (New Brunswick, N.J.: Transaction Publishing, 1992).

PETER BYRNE, *Ten Arguments for the Abolition of the Regulatory Takings Doctrine,* 22 ECOLOGY L.Q. 89 (1995).

CRAIG N. JOHNSTON, *An Essay on Environmental Audit Privileges: The Right Problem, the Wrong Solution,* 25 ENVTL. L. 335 (1995).

PAULA C. MURRAY, *The Environmental Self-Audit Privilege: Growing Movement in the States Nixed by EPA,* 24 REAL EST. L.J. 169 (1995).

PAULA C. MURRAY, Dolan v. City of Tigard: *Another Wrinkle on the Takings Doctrine,* 23 REAL EST. L.J. 275 (Winter 1995).

LYNDA J. OSWALD, *Cornering the Quark, Investment-Backed Expectations and Economically Viable Uses in Takings Analysis,* 70 WASH. L. REV. 91 (1995).

DANIEL RIESEL, *Criminal Prosecutions and Defense of Environmental Wrongs,* 15 ENVTL. L. REP. 10065 (March 1985).

ADAM D. SCHWARTZ, *The Law of Environmental Justice: A Research Pathfinder,* 25 ENVTL. L. REP. 10543 (October 1995).

ANDREW SZASZ. *Corporations, Organized Crime, and the Disposal of Hazardous Waste: An Examination of the Making of a Criminogenic Regulatory Structure,* 24 CRIMINOLOGY, (1) 1 (1986).

PETER YEAGER, THE LIMITS OF LAW: PUBLIC REGULATION OF PRIVATE POL-
LUTION (New York: Cambridge University Press, 1991).

ON THE INTERNET

http://thomas.loc.gov
A source for pending legislation, bill status, directory information about
members of the House and Senate

http://www.house.gov
The most comprehensive source of House of Representatives' legislative
data

http://www.fs.fed.us/land/envjust.html
A place to find the executive order on environmental justice

http://www.econet.org/lcv/home
League of Conservation Voters page providing information about legislators' votes

http://www.igc.apc.org/env/justice
Econet's resources on environmental racism

http://www.cruzio.com/~meuser/El/index.html
Contains bibliography of more than three hundred works about environmental justice

NOTES

1. THOMAS ARRANDALE, *The Mid-Life Crisis of the Environmental Lobby,* 32 GOVERNING, 36 (April 1992).
2. Ibid.
3. EPA, Office of Enforcement and Compliance Assurance, Enforcement and Compliance Assurance Accomplishment Report FY 1994, (May 1995).
4. EPA, Environmental Stewardship (May 1991), at 8.
5. EPA, note 3.
6. Ibid.
7. 421 U.S. 658 (1975).
8. 786 F.2d 1499 (1986).
9. Policy on Civil Penalties, Environmental Protection Agency, Feb. 16, 1984, 17 ELR 35083.
10. *Enforcement: Final Policy on Penalty Reductions Expanded to Include Due Diligence Systems,* 19 CHEMICAL L. REP. 1176 (Dec. 22, 1995).
11. VA. CODE ANN § 1001–1198(B) (1995).
12. Ibid.
13. Ibid
14. Ibid.
15. *More States Adopt Audit Privilege Laws; EPA calls Federal Legislation Ill-Advised,* ENVTL. L. REP. 2186 (March 10, 1995).

16. Ibid.

17. 452 U.S. 264 (1981).

18. 437 U.S. 617 (1978).

19. 112 U.S. 286 (1992).

20. 926 F.2d 1169 (1991).

21. NANCIE G. MARZULLA, The Property Rights Movement: How it Began and Where It Is Headed, in LAND RIGHTS 1–30 (Bruce Yandle, ed., 1995).

22. 114 S.CT. 2309 (1994).

23. MARIANNE LAVELLE & MARCIA COYLE, *Unequal Protection: The Racial Divide in Environmental Law,* NAT. L.J. 52 (Sept. 21, 1992).

24. Ibid.

25. Ibid.

26. Ibid.

27. Ibid.

28. WILLIAM K. REILLY, *EPA's Reilly Replies to "Unequal Treatment,"* NAT. L.J. 16 (Jan. 25, 1993).

29. CONGRESSIONAL RECORD, Dec. 20, 1969, at 40, 417.

30. 340 F. Supp. 532 (1972).

31. JOSEPH SAX, DEFENDING THE ENVIRONMENT: A STRATEGY FOR PUBLIC ACTION 163 (New York: Knopf, 1970).

32. 146 U.S. 387 (1892).

33. 263 N.E. 2d 11 (1970).

CHAPTER 2

The Litigation Process and Other Tools for Resolving Environmental Disputes

Environmental problems are not resolved simply by the passage of environmental regulations. Once regulations are passed, disputes often arise over how the laws should be applied and whether a particular behavior constitutes compliance with the law. Thus, it is important to understand the way laws are interpreted and enforced. In our society such interpretation and enforcement occur primarily through the use of an adversarial system we commonly refer to as *litigation*. The first sections of this chapter explain how this system works and also point out some of the system's flaws. Increasingly, however, litigation is being viewed as a last resort, and alternate methods of dispute resolution are favored. Thus, latter portions of this chapter discuss how various other dispute resolution processes work.

THE ADVERSARY SYSTEM

An Introduction to the Adversary System

Our system of litigation is often referred to as an *adversary system*. In an adversarial system a neutral fact finder hears evidence and arguments presented by both sides and then makes an objective decision based on the facts and the law as presented by the proponents of each side. Strict rules generally govern the types of evidence that the fact finder may consider.

Theoretically, the adversary system is the best way to bring out the truth, because each side aggressively seeks all the evidence that supports its position. Each side attempts to make the strongest possible arguments for its position and points out weaknesses of its opponent's arguments. No shred of evidence is overlooked, and no plausible argument is left unspoken. With all the best evidence and arguments presented, the truth, theoretically, is easily discernible.

Criticisms of the Adversary System

Many people criticize this system. They argue that because each side is searching for only the specific evidence that supports its position, a proponent who discovers evidence helpful to the other side will not bring such evidence to the attention of the court. This tendency to ignore contrary evidence prevents a fair decision, one based on all the available evidence. Another argument of the critics is that the adversary process is extremely time-consuming and costly.

Still others argue that the adversary system, as it functions in the United States, is unfair. Each party in the adversarial process is represented by an attorney. Having the most skillful attorney is a tremendous advantage. Because the wealthier party can afford a better attorney, the system unjustifiably favors the wealthy. In the environmental area, the impact of this disparity can be seen when you consider a group of local citizens banding together to sue a corporation. The corporation may have its own staff of attorneys; and even if the firm has to hire outside counsel, it has the money to do so. The citizens' group, however, must get its money from donations. Often, if a company can tie up a group with a lot of pretrial motions, the costs of attorneys' fees may be so high that the group may have to drop the lawsuit because it simply does not have the money to continue the action.

When used to resolve environmental disputes, the adversarial system is subject to these criticisms, as well as to others. However, perhaps the biggest criticism from environmentalists and some businesspersons is that the adversarial process promotes strife between the parties as each seeks to be the "winner." What is really needed in many environmental cases is not a legal winner but, rather, a creative compromise. Such compromises are generally not discovered in a trial. Litigation is ideally suited for a yes or no decision; either the plaintiff or the defendant wins. In many cases what the parties want is some other objective. The defendant may want to create an industrial park in an area that the plaintiff believes should be preserved. Unfortunately, those kinds of cases are not so easily resolved through our adversarial process.

THE U.S. DUAL COURT SYSTEM

Our adversary system is implemented through the court systems. As makes sense under federalism, we have a dual court system. The system is depicted in figure 2–1.

The Federal Court System

Federal Trial Courts. *Jurisdiction* is the power of a court to hear a case and to render a decision. There are many different types of jurisdiction. The trial court is the court of original jurisdiction. This designation means that it is the court that has the power to initially hear and decide the case. In

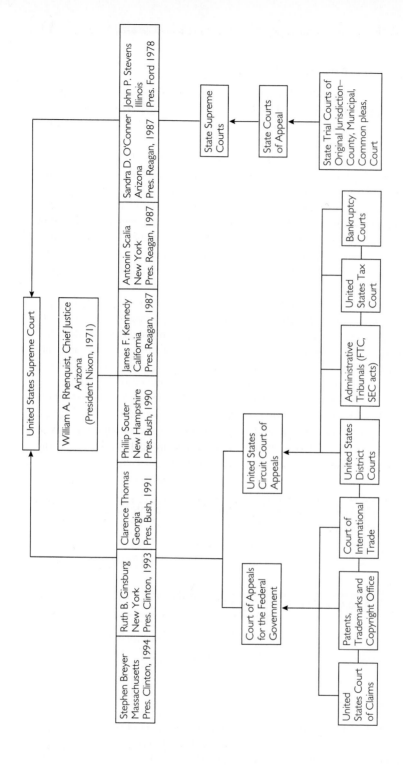

FIGURE 2-1 Our Dual Court System

Source: Kubasek, Nancy, Bartley Brennan, and M. Neil Browne, *The Legal Environment of Business: A Critical Thinking Approach*, page 38 (Prentice Hall, 1996).

the federal court system, the trial courts are the U.S. district courts. The United States is divided into ninety-six districts, and each district has at least one trial court. Almost all cases arising under the federal environmental laws are heard in the federal district courts. Figure 2–2 illustrates this federal system.

Intermediate Courts of Appeals.   The second level of courts in the federal system is made up of the U.S. circuit courts of appeals. The United States is divided into twelve geographic areas, including the District of Columbia, each of which has a circuit court of appeals. There are also federal circuit courts of appeals. Each circuit court of appeals hears appeals from all the district courts located within its area. Appeals from administrative agencies are heard by the federal circuit court of appeals.

Court of Last Resort.   The U.S. Supreme Court is the final appellate court in the federal system. In some instances, the Supreme Court also hears cases from the court of last resort in a state system. As previously noted, the Supreme Court also functions as a trial court in an extremely limited number of cases, such as suits against ambassadors of foreign nations.

The State Court System

There is no uniform state court structure because each state has devised its own court system. All states, however, follow a general structure similar to that of the federal court system.

State Trial Courts.   In state court systems, trial courts, or courts of original jurisdiction, are distributed throughout the state, usually by county. The names of these courts vary from state to state, including such titles as *courts of common pleas* or *county courts*. Cases involving state environmental laws and private tort claims involving environmental matters will generally be brought in these state trial courts of general jurisdiction.

Intermediate courts of appeals, similar to the federal circuit courts of appeals, exist in approximately half the states. These courts usually have broad jurisdiction, hearing appeals from courts of general and limited jurisdiction, as well as from state administrative agencies. The names of these courts also often vary by state. They may be called *courts of appeals* or *superior courts*.

Courts of Last Resort.   In almost all cases filed in the state court system, the last appeal is to the state court of last resort. This court is frequently called the *state supreme court*. In some states, it is known as the *court of appeals*. In approximately half the states, this is the second court to which an appeal can be made; in the other half, it is the only appellate court.

Geographical Boundaries of
United States Courts of Appeals and United States District Courts

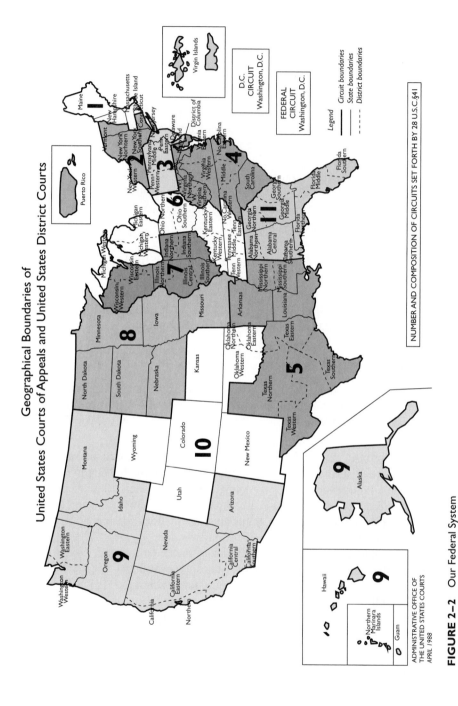

NUMBER AND COMPOSITION OF CIRCUITS SET FORTH BY 28 U.S.C.§41

Legend
—— Circuit boundaries
—— State boundaries
----- District boundaries

ADMINISTRATIVE OFFICE OF
THE UNITED STATES COURTS
APRIL 1988

FIGURE 2–2   Our Federal System

Source: Administrative Office of the United States Courts, April 1988.

Choice of Courts

Knowing that a case must be filed in a trial court does not tell the plaintiff which trial court will hear the case. The choice of which court system to enter is not purely a matter of deciding which forum would be the most desirable. Only in a limited number of cases does a party have the option to choose between the federal and state systems. Even if a party has that choice and chooses the state system, the other party may have the right to have the case removed to the federal system. The determination of which system may hear the case is a matter of subject matter jurisdiction. *Subject matter jurisdiction* is the power of the court to hear and render a decision in a particular type of case. Subject matter jurisdiction is extremely important because when a judge renders a decision in a case over which the court does not have subject matter jurisdiction, the decision is void, or meaningless. The parties cannot grant the judge such jurisdiction; it is determined by law as described in the following paragraphs. Figure 2–3 depicts the relationship among the types of jurisdiction.

Subject Matter Jurisdiction of State Courts. The state court system has jurisdiction over all cases not within the exclusive jurisdiction of the federal

**Exclusive
Federal Jurisdiction**
- Admiralty
- Bankruptcy
- Copyrights, Trademarks, Patents
- Claims against the U.S. Government
- Claims Arising under Statutes Providing for Exclusive Federal Jurisdictions
- Federal Criminal Prosecutions

Concurrent Jurisdiction
- Federal Question
- Diversity of Citizenship

State Court Jurisdiction
- All Cases Not under Exclusive Federal Jurisdiction

FIGURE 2–3 Subject Matter Jurisdiction

Source: Kubasek, Nancy, Bartley Brennan, and M. Neil Browne, *The Legal Environment of Business: A Critical Thinking Approach,* page 112.

court system. Those cases falling within the exclusive jurisdiction of the federal courts are enumerated in the next paragraph. Because the federal courts have exclusive jurisdiction over very few issues, unsurprisingly most litigation occurs in the state system.

Exclusive Federal Jurisdiction.   Cases that fall within the exclusive jurisdiction of the federal courts include such matters as admiralty, bankruptcy, federal criminal prosecutions, claims against the United States, and claims arising under those federal statutes that include a provision for exclusive federal jurisdiction. Cases brought under such statutes must be filed in the federal district court or the appropriate federal court of limited jurisdiction. Many federal environmental statutes grant exclusive jurisdiction to the federal courts.

Concurrent Federal Jurisdiction.   Many cases may be heard in either the federal or the state court. These cases are said to fall within the federal court's concurrent jurisdiction, meaning that both court systems have jurisdiction, so the plaintiff may file in the trial court of either system. There are two types of such cases. The first are federal question cases. If a case requires an interpretation of the U.S. Constitution, a federal statute, or a federal treaty, it is said to involve a federal question and may be heard in either state or federal court. Most federal statutes do not grant exclusive jurisdiction to the federal courts. Many federal environmental statutes give exclusive jurisdiction to the federal courts, but challenges to those that do not may be brought in state or federal court.

The second means by which a case may fall within the federal court's concurrent jurisdiction is through diversity of citizenship. If the opponents in a case are from different states, there is said to be diversity of citizenship. The diversity must be complete. If any two parties on opposing sides reside in the same state, diversity is lost. Also, when the basis for federal jurisdiction is diversity of citizenship, there must be at least $50,000 in controversy.

When a case falls within the federal court's concurrent jurisdiction because of either a federal question or diversity of citizenship, the suit may be filed in either state or federal court. If the case is filed in state court, the defendant has a right of removal, which means that he or she may have the case transferred to federal court. If the plaintiff files in federal court, the case must be heard in that court.

Why should both parties have the right to have such a case heard in federal court? In certain cases a party may fear local prejudice in a state court. Juries for a state court are generally drawn from the county in which the court is located. The juries for federal district courts are drawn from the entire district, which encompasses many counties. Juries in state court are usually more homogeneous than those of a district court. One problem that this homogeneity may present to the out-of-state corporate defendant occurs when the county in which the court is located is predominantly rural. If the case involves an injury to a member of this rural community, the defendant may feel that the jurors would be more sympathetic to the local injured party, whereas jurors drawn from a broader area, including cities, may be more likely to view the victim less sympathetically.

Some people believe that because federal judges have more experience in resolving questions that require an interpretation of federal statutes, they are better qualified to hear such cases. Finally, if a party anticipates that it may be necessary to appeal the case to the U.S. Supreme Court, bringing the case first in a federal district court may save one step in the appeals process.

Venue. Subject matter jurisdiction should not be confused with venue. Once it is determined which court system has the power to hear the case, venue determines which of the many trial courts in that system is appropriate. Venue, clearly prescribed by statute in each state, is a matter of geographic location. It is usually based on the residence of the defendant, the location of the property in dispute, or the location in which the incident out of which the dispute arose occurred. When there are multiple defendants who reside in various geographic locations, the party filing the lawsuit may usually choose from among the various locales. If a corporation is being sued or filing an action, its residence is the place of the corporate headquarters, as well as where the firm has plants or offices. Thus, if a plaintiff residing in Wood County sued a defendant residing in Lucas County over an accident that occurred in Huron County, venue would be appropriate in any of those three counties and the plaintiff may file the case in any of them.

If the location of the court in which the case is filed presents a hardship or inconvenience to one of the parties, that person may request that the case be moved under the doctrine of *forum non conveniens,* which simply means that the location of the trial court is inconvenient. This motion may be granted at the judge's discretion.

PRIMARY ACTORS IN THE LEGAL SYSTEM

An understanding of the structure of the legal system would be incomplete without an awareness of the primary actors within the legal system.

The Attorney

The party with whom environmental groups and business representatives usually have the most frequent contact is the attorney. Although the exact qualifications for being an attorney vary from state to state, most require that he or she have a law degree, have passed the state's bar examination, and be of high moral character. Attorneys are the legal representatives of the parties before the court. Some corporations have full-time attorneys, referred to as in-house counsel; other corporations send all their legal work to an outside law firm.

Attorneys are probably best known for representing clients in litigation, but they also provide other services. Attorneys represent their clients not only in courtroom litigation but also before administrative boards. Attorneys may serve as negotiators. For example, if a developer wants to undertake a project that the area's residents feel will not be environmentally sound, the residents may hire an attorney to negotiate with the developer to try to find an alternate plan. Attorneys also serve as advisers or counselors. Finally, the attorney may serve as a draftsperson, drawing up contracts and other legal documents.

Attorney-Client Privilege. The attorney can provide effective representation only when he or she knows all the pertinent facts. Clients who withhold information from their attorneys may cause irreparable harm if the hidden facts are revealed by the opposing side in court. To encourage client honesty, the attorney-client privilege was established. This privilege provides that information furnished in confidence to an attorney, in conjunction with a legal matter, may not be revealed by that attorney without permission from the client.

This protection also extends to the attorney's work product under what is known as the *work-product doctrine.* The work product includes those formal and informal documents prepared by the attorney in conjunction with the client's case. Thus, if a client fears that his or her company is violating an environmental law and hires an attorney to determine whether the corporate behavior is unlawful, the lawyer may not be called to testify as to the work performed in analyzing the company's behavior.

The Judge

Although few people actually come into contact with a judge, the role of the judge is especially important in our legal system. The judge's function changes, depending on whether he or she is a trial or appellate court judge. A trial court judge presides over the trial, rules on all motions made in the case, and decides all questions of law, such as what evidence is admissible and what items may be obtained through discovery. The judge explains the applicable law through the jury instructions. This judge makes sure that the case is heard with reasonable speed. If the parties waive their rights to a jury trial, or if, under the particular circumstances, they are not entitled to a jury, the judge also decides the facts in the case and renders a decision accordingly. A single judge presides over each case at the trial court level.

Although Thomas Jefferson said, "Ours is a government of laws, not of men," in reality, the "men" (and women) are as important as the laws. In an actual trial, the judge has a great deal of discretion when ruling on matters such as whether to admit a certain piece of evidence over the objection of opposing course. Thus, the careful litigant will always try to know something about the judge's ideology before bringing a case to trial. Certain courts earn reputations as being more pro- or antienvironment, and these reputations influence the types of cases brought to them. For example, the federal district court in Washington, DC, is known for being proenvironment, so environmental activists file cases there whenever possible. Louisiana district courts have the opposite reputation, so business interests file in these courts whenever possible. As new appointments are made, the ideological makeup of courts may change, so attorneys must keep track of changes in the appointees.

Appellate judges serve on panels. They review lower court cases to determine whether errors of law were committed. Their review consists primarily of reading the transcript of the trial, reading written arguments by counsel for both parties, and sometimes hearing oral arguments from both parties' attorneys.

Aside from ideological differences, not all judges have equivalent knowledge about environmental issues. In an attempt to remedy the problem of a lack of understanding of scientific issues related to the environment, the Flaschner Judicial Institute in Boston and the Environmental Law Institute in Washington, DC, have a two-day cram course in environmental law that they offer to judges all over the country.

State court judges are usually elected, although some are appointed, whereas federal court judges are appointed by the president with the advice and consent of the Senate. Federal court judges serve for life; state court judges generally serve definite terms, the length of which varies from state to state. Because of the lifetime tenure of federal judges, many people argue that the most powerful act of a president is the appointment of judges.

The Jury

The *jury* is the means by which citizens participate in our judicial system. It has its roots in ancient Greek civilization and is often considered the hallmark of democracy. A jury is a group of individuals, selected randomly from the geographic area in which the court is located, who will determine questions of fact. There are two types of juries: petit and grand.

Petit Juries.   *Petit juries* serve as the finders of fact for trial courts. Originally composed of twelve members, most juries in civil cases are allowed to have fewer members in many jurisdictions. Traditionally, jury decisions had to be unanimous. Today, however, more than half the jurisdictions no longer require unanimity in civil cases—a change made primarily to speed up trial procedures.

An important decision to be made by any party filing an action is whether to have a jury. In any civil action in which the plaintiff is seeking a remedy at law (money damages), a jury may hear the case. If both parties to the case agree, however, the jury may be waived and a judge decides the facts of the case. There is no rule about when a jury should be chosen, but a few factors should be considered. One is the technical nature of the case. If a case is highly technical, it may be one that can be more fairly decided by a judge, especially one with expertise in the area in dispute. Another factor is the emotional appeal of the case. If the case is one for which the opponent's arguments may have strong emotional appeal, a judge may render a fairer decision. In most environmental law cases, the remedy being sought is an equitable one, such as the granting of an injunction, and whenever a court order such as an injunction is being sought, no jury is allowed.

Grand Juries. *Grand juries* are used only in criminal matters. The Fifth Amendment requires that all federal prosecutions for infamous crimes (including all federal offenses that carry a term of imprisonment in excess of one year) be commenced with an indictment (a formal accusation of the commission of a crime, which must be made before a defendant can be tried for the crime) by a grand jury. This jury hears evidence presented by the prosecutor and determines whether there is enough evidence to justify charging a defendant.

Now that you understand how the court system is structured, and who the primary actors in the system are, it is time to examine how the court system works.

STEPS IN CIVIL LITIGATION

This section focuses on dispute resolution in the United States under the adversary system, in particular, examining the procedures used in a civil case. The rules that govern such proceedings are called the *rules of civil procedure.* There are federal rules of civil procedure, which apply in all federal courts, as well as state rules, which apply in the state courts. Most of the state rules are based on the federal rules. The procedures in a criminal case are very similar to those in a civil case except for the criminal issues of pretrial release of the defendant and sentencing. Figure 2–4 reviews the steps of the litigation process for you.

The Threshold Issues

Before instigating litigation, a party must be sure that his or her case meets certain threshold requirements. These requirements are said to ensure that only those cases really requiring adjudication are before the courts and that both sides of the case are properly represented. These objectives are met by the threshold requirements of standing, case or controversy, and ripeness. It is the requirement of standing that is of greatest importance in environmental cases, so we will discuss this requirement first and in the greatest detail.

Standing. *Standing* is said to be the legal right to bring a lawsuit. One who has standing is said to be a proper party to pursue the action. In most cases,

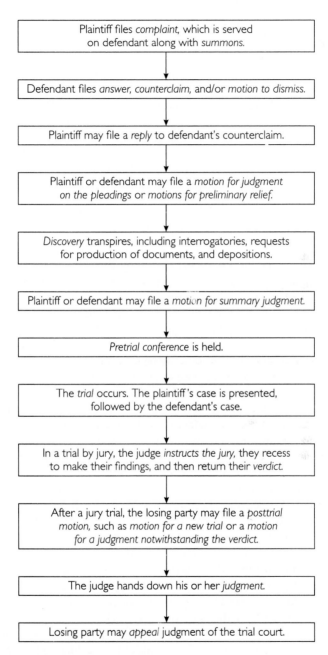

FIGURE 2–4 Anatomy of a Civil Lawsuit

Source: Kubasek, Nancy, Bartley Brennan, and M. Neil Browne, *The Legal Environment of Business: A Critical Thinking Approach,* page 131.

one has standing when he or she is personally affected by the outcome of a case. The personal involvement is believed necessary to stimulate the party to put forth the best possible case.

An important issue, once thought settled that is again controversial, is whether citizens' groups (as opposed to individual citizens) incur sufficient personal injury to have standing to bring an environmental case. The role of citizens' groups in bringing about enforcement of environmental legislation is undeniable. Almost all environmental lawsuits (except for those brought by the EPA) are filed by citizens' groups. During the "environmental decade," 1970 to 1980, when the initial environmental laws were first being interpreted, the most common lawsuit was a public interest group suing the government for allegedly abusing its discretion in administering environmental laws by not applying them with appropriate zeal.[1] These cases were heard only because a long line of cases have granted citizens' groups the right to bring lawsuits to enforce environmental statutes. However, with the more conservative, less activist courts ushered in by Reagan and Bush appointees, the broad standing granted to citizens' groups began to come under fire.

Conservatives have argued unsuccessfully for years that environmental groups should not be able to sue for harms that affect all citizens equally. Standing requires a particularized injury, and because everyone enjoys clean air and clean water, interest groups should not be allowed to sue to enforce these laws. This argument is now being heard anew.

The case that many had feared would begin the shrinking of the role of environmental interest groups in bringing environmental cases is *Lujan v. Defenders of Wildlife,*[2] argued before the U.S. Supreme Court on December 3, 1991. In that case, the Defenders argued that the Endangered Species Act of 1973 should apply to activities that the United States funds in foreign countries. The projects at issue involved the partial use of U.S. funds for an irrigation project in Sri Lanka and funds to rebuild the Aswan Dam on the Nile River, projects that threatened the endangered elephant in Sri Lanka, the crocodile in Egypt, and other species in the areas. Besides arguing on the merits, Lujan raised the standing issue, arguing that, at minimum, a group must show an injury-in-fact caused by the regulation that it is challenging. The Defenders argued that they have standing because they represent members of their organization who had personally visited the sites under regulation to study the endangered species that are to be regulated under the act, a basis for standing that would be sufficient under the traditional definition of standing recognized since the Supreme Court case of *Sierra Club v. Morton.*[3]

In *Sierra Club v. Morton,* the Sierra Club challenged a decision of the Forest Service and Department of the Interior to consider a proposal of Walt Disney Enterprises, Inc., to turn the Mineral King Valley, a national game refuge and quasi-wilderness area, into a resort. The Sierra Club alleged it had standing to seek the injunctions against granting the permits because its membership corporation had "a special interest in the conservation and the sound maintenance of the national parks, game refuges, and forests of the country." The High Court denied standing to the Sierra Club in that case, but the Court's reason for the denial set the basis for the broad interpretation of the standing requirement. The Court denied standing because the Sierra Club "failed to allege that it or any of its members would be affected in any of their activities or pastimes by the Disney development. Nowhere in the pleadings or affidavits did the Club state that its members used Mineral King for any purpose, much less that they use it in any way that would be significantly affected by the proposed actions of the respondents."

Thus, the holding in *Sierra Club v. Morton* made it clear that an organization whose members would be adversely affected by failure to comply with an environmental statute would have standing, and that the requirement of a "particularized injury" was not going to mean that the petitioners had to be the only ones affected by the action. This holding was subsequently reinforced in *United States v. Students Challenging Regulatory Agency Procedures* (SCRAP 1).[4] In SCRAP 1, an unincorporated student group sought an injunction prohibiting the Interstate Commerce Commission from allowing the railroads to collect a 2.5 percent surcharge on goods being transported for purposes of recycling without first filing an environmental impact statement. The commission challenged the standing of the organization to bring the action.

The Supreme Court found a sufficient basis for standing in the student group's allegations that each of its members "suffered economic, recreational and aesthetic harm directly as a result of the adverse environmental effect of the railroad freight structure." The specific harms allegedly suffered were that members had to "pay more for finished products," and that each used "the forest, rivers, streams, and other natural resources surrounding the Washington Metropolitan area and at his legal residence, for camping, hiking, fishing, sightseeing, and other recreational and aesthetic purposes" and these uses were adversely affected by the increased freight rate. The group also alleged that members breathed air that was more polluted because of the rate increase, and that each member had to pay increased taxes because sums had to be expended to dispose of otherwise reusable waste materials. The Court found that the allegations of those specific harms were sufficient to deny a motion to dismiss for lack of standing.

Looking at these two primary precedent-setting cases on the issue of standing in environmental cases, many felt that the defenders' position in *Lujan* would prevail. However, the Supreme Court today is very different from the Court of the 1970s; the *Lujan* court chose to restrict the right of citizens to challenge the enforcement of environmental statutes by restricting the definition of standing. Applying a rigorous standing test advocated by the Bush administration, the opinion of the seven to two majority, written by Justice Antonin Scalia, said that the environmental group did not show that it would suffer an "injury in fact" or demonstrate "redressability." The High Court said that the group needed to demonstrate "not only that the listed species were in fact threatened by funded activities abroad, but also that one or more of [their] members would thereby be 'directly' affected from their 'special interest' in the subject." The Court held that it failed to demonstrate the latter.

Reaction to the decision from environmentalists matched the feelings expressed by the dissent. Justice Blackmun, joined by Justice O'Conner, wrote that the decision was "a slash and burn expedition through the law of environmental standing." He expressed fear that the decision would impose "fresh limitations" on Congress's authority to allow citizens' suits in federal courts for injuries that were "procedural" in nature.[5] Losing counsel for the Defenders was quoted as saying, "I've been in the environmental litigation business for 18 years, and this is an attempt by the Supreme Court to put us all out of business."[6] Three years after his "dire prediction," most commentators agree that the case has not significantly cut back on environmental litigation by citizens' groups.

Case or Controversy.   The requirement that the courts render a decision only when there is a case or controversy before them may seem like a relatively simple matter. In actuality, though, the term *case or controversy* is very imprecise and thus has been subject to changing interpretations. Today, the requirement appears to demand that the case have three essential characteristics. First, the affected parties must be in an adverse relationship to each other. Second, actual or threatened events must give rise to a live legal dispute. Finally, the courts must have the ability to render a final and meaningful judgment. Thus, the courts may give only judgments that solve an existing problem. They cannot provide advisory opinions or provide rulings with respect to hypothetical situations.

Ripeness.   *Ripeness* simply means that there exists a present controversy for which a decision is needed. In other words, the decision must have the capacity to affect the parties immediately. This issue most often comes into play when one party argues that the issue is moot, or no longer ripe. For example, if a party wanted to stop a development because it would cause the loss of an endangered species habitat, but the project had already begun to the extent that the habitat had already been destroyed, the issue would be moot, so the court would not hear the case.

Pretrial

Informal Negotiations.   For anyone involved in a dispute, the first step is to discuss the dispute with an attorney. It is important that the attorney be given all relevant information, even if it does not make the client look good. The more relevant facts the attorney has, the better his or her advice will be. Together, the attorney and the client may be able to resolve the dispute informally with the other party.

Initiation of a Legal Action.   Once a party decides that an informal resolution is not possible, the parties enter what is often called the *pleading stage* of a lawsuit. Pleadings are papers filed by a party in court and then served on the opponent. The basic pleadings (described in detail later) are the complaint, the answer, the counterclaim, and the motion to dismiss. The attorney of the person who feels he or she has been wronged initiates a lawsuit by filing a complaint in the appropriate court. A *complaint* is a document that states the names of the parties to the action, the basis for the court's subject matter jurisdiction, the facts on which the party's claim is based, and the relief that the party is seeking. The party on whose behalf the complaint is filed is the *plaintiff.* The *defendant* is the party against whom the action is being brought. In most environmental cases, the plaintiff is a government agency. The second most common plaintiff is a citizens' group. The most common defendants are also government agencies, and second are corporations.

In determining the appropriate court in which to file the complaint, the attorney must determine which court has subject matter jurisdiction over the case. Once that determination has been made, the attorney must ascertain the proper venue for the case. The means used by the attorney to determine subject matter jurisdiction and venue were discussed earlier in this chapter.

The Court's Acquisition of Jurisdiction over the Person.   Once the complaint is filed, the court serves a copy of the complaint and a summons on the defendant. Service is the procedure used by the court to ensure that the defendant actually receives a copy of the summons and the complaint. The *summons* is an order of the court notifying the defendant of the pending case and telling him or her how and when to respond to the complaint.

Personal service, whereby a sheriff or other person appointed by the court hands the summons and complaint to the defendant, has been the traditional method of service. Today, other types of service are more common. Residential service may be used, whereby the summons and complaint are left by the representative of the court with a responsible adult at the home of the defendant. Certified mail or, in some cases, ordinary mail is also used to serve defendants. When one thinks about how the rules of service would apply to a suit against a corporation, the question arises: How do you serve a corporation? The legal system has solved that question. Most states require that corporations appoint an agent for service when they are incorporated. This agent is a person who has been given the legal authority to receive service for the corporation. Once the agent has been served, the corporation is served. In most states, service on the president of the corporation also constitutes service on the corporation.

The purpose of service of the summons and the complaint is to give the defendant *notice* of the pending action. It also gives the court *jurisdiction over the person* of the defendant. This jurisdiction means that the court has the power to render a decision that is binding on the defendant.

Defendant's Response.   Once the defendant has been properly served, he or she files an answer and possibly a counterclaim. An *answer* is a response to the allegations in the plaintiff's complaint. The answer must admit, deny, or state that the defendant has no knowledge about the truth of each of the plaintiff's allegations. The answer may also contain *affirmative* defenses, which consist of facts that were not stated in the complaint that would provide justification for the defendant actions *and* a legally sound reason to deny relief to the plaintiff. These defenses must be stated in the answer. If they are not raised in the answer, the court may not allow the defenses to be raised later. The defendant is required to plead his or her affirmative defenses in the answer in order to give the plaintiff notice of all the issues that will be raised at the trial.

When a defendant, on receiving the complaint, believes that even if all of the plaintiff's factual allegations were true the plaintiff would not be entitled to a favorable judgment, the defendant may file a *motion to dismiss*. There are no factual issues being debated, so the judge accepts the facts as stated by the plaintiff and makes a ruling on the legal questions in the case. Judges are generally not receptive to such motions.

If the defendant believes that he or she has a cause of action against the plaintiff, this will be included as a *counterclaim*. The form of a counterclaim is just like that of a complaint: The defendant states the facts supporting his or her claim and asks for the relief to which he or she feels entitled. If the defendant files a counterclaim, the plaintiff generally files a reply. A *reply* is simply an answer to a counterclaim. In the reply the plaintiff admits, denies, or states that he or she is without knowledge of the truth of the facts asserted by the defendant in the counterclaim. Any affirmative defenses that are appropriate must be raised in the reply.

After the pleadings have been filed, either party can file a *motion for judgment on the pleadings*. When such a motion is filed, the party is saying that even if all the facts are as alleged by the opposite side's pleadings, the filer should still win the case. Such motions are rarely granted.

Pretrial Motions.   The early pleadings just described serve to establish the legal and factual issues of the case. Once these issues have been established, either the plaintiff or the defendant may file a motion designed to bring the case to an early conclusion or to gain some advantage for the party filing the motion. A *motion* is simply a request by a party for the court to do something. A party may request, or move, that the court do almost anything pertaining to the case.

Discovery.   Once the initial pleadings and motions have been filed, the parties gather information from each other through *discovery*. At this stage a party is frequently asked by her or his attorney to respond to the opponent's requests for information about the case. There are a number of tools of discovery through which these requests are made. One of the most common is *interrogatories*—a series of written questions that are sent to the opposing party, who must truthfully answer them under oath. Interrogatories are frequently accompanied by a *request to admit certain facts.* The attorney and the client work together to answer these interrogatories and requests for admission of facts.

A *request to produce documents* or other items is another tool of discovery. Unless the information requested is privileged or is irrelevant to the case, it must be produced. Photographs, contracts, written estimates, and forms that must be filed with governmental agencies are among the items that may be requested. One party may also request that the other party submit to a mental or physical examination. This motion will be approved only when the party's mental or physical health is at issue in the case.

Finally, testimony before trial may be obtained by the taking of a deposition. At a deposition, a witness is examined under oath by the attorneys. A court reporter (stenographer) records every word spoken by the attorneys and witnesses. The testimony is usually transcribed so that both parties have a written copy. When a person is to be deposed in a case, it is very important that he or she and the attorney talk extensively about what kinds of questions may come up at the deposition and how such questions are to be answered. The party who requested the deposition is not only seeking information but is also laying the groundwork for identifying any inconsistencies that may arise between a person's testimony at the deposition and in court. If such inconsistencies exist, they will be brought to the attention of the fact finder and may result in a loss of credibility for the courtroom testimony.

Depositions may also be used when a potential witness is old or ill and may die before the trial. They are useful if witnesses may be moving or for some other reason may not be available at the time of the trial.

As a result of discovery each party should have knowledge of most of the facts surrounding the case. This process is supposed to prevent surprises from occurring in the courtroom. Parties must comply with requests for discovery, or the court may order that the facts sought to be discovered be deemed admitted as if they had been proved. An attorney who feels that certain material should not be discovered makes arguments about its lack of relevance to the case, but if the court disagrees, the information must be supplied.

Pretrial Conference.   If the judge finds that questions of fact exist, he or she usually holds a pretrial conference. This is an informal meeting of the judge with the lawyers representing the parties. At this meeting, they try to narrow the legal and factual issues and to work out a settlement if possible. When the lawsuit begins, there are many conflicting assertions as to what events led to the lawsuit. Questions about what actually happened are referred to as questions of fact. Many times, as a result of discovery, parties come to agree on most of the facts. Remaining factual disputes may often be resolved at the conference. Then the only questions left are how to apply the law to the facts and what damages, if any, to award. If no settlement can be reached, the attorneys and the judge discuss the administrative details of the trial, its length, the witnesses, and any pretrial stipulations of fact or law to which the parties can agree.

The Trial

Once the pretrial stage has concluded, the next step is the trial. As noted earlier, if the plaintiff is seeking a legal remedy (money damages), he or she is usually entitled to a jury trial. The judge is the fact finder when an equitable remedy (an injunction or other court order) is being sought or the parties have waived their right to a jury. For example, when a plaintiff in a negligence action against a manufacturer that produced a toxic substance requests a judgment for $10,000 in medical expenses, he or she is seeking a legal remedy and is entitled to a jury trial. But a plaintiff seeking an injunction to prohibit the construction of a dam that would destroy the habitat of an endangered species is requesting an equitable remedy and is not entitled to a jury. It is important for a person filing an action to determine at the outset whether a jury is desirable, because a jury must be demanded in the complaint.

The stages of a trial are jury selection, opening statements, plaintiff's case, defendant's case, conference on jury instructions, closing arguments, and posttrial motions.

Jury Selection.   An important part of a jury trial is the selection of the jury. A panel of potential jurors is selected randomly from a list of citizens. In the federal court system, voter lists are used. In a process known as *voir dire,* the attorneys and/or the judge question potential jurors to determine whether they could render an unbiased opinion in the case. In most states each attorney is allowed to reject a minimal number of potential jurors without giving a reason. These rejections are called *peremptory challenges.* Attorneys are given an unlimited number of challenges for cause. *For cause* dismissals are used when questioning reveals a fact that would make it difficult for the potential juror to be impartial.

Jury selection is deemed so crucial to the litigation process that some law firms hire psychologists or jury selection professionals to assist them in the voir dire process. In fact, there is a great deal of debate about whether jury selection is a science, and what impact jury selection has on the outcome of a case. If jury selection is indeed a science, and the use of jury selection consultants can influence the outcome of a case, there are important implications for environmental litigation. The party with the greater financial resources would enjoy a distinct advantage in the courtroom. In most cases the advantaged party would be a corporate defendant. In any event, enough people believe that jury selection is a science that jury consultant firms are springing up across the country.

Opening Statements.   Once a jury has been impaneled, or selected, the case begins with the opening statements. Each party's attorney explains to the judge and the jury what facts he or she intends to prove, the legal conclusions to which these facts will lead, and how the case should be decided.

Plaintiff's Case. The plaintiff then presents his or her case, which consists of examining witnesses and presenting evidence. The procedure for each witness is the same. First, the plaintiff's attorney questions the witness in what is called *direct examination.* Then the opposing counsel may *cross-examine* the witness; only questions pertaining to the witness's direct examination may be asked. The plaintiff's attorney then has the opportunity for redirect examination, to repair any damage done by the cross-examination. The opposing counsel then has a last opportunity to cross-examine the witness to address facts brought out in redirect examination. This procedure is followed for each of the plaintiff's witnesses.

Immediately following the plaintiff's case, the defendant may make a *motion for a directed verdict.* In making such a motion, the defendant is stating to the court that even if all the plaintiff's factual allegations are true, the plaintiff has not proved his or her case. For example, as will be discussed in chapter 4, to prove a case of nuisance, the plaintiff must prove that the defendant used his own property in a manner that interfered with the plaintiff's use or enjoyment of her property. If the plaintiff offers no evidence of how her use or enjoyment of her land has been diminished, then there can be no judgment for the plaintiff. In such a case a motion for a directed verdict would be granted and the case dismissed. Such motions are rarely granted because the plaintiff will usually introduce some evidence of every element necessary to establish the existence of his or her case.

Defendant's Case. If the defendant's motion for a directed verdict is denied, the trial proceeds with the defendant's case in chief. The defendant's witnesses are questioned in the same manner as were the plaintiff's, except that the defendant's attorney does the direct and redirect examination and the plaintiff's attorney is entitled to cross-examine the witnesses.

Conference on Jury Instructions. If the case is being heard by a jury, the attorneys and the judge then retire for a conference on jury instructions. Jury instructions are the court's explanation to the jury of what legal decision they must make if they find certain facts to be true. Each attorney presents to the judge the set of jury instructions he or she feels will enable the jury to accurately apply the law to the facts. The judge confers with the attorneys regarding their proposed instructions and then draws up the instructions for the jury. Attorneys listen very carefully to the instructions the judge gives because one basis for appeal of a decision is that the judge improperly instructed the jury.

Closing Arguments. The attorneys' last contact with the jury then follows when the attorneys present their closing arguments. The party who has the burden of proof, the plaintiff, presents the first closing argument; the defendant's closing argument follows. Finally, the plaintiff is entitled to a rebuttal. The judge then reads the instructions to the jury, and the jurors retire to the jury room to deliberate. When they reach a decision, the jurors return to the courtroom, where their verdict is read.

Posttrial Motions. The party who loses has a number of options. A *motion for a judgment notwithstanding the verdict* (*judgment* N.O.V.) may be made. This is a request for the judge to enter a judgment contrary to that handed down by the jury on the ground that as a matter of law the decision could only have been different from that reached by the jury. For example, if a plaintiff requests damages of $500 but introduces evidence of only $100 worth of damages, the jury cannot award the plaintiff $400 in damages. If they do so, the defendant would file a motion for a judgment notwithstanding the verdict. Alternately, the dissatisfied party may file a motion for a new trial on the ground that the verdict is clearly against the weight of the evidence. If neither of these motions is granted and the judge enters a judgment in accordance with the verdict, the losing party may appeal the decision.

Appellate Procedure

As discussed previously, the court to which the case is appealed depends on the court in which the case was originally heard. A case heard in a federal district court is appealed to the U.S. circuit court of appeals for the geographic region in which the district court is located. If heard in a state trial court, the case is appealed to that state's intermediate appellate court or, if none exists, to the state's final appellate court.

To appeal a case, the losing party must allege that a prejudicial error of law occurred during the trial. A *prejudicial error* is one that is so substantial that it could have affected the outcome of the case. For example, the judge may have ruled as admissible in court certain evidence that had a major impact on the decision, when that evidence was legally inadmissible. Or the party may argue that the instructions the judge read to the jury were inaccurate and resulted in a misapplication of the law to the facts.

When a case is appealed, there is not a new trial. The attorney for the appealing party (the appellant) and the attorney for the party who won in the lower court (the appellee) file briefs, or written arguments, with the court of appeals. They also generally present oral arguments before the appeals court. The court considers these arguments, reviews the record of the case, and renders a decision. The decision of the appellate court can take a number of forms: The court may accept the decision of the lower court and *affirm* that decision. Alternately, the appellate court may conclude that the lower court was correct in its decision, except for granting an inappropriate remedy, and so it will *modify* the remedy. If the appellate court decides that the lower court was incorrect in its decision, that decision will be *reversed*. Finally, the appeals court may feel that an error was committed, but it does not know how that error would have affected the outcome of the case, so it will *remand* the case to the lower court for a new trial.

Although the appeals procedure may sound relatively simple compared to the initial trial procedure, appeals require a great deal of work on the part of the attorneys. They are consequently expensive. Thus, when deciding whether to appeal, a party must consider how much money he or she wishes to spend. In some cases, it may be less expensive to pay the judgment than to appeal.

However, a more important factor to consider when deciding whether to appeal may be the precedential value of the case. The case may involve an important new issue of law that a party hopes may be decided in her or his favor by an appeals court. If she or he anticipates similar prospective suits, it may be important to get a favorable ruling. If the case appears to be strong, an appeal may be desirable. If the case is weak, the wiser move may be to accept the lower court decision and wait for another opportunity to get an appellate ruling. Remember, an appellate precedent carries more weight than a trial court decision.

Appellate courts, unlike trial courts, are usually composed of at least three judges. There are no juries. The decision of the court is determined by the majority of the judges. One of the judges who votes with the majority records the court's decision and their reasons in what is called the *majority opinion*. These have precedential value and are used by judges to make future decisions and by attorneys in advising their clients as to the appropriate course of behavior in similar situations. If any of the judges in a case agrees with the ultimate decision of the majority but for different reasons, he or she may write a *concurring opinion,* stating how this conclusion was reached. Finally, the judge or judges disagreeing with the majority may write their *dissenting opinion,* giving their reasons for reaching a contrary conclusion.

In many important U.S. Supreme Court cases, there is one majority opinion accompanied by several concurring and dissenting opinions. A case that has only one majority opinion signed by all the judges is considered much stronger, and potentially longer lasting, than a majority opinion accompanied by numerous concurring and dissenting opinions. For most cases only one appeal is possible. In some states, where there is both an intermediate and a superior court of appeals, a losing party may appeal from the intermediate appellate court to the state supreme court. In a limited number of cases a losing party may be able to appeal from a state supreme court or a circuit court of appeals to the U.S. Supreme Court.

Appeal to the U.S. Supreme Court.   There are two types of appeals to the U.S. Supreme Court: appeal by writ of certiorari and appeal as of right. The former is the more common type of appeal. To appeal by writ of certiorari, the losing party files a petition with the Supreme Court in which he or she argues that the issue on which the appeal is based either presents a substantial federal question or involves a matter that has produced conflicting decisions from the various circuit courts of appeal and is in need of resolution. The Supreme Court reviews the petition and may decide to review the case if at least four justices are convinced that it is a matter in need of resolution.

It is often difficult to predict whether the Court will hear a case. A federal question is simply an issue arising under the federal Constitution, treaties, or statutes. Substantiality is more difficult to define. If the decision would affect a large number of people, or is likely to arise again if not decided, it may be considered substantial. If the Supreme Court refuses to hear a case, such refusal has no precedential effect.

In a limited number of cases the losing party is entitled to nondiscretionary appeal as of right. When parties are entitled to an appeal as of right, they file a notice of appeal, and the Supreme Court must review the case on its merits. For example, if a state supreme court holds that a federal statute is unconstitutional, this ruling can be appealed as of right. In both appeals by writ and as of right, the appeal may be limited to the Court's simply reviewing the transcript of the lower court case. It is up to the Court to determine whether it wants to hear oral arguments and read written briefs.

ALTERNATIVES TO CIVIL LITIGATION

The litigation process seems extremely time-consuming and expensive to many people, so unwieldy that they have turned to other means to resolve their disputes. In the environmental arena the two main alternatives are arbitration and mediation. Both these alternate methods share certain advantages over litigation. Generally, they are less expensive and less time-consuming, and the formal hearing times and places can be set at the parties' mutual convenience. The persons presiding over the resolution process can be chosen by the parties and, in many cases, are more familiar with the area of law over which the dispute arose than would be a randomly assigned judge. These alternatives may also prevent adverse publicity, which could be ruinous to a business. They may also result in the preservation of confidentiality, which may be extremely important when a company's trade secrets are involved.

The following detailed examination of these alternate dispute-resolution methods should help you understand the types of situations wherein each of these alternatives may be preferable to litigation. One problem that sometimes arises in the decision to use an alternate form of dispute resolution is that in many cases arbitration or mediation may benefit one party, whereas litigation may be more beneficial to the other.

Arbitration

Arbitration—the resolution of a dispute by a neutral third party outside the judicial setting—is one of the most well-known alternatives to litigation, although not the most common form used to resolve environmental matters. The arbitration hearing is somewhat similar to a trial, but there is no prehearing discovery process. The stringent rules of evidence applicable in a trial are generally relaxed in arbitration. Each side presents witnesses and evidence, and the parties are given the opportunity to cross-examine their opponent's witnesses. The arbitrator frequently takes a much more active role in questioning witnesses than would a judge. An arbitrator who needs to know more information will generally ask for that information from witnesses.

Differing from a trial, there is usually no official record of the hearing. However, the parties and the arbitrator may agree to have a stenographer record the proceedings at the expense of the parties. Often, to save money, a party may consult an attorney to help plan the arbitration strategy, but the party appears at the arbitration without the lawyer. Individuals may represent themselves or may have someone else represent them. In some cases, the arbitrator may request written arguments from the parties. These documents are called *arbitration briefs.*

The arbitrator usually provides a decision for the parties within thirty days of the hearing. He or she may provide the reasons for the decision but is not required to do so. The decision rendered by the arbitrator is much more likely to be a compromise decision than is the decision handed down by a court, for a number of reasons. First, the arbitrator is not as constrained by precedent as are judges, although of course he or she cannot render a decision that is clearly contrary to the law. Second, the arbitrator may be more interested than a judge in preserving an ongoing relationship with the parties. A compromise is much more likely to achieve this result than is a clear win-or-lose decision. Finally, because an arbitrator frequently decides cases in a particular area, he or she wants to maintain a reputation of being fair to both sides so as to be selected to decide future cases.

The decision rendered by the arbitrator is legally binding. The decision may be appealed through the court system, but judges will only rarely overturn an arbitrator's decision. Usually the only basis for overturning the decision is that the arbitrator exceeded the bounds of his or her authority. Such a high standard for review may seem to give an arbitrator more power than the trial court.

Methods of Securing Arbitration. There are three basic methods by which parties can secure arbitration. One means is by inclusion of a binding arbitration clause in a contract. Such a clause provides that all or certain disputes arising under the contract are to be settled by arbitration. The clause should also include the means by which the arbitrator is to be selected.

If no arbitration clause is included in a contract and a dispute arises over its terms, the parties may secure arbitration by entering into a submission agreement. This is a written contract stating that the parties wish to settle their dispute by arbitration. It usually also states the means by which the arbitrator will be selected and the limits of the arbitrator's authority.

If the parties have entered into a submission agreement or have included an arbitration clause in their contract, they will be required to resolve their disputes through arbitration. Both federal and state courts must defer to arbitration if the contract in dispute contains a binding arbitration clause.

Selection of an Arbitrator. Once the decision to arbitrate has been made, an arbitrator must be selected. Arbitrators are generally lawyers, professors, or other professionals. They are frequently selected on the basis of their special expertise in some area. If the parties have not agreed on an arbitrator before a dispute, they generally use one of two sources for selecting an arbitrator: the Federal Mediation and Conciliation Service (FMCS), a governmental agency, or the American Arbitration Association (AAA), a private, nonprofit organization.

When the disputants contact one of these agencies, they receive a list of arbitrators along with a biographical sketch of each. Once the arbitrator has been selected, the parties and the arbitrator agree on the time, date, and location of the arbitration. They also agree on the substantive and procedural rules to be followed in the arbitration.

Disadvantages of Arbitration. The most significant reason for not using arbitration would probably be that the decision does not create a legally binding precedent, which may be important in many cases. Less importantly, a party may want the publicity generated by a lawsuit, which arbitration does not usually provide. Another problem with arbitration is that the lengthy court procedures that arbitration omits serve to protect parties from surprise and unfair admission of questionable evidence. The protection of thorough review on appeal is also lost.

Mediation

Since the mid-1970s, mediation has been used increasingly to resolve environmental disputes, especially those involving complex issues and multiple parties with different interests. Between 1974 and 1984, mediation was used to solve approximately 160 environmental disputes involving matters that ranged from air quality to land use to toxic waste. Mediation differs from arbitration and litigation in that the mediator makes no final decision. The mediator is simply a facilitator of communication between disputing parties. Mediation is an informal process in which the two disputants select a party, usually one with expertise in the disputed area, to help them reconcile their differences. Although there is no guarantee that a decision will be reached through mediation, if a decision is reached, the parties generally enter into a contract that embodies the terms of their settlement. If one party does not live up to the terms of the settlement, that party can then be sued for breach of contract.

Advantages of Mediation.   Among environmentalists, agency employees, and businesspersons, mediation has both its supporters and its detractors. Although not all environmental issues are suitable for mediation, clearly all environmental issues are not appropriate for litigation, either. The primary advantage of mediation is that because of its nonadversarial nature, it tends to preserve the relationship between the parties to a greater extent than would a trial or an arbitration. Thus, it is used more and more frequently in cases in which the parties will have an ongoing relationship once the immediate dispute is settled. Many times in community disputes, parties will find themselves in conflict; conceivably, mediation could help each understand the other a little better, so future disagreements might be resolved more easily.

A second advantage is that mediation can be quicker. With the ever-increasing federal court caseload, delays are inevitable. Mediation can be almost instantaneous, once a mediator is chosen. Because many environmental issues demand a quick response, mediation may be desirable. Mediation may be less expensive than litigation. At minimum, mediation eliminates the cost of hiring expensive expert witnesses to testify at the trial. An extremely complex mediation may cost thousands of dollars, but an expensive lawsuit may run into the millions.

Another reason why mediation may be desirable for environmental problems is that in many cases the environmental issue does not fit neatly into the two-party, right-wrong mode of litigation. Often the environmental matter may involve numerous groups with varying interests. A creative solution that takes into account multiple interests is needed. Mediation provides a forum in which an unlimited number of interests can be heard, and a solution other than a "winner takes all" judgment for the plaintiff or no liability for the defendant can be attained. Even if a solution cannot be reached, mediation will have at least served to help educate the parties as to the other's position. And in the future, if the parties have to deal with each other, they may be a little more understanding and be able to work out problems together.

Disadvantages of Mediation.   Sometimes mediation is clearly inappropriate. If you want to establish a precedent-setting interpretation of a case, you have no choice but to go to court. A related problem is that mediation may produce more inconsistent outcomes. Arguably, this disparity of outcomes could be considered unfair.

Also, if part of a party's objectives include getting publicity that it hopes will turn public opinion against a project strongly enough to block the project, then, again, mediation is not appropriate. In many environmental disputes, the greatest benefit of litigation for a citizens' group may be in creating public awareness that it hopes will lead to public pressure to prohibit some action.

Finally, no one can be forced to mediate. If one person whose interests are affected chooses to not mediate, even if twenty other affected interests agree to a mediated solution, the party who did not participate may still raise the issue through litigation. Sometimes those involved in the mediation may not be aware of an affected party who consequently is not included in the mediation. That party may later litigate. Even worse, a party who wants to tie up a project may agree to mediation and go through the process, fully intending not to reach any agreement. The party is simply "tying the case up" in mediation. Once the other party realizes what is going on, the case may then be litigated, but by that time there has been a costly delay.

Critics of mediation often argue that the informal nature of the process represses and denies certain irreconcilable structural conflicts, such as the inherent strife between developers and environmentalists. They also argue that this informal process tends to create the impression of equality between the disputants when no such equality exists. The resultant compromise between unequals is an unequal compromise, but it is clothed in the appearance of equal influence. Despite these criticisms, mediation has its place in the resolution of environmental disputes. It will probably always be a supplement to, and not a replacement for, litigation.

CONCLUDING REMARKS

You now understand how the U.S. dual court system is structured and functions. Dispute resolution through our courts is an adversarial process, so disputes are managed by two conflicting parties, represented by lawyers, each of whom tries to bring out the strongest evidence and make the best argument for his or her side. A neutral third party, either a judge or jury, will decide who is the winner.

This adversarial process, however, is not well suited for many disputes, especially environmental ones. It is time-consuming, publicity-generating, does not lead to compromise resolutions, and often worsens the relationship between two parties who must work with each other in the future. Because of these problems, alternatives to litigation increasingly are being used to resolve environmental disputes. Some of the more common alternatives include arbitration and mediation. Mediation is probably the most common because it preserves the parties' relationship and also allows the easiest inclusion of a multiplicity of interests.

Once you appreciate how the dispute resolution systems function, there is only one more area of the American legal system that you need to understand before you are ready to explore environmental law: administrative law. Chapter 3 introduces this important system of law.

QUESTIONS FOR REVIEW AND DISCUSSION

1. Explain what is meant by an *adversary system* and justify the use of such a system.
2. Explain the problems associated with reliance on the adversarial process to resolve environmental disputes.
3. Distinguish subject matter jurisdiction from jurisdiction over the person.
4. Explain the various roles a lawyer may play.
5. Distinguish a grand jury from a petit jury.
6. Explain the significance of the standing cases such as *Lujan v. Defenders of Wildlife* and *Sierra Club v. Morton.*
7. Trace the steps of a civil lawsuit.
8. Explain and critique the primary alternatives to litigation.

FOR FURTHER READING

Comment, *Calm after the Storm: Grandmother of Environmental Lawsuits Settled by Mediation,* 11 ENVTL. L. REP. 10074 (1981).

WILLIAM FUNK, *Justice Breyer and Environmental Law,* 8 ADMIN. L.J. AM. U. 735 (1995).

THOMAS HOBAN & RICHARD BROOKS, GREEN JUSTICE: THE ENVIRONMENT AND THE COURTS (Boulder, Colo.: Westview Press, 1987).

JAN MCDONALD, *Public Interest Environmental Litigation—Chipping Away at Procedural Obstacles,* 12 ENVTL. PLAN. L.J. 140 (1995).

Note, Lujan v. National Wildlife Federation: *The Supreme Court Tightens the Reins on Standing for Environmental Groups,* 40 CATH. U.L. REV. 443 (1991).

J. SAX, *The Public Trust Doctrine in Natural Resource Law: Effective Judicial Intervention,* 68 MICH. L. REV. 471 (1970).

D. SINGER, *The Use of ADR Methods in Environmental Disputes,* 47 ARB. L.J. 55 (March 1992).

DAVID SIVE, *Environmental Standing,* 11 NAT. RESOURCES ENV'T. 49 (Fall 1995).

CHRISTOPHER STONE, SHOULD TREES HAVE STANDING? TOWARD LEGAL RIGHTS FOR NATURAL OBJECTS (Los Altos, Calif.: William Kaufmann, 1974).

PETER WENZ, ENVIRONMENTAL JUSTICE (Albany: State University of New York Press, 1988).

MATTHEW M. WERNER, *Mootness and Citizen Suit Civil Penalty Claims under the Clean Water Act: A Post Lujan Reassessment.* 25 ENVTL. L. 801 (1995).

ROBERT WIYGUL, *Eight Years Later: Proving Jurisdiction and Article III Standing in Clean Water Act Citizen Suits,* 8 TUL. ENVTL. L.J. 435 (1995).

ON THE INTERNET

http://www.gama.com/director.htm
A directory of ADR providers and organizations

http://www.dnai.com/tvlf/vlf_arbitration.html
Information about alternative dispute resolution

http:/www.adr.org/
Home page of the American Arbitration Association

NOTES

1. LETTIE WENNER, THE ENVIRONMENTAL DECADE IN COURT (Bloomington: Indiana University Press, 1982).
2. 405 U.S. 727 (1972).
3. 405 U.S. 727 (1972).
4. 412 U.S. 669 (1973).
5. M. COYLE & M. HAVELLE, *Eco-Groups' Standing Curtailed,* NAT'L. L.J. 3 (June 1992).
6. Ibid.

CHAPTER 3

Administrative Law and Its Impact on the Environment

Environmental law is classified as a branch of administrative law. This classification means that these laws are overseen by a body known as an administrative agency, and that many of the specific regulations in this area are also established by this agency. Because environmental law falls within this classification, some basic understanding of administrative law is necessary.

The first part of this chapter explains how administrative agencies are created. Next, their primary functions, rule making, adjudication, and administrative activities, are described. The third section focuses on the ways in which the primary branches of the U.S. government control these agencies. The chapter concludes with a description of some of the major agencies affecting the environment.

The first federal administrative agencies were created by Congress near the end of the nineteenth century and the beginning of the twentieth. They were the Interstate Commerce Commission (ICC) and the Federal Trade Commission (FTC). Congress felt that the anticompetitive conduct of railroads and other corporations could best be controlled by separate regulatory bodies with defined statutory mandates. Following the crash of the stock market and the Great Depression of the 1930s, Congress saw a need for additional agencies that could assist in guiding market decisions in the public interest. Since then, numerous agencies have been created whenever Congress believed there was an area that required more intense regulation than Congress could provide.

An administrative agency is generally defined as any body created by a legislative branch (e.g., Congress, a state legislature, or a city council) to carry out specific duties. Most agencies, however, are not situated entirely in the legislative, the executive, or the judicial branch of government. They generally have legislative power to make rules for an entire industry, judicial power to adjudicate (decide) individual cases, and executive power to investigate corporate misconduct. Numerous agencies play a role in creating and enforcing environmental regulations; especially important is the Environmental Protection Agency (EPA).

CREATION OF ADMINISTRATIVE AGENCIES

Congress creates most administrative agencies through statutes called *enabling legislation,* although the president sometimes creates administrative agencies through an executive reorganization plan. Generally, the enabling statutes contain broad delegations of congressional legislative power to agencies for the purpose of serving the "public interest, convenience, and necessity." This power to create rules is sometimes referred to as *quasi legislative* because the agency's rule-making authority is limited in scope to the authority it is granted by Congress. Using this mandate, a particular administrative agency issues rules that control individual and business behavior. In many instances, such rules carry civil, as well as criminal, penalties.

When passing an enabling statute, Congress also delegates executive power to agencies to investigate potential violations of rules or statutes. Through enabling stat tes, Congress also delegates judicial power to settle or adjudicate individual disputes that an agency may have with businesses or individuals. For example, the EPA administrator, using the congressional mandate under the Clean Air Act, sets forth rules governing the amount of certain hazardous air pollutants that may be emitted into the atmosphere. Using these standards, another branch of the EPA sends investigators to inspect a plant suspected of violating the act. If the inspector finds a violation and the EPA imposes a penalty, the plant operator will most likely contest the imposition of the fine, and a hearing will be held before an administrative law judge employed in another division of the EPA.

Because legislative, executive, and judicial powers have traditionally been placed in separate branches of government by the Constitution, the role of administrative agencies has led some to state that an unofficial "fourth branch of government" really exists. Although there is a semblance of truth to that characterization, administrative agencies are not in fact another branch, primarily because all their authority is simply delegated to them and they remain under the control of the three traditional branches of government. They are not as independent as the term *fourth branch of government* might imply.

FUNCTIONS OF ADMINISTRATIVE AGENCIES

Administrative agencies perform the following functions: rule making; adjudication of individual cases brought before administrative law judges by the staff of an agency; and administrative activities.

Rule Making

Americans are probably most familiar with administrative agencies because of their rule-making powers. Administrative agencies are granted the authority to perform the legislative function of making rules or regulations by the enabling statutes that bring them into existence. For example, the enabling statute creating the Occupational Safety and Health Administration gave the secretary of labor authority to set "mandatory safety and health standards applicable to businesses affecting interstate commerce." The secretary was given the power to "prescribe such rules and regulations that he may deem necessary to carry out the responsibilities under this act." In some cases, the procedures for implementing the rule-making function are spelled out in the enabling act. When this is not done, one of three alternate models for rule making may be used: informal, formal, or hybrid.

One reason for the creation of administrative agencies has been the idea that they could be staffed with people who had expertise in the area the agency was regulating and therefore would be capable of knowing what types of regulations were necessary to protect citizens. Also, because they were not elected, agency employees, in their rule-making capacity, would not be subject to political pressure. Agencies would also be able to act more swiftly than Congress in enacting laws. Today, administrative agencies actually create more rules than Congress and the courts combined.

As you read about the administrative rule-making procedures, compare them to the legislative process; it is much easier for the public to participate in agency rule making. One reason for the relatively great opportunity for public participation is concern on the part of Congress that people would be upset about laws being made by unelected individuals.

Informal Rule Making.   The primary type of rule making used by administrative agencies is informal, or notice-and-comment, rule making. As provided by Section 553 of the Administrative Procedure Act (APA), informal rule making applies in all situations in which the agency's enabling legislation or other congressional directives do not require another form. An agency initiates informal rule making by publishing in the *Federal Register* the proposed rule, along with an explanation of the legal authority for issuing the rule and a description of how one can participate in the rule-making process. Following this publication, opportunity is provided for all interested parties to submit written comments. These comments may contain data, arguments, or other information a person believes might influence the agency in its decision making. Although the agency is not required to hold hearings, it has the discretion to receive oral testimony if it wishes to do so. After considering the comments, the agency publishes the final rule, with a statement of its basis and purpose, in the *Federal Register.* This publication also includes the date on which the rule becomes effective, which must be at least thirty days after publication. Figure 3–1 depicts this process.

Informal rule making is most often used because it is more efficient for the agency in terms of time and cost. No formal public hearing is required, and no formal record need be established, as would be true in formal rule making. Some people, however, believe that informal rule making is unfair

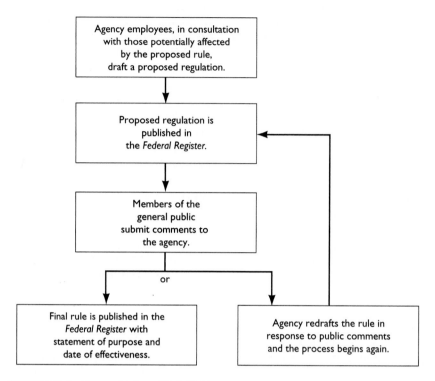

FIGURE 3–1 Stages of Informal Rule Making

because parties who are interested in the proposed rule have no idea what types of evidence the agency has received from other sources with respect to that rule. Thus, if the agency is relying on what one party might perceive as flawed or biased data, that party has no way to challenge those data. A second type of rule making, formal rule making, avoids that problem.

Formal Rule Making.　Section 553(c) of the APA requires formal rule making when an enabling statute or other legislation requires that all regulations or rules be enacted by an agency as part of a formal hearing process that includes a complete transcript. This procedure is initiated in the same manner as is informal rule making, with publication of a notice of proposed rule making by the agency in the *Federal Register.* The second step in formal rule making is a public hearing at which witnesses give testimony on the pros and cons of the proposed rule and are subject to cross-examination. An official transcript of the hearing is kept. Based on information received at the hearing, the agency makes and publishes formal findings. On the basis of these findings, an agency may or may not promulgate a regulation. If a regulation is adopted, the final rule is published in the *Federal Register.* Because of the expense and time involved in obtaining a formal transcript and record, most enabling statutes do not require a formal rule-making procedure when promulgating regulations.

Hybrid Rule Making. After agencies began regularly making rules in accordance with the appropriate procedures, the flaws of each type of rule making became increasingly apparent. In response to these problems a form of hybrid rule making became acceptable to the courts and legislature. Hybrid rule making is an attempt to combine the best features of both. The starting point, publication in the *Federal Register,* is the same. This publication is followed by the opportunity for submission of written comments and then an informal public hearing with a more restricted opportunity for cross-examination than in formal rule making. The publication of the final rule is the same as for other forms of rule making.

Exempted Rule Making. Section 553 of the APA contains an exemption from rule making that allows an agency to decide whether public participation will be allowed. The APA exempts public rule-making proceedings with regard to "military or foreign affairs" and "agency management or personnel." Exemptions are also granted for rule-making proceedings relating to "public property, loans, grants, benefits or contracts" of an agency.

Also exempted from the rule-making procedures are interpretive rules and general policy statements. An interpretive rule is a rule that does not create any new rights or duties but is merely a detailed statement of the agency's interpretation of an existing law. These interpretive rules are generally very detailed, step-by-step statements of what actions a party would take to be considered in compliance with an existing law. Policy statements are general statements about directions in which any agency intends to proceed with respect to its rule-making or enforcement activities. Again, these statements have no binding impact on anyone; they do not directly affect anyone's legal rights or responsibilities.

A final exemption is when public notice and comment procedures are "impracticable, unnecessary, or contrary to the public interest." This exemption is used most commonly when either the issue is so trivial that there would probably be very little, if any, public input or when the nature of the rule necessitates immediate action. Whenever an agency chooses to use this exception, it must make a "good cause" finding and include in its publication of the final rule a statement explaining why there was no public participation in the process.

Judicial Review of Rule Making. Following the promulgation of a regulation by an administrative agency and its publication in the *Federal Register,* the regulation becomes law. Often, however, regulated interests may not be happy with a law that an agency promulgates. These disgruntled parties have two options. First, they may immediately bring an action in the federal district court to have the law invalidated. An alternate approach is just to ignore the law. When the agency tries to fine the party for violating the law, the party's defense would be that the rule was not valid. If the administrative law judge upholds the rule, the party may appeal the case to the federal district court and on through the appeals process.

Generally, appellate courts have accepted an agency-promulgated regulation as law unless a business, other groups, or individuals affected can prove it is invalid for one of four reasons. One reason is that the congressional delegation of legislative authority in the enabling act was unconstitutional because it was *too vague* and did not properly limit the agency's actions in any way. A second claim is that an agency action *violated a constitutional standard,* such as the right to be free from unreasonable searches and seizures under the Fourth Amendment. For example, if an agency like OSHA promulgated a rule that allowed its inspectors to search a business property at any time without permission of the owners, and without an administrative search warrant, this law would be struck down as a violation of the Fourth Amendment.

A third alternative is to show that the act of an agency was *beyond the scope of power* granted to it by Congress in its enabling legislation. In other words, the agency passed a rule that it had no authority to delegate. Finally, a party could demonstrate that the agency *did not follow the proper procedures* in promulgating the rule. For example, the agency was required by its enabling statute to engage in formal rule making but instead followed informal rule-making procedures.

You are correct if you believe that these four circumstances seem highly unlikely. It is very unusual for a court to strike down an administrative rule. Despite the low success rate of such challenges, firms continue to challenge agency rules. For example, approximately 80 percent of the rules made by the EPA from 1987 through 1991 have been challenged in court. Even if such a challenge is not successful, it still buys time for the firm. The firm may be able to get a temporary injunction prohibiting enforcement of the law until there is a final decision in the case. Many times the appeals process will last for years; the resulting delay can save a firm a substantial amount of money, especially when the cost of compliance is high.

Regulated Negotiation.   The exceedingly high number of challenges to regulations, as well as a growing belief that structured bargaining among competing interest groups might be the most efficient way to develop rules, has stimulated interest in a number of agencies in a relatively new form of rule making, often referred to as *reg-neg*. Each concerned interest group and the agency itself send representatives to bargaining sessions led by a mediator. After the parties achieve a consensus, that agreement is forwarded to the agency.

The agency is then expected to publish the compromise as a proposed rule in the *Federal Register* and follow through with the requisite rule-making procedures. The agency, however, is not bound to do so. If it does not agree with the proposal the group negotiated, the agency is free to try and promulgate a completely different rule or a modification of the one obtained through the negotiation. The reasoning behind reg-neg is similar to that supporting the increased use of mediation. The parties who hammer out an agreement have a stake in making it work because they helped to create it.

Admittedly, reg-neg is not possible in all situations. If, for example, there were an unmanageably large group of interests that would have to be represented, if any possible compromise would have to result from one group backing away from a fundamental principle, or if two groups feel so antagonistic toward each other that they are unable to rationally sit down and talk, reg-neg would probably not be worth trying.

Problems Associated with Rule Making.   Although there is an expediency associated with this process of rule making, critics are quick to point out that some problems are associated with this process. Agency employees are not subject to the same political pressures as legislators, but they are not necessarily unbiased "scientists." Many of the people with the necessary expertise to regulate specific areas come from the industry they are now going to be regulating. Many people believe that it will be difficult for regulators to ignore their past and potential ties to industry and pass the regulations that are in the public interest, especially when the regulations would increase costs to the industry or are opposed by the industry for other reasons. When people are discussing an agency in which they perceive this problem as existing, they will often refer to the agency as being a "captured" agency. The counterargument is that those who have been deeply involved in an industry know it best.

Rule making in the environmental area is especially difficult, because there is so much uncertainty surrounding the causes and consequences of pollution. There is often a significant lag between exposure and the resultant detrimental health effects or ecological changes, making it difficult to ascertain the impact of a given pollutant. There is very little agreement as to how much certainty is needed before a regulation should be imposed. Even when we have a little knowledge about a single pollutant's effects, we know less about synergistic effects, that is, the effects brought about by the interactions of various pollutants.

Another problem associated with environmental rule making is that though many of the costs of regulation are borne immediately, the benefits flow primarily to future generations. Thus, many people question how much the present generation can be asked to sacrifice for future generations. This question becomes complicated by the fact that sometimes those costs are borne by those with the least economic and political power.

Regulators in the environmental area are confronted with a difficult task. With respect to almost every standard they set, they must balance the risk to society with the cost of expenditures for pollution-control equipment. And they know that almost every standard they set is going to be challenged in court by the regulated industries, which will see the standards as too stringent, and the environmental groups, which will see them as too weak.

An issue that has been increasingly arising in debates over environmental policies is the impact that the costs of compliance will have on the competitiveness of U.S. firms in a global economy. Yet the effects of pollution-control compliance on global competitiveness are unknown. We can gather data on costs of pollution-control equipment in the United States, but we do not know how much other nations' industries spend. Nor do we know how much increased efficiency the pollution-control equipment generates.

As you will read in chapter 10, differences in environmental regulation have become important in trade agreements. We know that some firms have left the United States to go to less-developed countries where there are less-stringent pollution-control regulations. However, not all firms that move do so just to avoid environmental regulations; some may also be seeking cheaper labor or material costs.

Finally, regulators must be sensitive to the role the economy plays in the public's willingness to accept or support environmental regulations. When the economy is flourishing and unemployment is low, there is much greater acceptance of regulations. When unemployment is high, people are more reluctant to accept regulations that they believe might cause some workers to lose their jobs and/or cause the prices of products to rise.

Adjudication

In addition to rule making, adjudication of individual cases is another important agency activity. The number of cases heard by administrative law judges is extremely high: In 1983, one-third more cases were referred to administrative law judges than were filed in the federal district courts. The APA again sets forth the steps for adjudication, which can be modified by an agency's enabling statute. APA Sections 554, 556, and 557 set out the minimal standards for adjudication whenever an agency's adjudication is "required by statute to be determined on the record after opportunity for an agency hearing."

An agency adjudication is generally preceded by an investigation and the filing of a complaint with an administrative law judge (ALJ) by the agency staff. The party against which the agency is taking the action is entitled to notice of the time and place of the hearing, the authority the agency is relying on, and the "matters of fact and law asserted." A hearing is then conducted by the ALJ, followed by an initial decision. An appeal to the full commission or the head of an agency may then be filed. That decision may then be appealed to the circuit court of appeals. Figure 3–2 illustrates the steps of this administrative adjudication process.

The Environmental Protection Agency (and approximately eight other federal agencies) has so many appeals that a special board has been set up within the agency to handle certain types of appeals. On March 1, 1992, a special three-person board began operation to handle appeals of penalty deci-

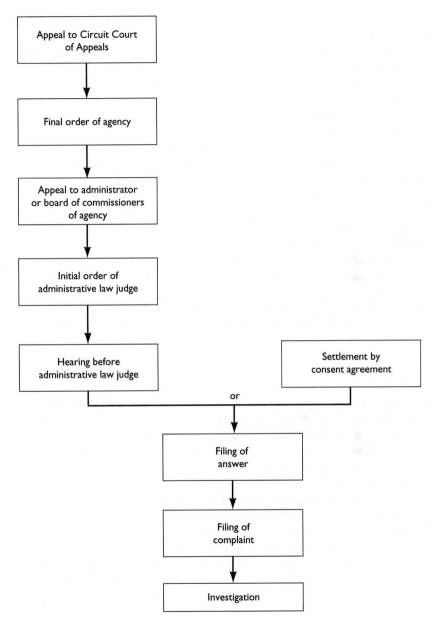

FIGURE 3-2 Steps in Administrative Adjudication

sions made by EPA administrative law judges and appeals of permit decisions in the EPA's ten regions. This board was created in anticipation of a crush of environmental disputes that are expected to be heard by administrative law judges and then appealed in the mid- and late-1990s.

The administrative adjudication process is extremely important because most agencies rely primarily on administrative actions to enforce their regulations. This enforcement strategy is especially true in the environmental area. Administrative actions are often preferred to taking a violator to trial because they are generally quicker, less expensive, and less resource-intensive than a trial. An administrative proceeding may be handled by an agency employee, whereas in order to prosecute a violator in court, a federal agency must turn the case over to the Justice Department and a state agency must refer the case to the state attorney general.

As a result of an administrative action, an agency can issue a compliance order, which may require immediate action by a violator, or a timetable that must be followed in moving toward compliance. The order may contain daily penalties for noncompliance or include provisions for suspension or revocation of a violator's operating permit under appropriate circumstances.

Administrative agencies may also issue corrective orders. These orders are comparable to court orders for specific performance. For example, a corrective order may require a violator that has released water containing waste into a river to install equipment that would filter out the waste before the water is released.

Penalties for Noncompliance.   Each of the environmental laws that you will be reading about contains provisions for administrative, civil, and criminal actions. Generally, administrative penalties are less than civil and criminal penalties. By providing lesser penalties for administrative actions, violators are encouraged to settle early. In one EPA case, a violator was encouraged to settle for a $200 agency fine. The violator refused, and the case was turned over to the Justice Department. The federal district court awarded the statutory penalty of $10,000.[1]

In light of the substantial difference between administrative penalties and civil and criminal awards, it is not surprising that violators are often willing to settle for small administrative penalties. Table 3–1 shows the difference between judicial and administrative penalties assessed for fiscal years 1978 through 1989.

Citizen Rewards.   As you will discover as you read more about specific environmental laws, often violations are discovered not by the agencies themselves but by citizens. In order to motivate citizens, most federal and state agencies involved in environmental enforcement have various types of reward programs to encourage them to bring forth evidence of environmental violations. The EPA, for example, administers Superfund Citizen Award Provision, paying up to $10,000 for information leading to a successful criminal prosecution.

TABLE 3-1 Penalty Assessments in Civil Cases Relating to Environmental Law, Fiscal Years 1978-1989

Year	Civil Judicial	Administrative	FY Total
FY78	1,313,873	25,000	1,338,873
FY79	4,028,469	56,800	4,085,269
FY80	10,570,040	159,110	10,729,150
FY81	5,634,325	742,910	6,377,235
FY82	3,445,950	949,430	4,395,380
FY83	5,461,583	2,419,898	7,881,481
FY84	3,497,579	3,385,344	6,882,923
FY85	13,071,530	9,707,480	22,779,010
FY86	13,178,414	7,449,993	20,628,407
FY87	17,507,499	6,818,374	24,325,873
FY88	24,976,221	11,786,300	36,762,521
FY89	20,700,000	12,900,000	33,600,000
FY94	65,635,930	48,021,941	113,657,871

Source: U.S. Environmental Protection Agency, Office of Enforcement and Compliance Monitoring, Information Sheet (Washington, D.C., 1990); U.S. EPA Office of Enforcement and Compliance Assurance Accomplishments Report, May 1995.

Administrative Activities

Executive and independent agencies perform a variety of less well-known but equally important tasks. These include advising, conducting research, issuing permits, and managing property.

One of the most common ways individuals come into contact with agencies is when agencies *advise* businesses and individuals as to whether the agency considers an activity legal or illegal. Agencies also *conduct studies* of industry and markets. For example, the FTC, OSHA, and FDA conduct studies to determine the level of economic concentration, safety in the workplace, and whether drugs are harmful to the public. Also, agencies *provide information* to the general public on various matters through hotlines (see table 3-2), publications, and seminars. Agencies also devote much of their time to *issuing licenses or permits.* The EPA, for example, helps protect the environment by requiring certain environmentally sound activities before granting permits. Finally, agencies often are responsible for *managing property.*

LIMITATIONS ON AGENCY POWERS

Statutory Limitations

Certain federal statutes restrict the power of administrative agencies. One of these limiting statutes, the Administrative Procedure Act, has been discussed

TABLE 3–2 Environmental Hotlines for Federal Government Agencies	
Consumer Product Safety Commission For information or to report a product with an actual or potential hazard	(800) 638-2772
National Institute for Occupational Safety and Health (NIOSH) For questions concerning workplace health hazard evaluations	(800) 35-NIOSH
National Response Center Hotline To report a release or spill of oil or hazardous waste materials anywhere nationwide	(800) 424-8802
Occupational Safety and Health Administration (OSHA) To register a complaint about health or safety violations in the workplace	(800) 582-1708
U.S. Environmental Protection Agency Safe Drinking Water Hotline For questions about drinking water standards and contaminants	(800) 426-4791
RCRA - Superfund Hotline For general information on Superfund sites and hazardous waste laws	(800) 424-9346
Emergency Planning and Community Right-to-Know For questions about the national right-to-know law and state and local emergency planning efforts	(800) 535-0202
U.S. Federal Bureau of Investigation To report potential criminal violations of environmental laws	(800) 582-1766

previously. Its rule-making procedures, for example, mandate public involvement. Two other acts are especially helpful in keeping agency action open to the public and preventing secret, arbitrary, or capricious activity: the Freedom of Information Act of 1966, as amended in 1974 and 1976, and the Government in Sunshine Act.

The Freedom of Information Act requires federal agencies to publish in the *Federal Register* places where the public can get information from the agency. The act requires similar publication of proposed rules and policy statements. Finally, it requires the agencies to make such items as staff manuals and interpretations of policies available for copying to individuals, upon request. The Government in Sunshine Act requires agency business meetings to be open to the public if the agency is headed by a collegiate body. A collegiate body consists of two or more persons, the majority of whom are appointed by the president with the advice and consent of the Senate. This open-meeting requirement applies only when a quorum is present. The law also requires agencies to keep records of closed meetings.

In addition, private citizens can sue the government for damages caused by improper acts of employees of federal administrative agencies through the Federal Tort Claim Act of 1946. This act forces an agency to waive sovereign immunity for its tortious actions and those of its employees. Tortious actions under this act include assault, battery, abuse of prosecution, and false arrest. For example, if an inspector from the EPA illegally enters a business property and pushes the owner who is trying to block the door, and if the owner is injured from the assault, the EPA inspector, as well as the agency, may be held liable.

Institutional Limitations

Executive Branch.   The power of administrative agencies is limited by the executive branch through (1) the power of the president to appoint the heads of the agencies; (2) the power of the Office of Management and Budget (OMB) to recommend a fiscal year budget for each agency; and (3) presidential executive orders. As already discussed, the president appoints the head of each agency, as well as some lower-level heads of departments and divisions that do not fall under the federal civil service system. Presidential appointees usually have the same philosophical bent as the chief executive and are often of the same party.

As you will see in greater detail later in this chapter, the chief executive's ability to appoint an agency's head and to make recommendations can have a powerful, long-lasting effect on an agency. It is the agency's head who sets the tenor of the agency. The importance of the heads of agencies is reflected by the vigor with which interested parties lobby the president when he is making such appointments.

The executive branch also restricts agencies through its Office of Management and Budget. This office reviews agencies' budgets and makes recommendations with respect to their need for greater or lesser funding. Two of the most powerful agencies with respect to enforcing environmental policies, the Environment Protection Agency and the Council on Environmental Quality, were forced to curtail their actions severely as a result of President Reagan's budget and personnel decisions for 1980 through 1988.

The issuance of executive orders can also have a major impact on agencies' activities. One of the most significant of such orders is Executive Order 12291, issued by President Reagan on February 17, 1981. This order mandated that a cost-benefit analysis be performed by executive agencies for every regulation they enacted.

Soon after taking office in 1989, President Bush found an additional way for the executive branch to influence administrative agencies. He created the White House Council on Competitiveness. Headed by Vice President Dan Quayle, and consisting of several high-ranking cabinet officials, the council ostensibly was designed to enable the administration to "speak with one voice on issues involving international competitiveness."[2] During the summer of 1990, President Bush gave the council a mandate to push for deregulation. The council was to review new regulations, and any that would impose more costs on business than the benefits generated to the rest of society were to be held up or revised.

Although some Democrats labeled the Council on Competitiveness "sinister," and others claimed its actions were "Orwellian," "nothing short of treason, and perhaps illegal," defenders of the council claimed the body has clear authority to review regulations under Executive Order 12291. Regardless of one's attitude toward the legitimacy of the council, no one would attempt to deny its impact. Some claim it became a forum for appeals on any rules that were the subject of disputes between the EPA and other agencies. The council, either alone or in concert with other agencies, helped to kill a proposal to require recycling at municipal incinerators, softened a plan to improve visibility at the Grand Canyon by reducing sulfur dioxides from a nearby power plant, and postponed an EPA plan to discourage the incineration of lead batteries, a source of toxic pollution.[3]

Legislative Branch. Congress limits the authority of administrative agencies through (1) its oversight power; (2) its investigative power; (3) its power to terminate an agency or amend its enabling statute; (4) its power to approve or disapprove budgets; and (5) its power to advise and consent on the president's nominations for heads of administrative agencies.

When Congress creates an agency, it delegates its legislative power over a narrow area of commerce or human rights. Each year, using its oversight power, it determines, through one of its oversight committees, whether the agency has been carrying out its mandated function. As we shall discuss, during the 1980s, there were numerous committee hearings at which the head of the EPA was called to testify as to why the agency did not appear to be fulfilling the tasks assigned to it.

The greatest limitation on agency power by Congress, however, lies in its right to approve or disapprove any agency's budget. If Congress disagrees with the agency's action or the OMB's proposed budget, it can slash the budget, raise it, or refuse to fund the agency. The latter action shuts the agency down.

Judicial Branch. As explained earlier in this chapter, the courts can curb excesses of the administrative agencies' rule-making and adjudication functions by reversing or modifying such actions. The U.S. Supreme Court case of *Citizens of Overton Park v. Volpe*[4] clearly stated that all agency action is subject to judicial review unless there is a statutory prohibition or "agency action is committed to agency discretion by law." This agency discretion exception has been interpreted very narrowly. The scope of review set forth in this case is that agency action must be set aside if it is arbitrary or capricious, unconstitutional, outside the scope of the agency's authority, or in violation of procedural requirements.

The power of the judiciary to control the rule-making actions of administrative agencies was demonstrated by a recent U.S. Court of Appeals ruling in *AFL-CIO v. OSHA*.[5] In that case, OSHA had undertaken its most extensive rule-making effort ever, promulgating permissible exposure limits (PELs) for 428 toxic substances. OSHA had promulgated only twenty-four substance-specific health regulations by 1989. In an effort to speed up its rule making, OSHA attempted to engage in "generic rule making."

Section 3(8) of the Occupational Safety and Health Act (OSH Act) defines an "occupational health and safety standard" as "a standard which requires conditions or the adoption or use of one or more practices, means, methods, operations, or processes, reasonably necessary or appropriate to provide safe or healthful employment and places of employment." The Supreme Court interpreted that provision to require that, before the promulgation of any new permanent health standard, OSHA make a threshold finding that a significant risk of material health impairment exists at the current levels of exposure to the toxic substance in question, and therefore a new, lower threshold is reasonably necessary or appropriate to provide safe or healthful employment. Any subsequent standard the EPA promulgates must also comply with Section 6(b)5 of the act, which requires that a standard adopted must prevent material impairment of health "to the extent feasible."

Industry petitioners argued that OSHA's use of generic findings, its lumping together of so many substances in one rule making, and the short time for public comment created a record that was inadequate to support the rule making. The union argued that the procedure resulted in standards that were inadequate to protect employee health.

The Court, in looking at OSHA's record, agreed with the industry position. It said that OSHA had a responsibility to quantify, or explain to a reasonable degree, the risk posed by each toxic substance. OSHA's discussions of individual substances contained summaries of various studies of that substance and the health effects found at various levels of exposure but made no estimate of the risk of contracting those health effects; instead, OSHA provided a conclusory statement that the new limit would reduce the "significant" risk of material health effects, without any explanation of how the agency determined what was significant. The Court also faulted OSHA for failing to establish the economic and technical feasibility for each standard.

Thus, though the courts do not tend to scrutinize carefully the evidence agencies rely on, agencies must act in accordance with their statutory mandates. As the Supreme Court said in *AFL-CIO v. OSHA,* an agency cannot shortcut the proper rule-making procedures by attempting to combine multiple substances in a single rule making. Besides demonstrating the courts' power over agencies, this case also points out one of the dilemmas agencies sometimes face. They are often given a tremendous number of standards to set, and in order to save valuable time, they may wish to act with less than the maximum attainable evidence. Yet, in their haste to regulate, they may find that they have overstepped their authority.

IMPORTANT AGENCIES AFFECTING THE ENVIRONMENT

Currently more than one hundred federal agencies are in operation, as well as countless state agencies. Often, when there is a federal agency, there will also be comparable state agencies to which the federal agency will delegate much of its work. For example, the most important federal agency affecting environmental matters is the Environmental Protection Agency. Every state has a state environmental protection agency to which the federal EPA delegates primary authority for enforcing environmental protection laws. However, if at any time the state agency fails to enforce these laws, the federal EPA will step in to enforce them. Because the EPA is the primary agency responsible for enforcement of environmental laws, we devote the greatest attention to that agency. Other agencies that affect the environment are briefly introduced, either in the text or in Table 3–5.

Executive vs. Independent Agencies

Agencies are classified as either executive or independent. *Executive agencies* are sometimes seen as less stable in terms of their regulatory policies because the administrators of these agencies, who are appointed by the president with the advice and consent of the Senate, may be discharged by the president at any time, for any reason. Generally, whenever a new president is elected, he will place his appointees in charge of executive agencies. These agencies are generally located within the executive branch, under one of the cabinet-level departments. Hence, executive agencies are often referred to as cabinet-level agencies.

Although executive agencies are usually led by an administrator, it is a board of commissioners, one of whom is the chair, that is generally in charge of an independent agency. The president likewise appoints the commissioners of *independent agencies* with the advice and consent of the Senate, but these commissioners serve fixed terms and cannot be removed except for cause. No more than a simple majority can be members of any single political party. Serving fixed terms is said to make them less accountable to the will of the executive. These agencies are generally not located within any department.

One other difference between these two types of agencies is the scope of their regulatory authority. Executive agencies are responsible for making rules covering a broad spectrum of industries and activities. Independent agencies, often called commissions, tend to have more narrow authority over many facets of a particular industry. Executive agencies focus more on "social" regulation, whereas independent agencies more often concentrate on what we refer to as primarily "economic" regulation.

Hybrid Agencies. Some agencies do not fall clearly into one classification or the other. Created as one type of agency, the body may share characteristics of the other. The EPA, for example, was created as an independent agency, not located within any department of the executive branch. Yet it is headed by a single administrator who serves at the will of the president. During the early 1990s, in fact, there were discussions of the need to transform the EPA into a cabinet-level executive agency. (These initiatives did not succeed.) Another example is the "independent" Federal Energy Regulation Commission, which has the typical structure of an independent agency, yet is located within the Department of Energy.

The Environmental Protection Agency

History. By a presidential reorganization order, the Environmental Protection Agency was created in 1970 as an independent agency. This new agency was to take over functions that were formerly carried out by the Federal Water Quality Administration in the Department of the Interior; the National Air Pollution Control Administration and the Food and Drug Administration in the Department of Health, Education, and Welfare; and the Atomic Energy Commission, among others. Its mission was to control and abate pollution in the areas of air, water, solid waste, pesticides, radiation, and toxic substances. Its mandate was to mount an integrated, coordinated attack on environmental pollution in cooperation with state and local governments. In 1973, the EPA had 8,200 employees. By 1982, it had grown to be one of the largest federal agencies, with 12,623 employees, and by 1992, it had more than 17,000 employees. It has also been one of the most controversial agencies, having most of its actions criticized by either business groups, environmentalists, or both. The EPA has often been in conflict with the executive branch and with Congress.

The EPA's first head was William Ruckleshaus, under whose three-year tenure the agency served as a vigorous enforcer of air and water quality standards. As Congress passed more and more environmental regulations, the agency expanded and was given increasing amounts of responsibility. In September 1973, Ruckelshaus was succeeded by Russell Train, who ran the agency during three more years of growth. Next, under the leadership of Carter appointee Douglas Costle, the EPA continued to grow as the new administrator attempted to streamline its regulatory process and make the agency more cost-effective.

President Reagan's tenure demonstrated how effectively an agency can be gutted by an executive hostile to the agency's mission. During his first three years in office, Reagan cut the EPA's research budget by 50 percent, cuts from which the agency has not yet recovered. He also appointed Anne Burford (then Anne Gorsuch) to head the agency. Burford requested budget cuts for the agency, and reduced the number of enforcement actions. Fewer new regulations were issued under her leadership, and many long time employees of the agency resigned. Conflicts arose between Congress and the agency, as Congress tried to push the agency back on its former course; between October 1981 and July 1982, officials of the agency were called to testify before congressional oversight committees more than seventy times. Alleged mismanagement at the EPA continued until finally, in February 1983, several top EPA officials were fired.[6]

In March of 1983 Anne Burford was replaced by the former administrator William Ruckelshaus, who was followed in 1984 by Lee Thomas, who began once again to increase the number of agency enforcement orders and environmental regulations. Thomas was followed by William Reilly, the former head of the Conservation Foundation and World Wildlife Federation. The EPA's budget improved somewhat under the Bush administration, although the agency's 1990 budget, in constant dollars, actually increased by less than 20 percent over 1972 levels. This increase, however, is very modest indeed in light of all of the new environmental regulations the EPA has been given responsibility for since 1972. If we exclude the staff employed under the Superfund, the EPA's staff was actually smaller at the end of the 1980s than at its inception.

Where exactly is the EPA now? The agency, even in the best of times, has tended to be reactive, responding to the public's concerns as revealed through congressional enactments. Generally the agency has seen its role as enforcing specific pollution-control laws, not as being in the forefront of generating new policies to prevent problems from arising. A report of the Science Advisory Board (SAB) to the director of the EPA, completed in September 1990, may help the agency become more effective. The SAB made ten recommendations in its report (see table 3–3).

In January 1993, President Clinton nominated Carol M. Browner to head the EPA in what is hoped to be an era of greater cooperation among Congress, the executive branch, and the agency. Browner was the former head of the Florida EPA, as well as the legislative director for Vice President Gore when he was a senator. At Browner's confirmation hearing, Max Baucus, chair of the Senate Environment and Public Works Committee stated, "For the past several years, Congress and the Administration have been paralyzed by gridlock, particularly when it comes to environmental policy. . . . Now the American people expect all that to change."[7] The only promise that the new administrator seemed to give was to provide a regulatory climate not hostile to business. Depicted as practicing a pragmatic, cost-conscious brand of environmentalism, she may have been chosen for her appearance of "balance." By not being clearly aligned with either environmental or business extremists, she may be perceived as being able to balance the interests of the two groups and thereby turn the agency into a more effective regulator. She claims that her experience with the Florida EPA has taught her that we can "ease the regulatory burden on business without compromising the environment."

Evidence of Browner's intent to do just that came from her Common Sense Initiative, launched in July 1994. The initiative is her attempt to improve environmental regulations and streamline permitting, while developing antipollution alternatives such as prevention and new environmental technologies.

In March 1994, the EPA adopted a "place based" or "community based" strategy. This strategy is an effort to see how the EPA can initiate or support cross-media activities designed for specific places. The idea is to

TABLE 3–3 Recommendations of the Science Advisory Board

1. *EPA should target its environmental protection efforts on the basis of opportunities for the greatest risk reduction.* Since this country already has taken the most obvious actions to address the most obvious environmental problems, EPA needs to set priorities for future actions so the Agency takes advantage of the best opportunities for reducing the most serious remaining risks.

2. *EPA should attach as much importance to reducing ecological risk as it does to reducing human health risk.* Because productive natural ecosystems are essential to human health and to sustainable, long-term economic growth, and because they are intrinsically valuable in their own right, EPA should be as concerned about protecting ecosystems as it is about protecting human health.

3. *EPA should improve the data and analytical methodologies that support the assessment, comparison, and reduction of different environmental risks.* Although setting priorities for national environmental protection efforts always will involve subjective judgments and uncertainty, EPA should work continually to improve the scientific data and analytical methodologies that underpin those judgments and help reduce their uncertainty.

4. *EPA should reflect risk-based priorities in its strategic planning processes.* The Agency's long-range plans should be driven not so much by past risk reduction efforts or by existing programmatic structures, but by ongoing assessments of remaining environmental risks, the explicit comparison of those risks, and the analysis of opportunities available for reducing risks.

5. *EPA should reflect risk-based priorities in its budget process.* Although EPA's budget priorities are determined to a large extent by the different environmental laws that the Agency implements, it should use whatever discretion it has to focus budget resources at those environmental problems that pose the most serious risks.

6. *EPA—and the nation as a whole—should make greater use of all the tools to reduce risk.* Although the nation has had substantial success in reducing environmental risks through the use of government mandated end-of-pipe controls, the extent and complexity of future risks will necessitate the use of a much broader array of tools, including market incentives and information.

7. *EPA should emphasize pollution prevention as the preferred option for reducing risk.* By encouraging actions that prevent pollution from being generated in the first place, EPA will help reduce the costs, intermediate transfers of pollution, and residual risks so often associated with end-of-pipe controls.

8. *EPA should increase its efforts to integrate environmental considerations into broader aspects of public policy in as fundamental a manner as are economic concerns.* Other Federal agencies often affect the quality of the environment, e.g., through the implementation of tax, energy, agricultural, and international policy, and EPA should work to ensure that environmental considerations are integrated, where appropriate, into the policy deliberations of such agencies.

9. *EPA should work to improve public understanding of environmental risks and train a professional workforce to help reduce them.* The improved environmental literacy of the general public, together with an expanded and better-trained technical workforce, will be essential to the nation's success at reducing environmental risks in the future.

10. *EPA should develop improved analytical methods to value natural resources and to account for long-term environmental effects in its economic analyses.* Because traditional methods of economic analysis tend to undervalue ecological resources and fail to treat adequately questions of intergenerational equity, EPA should develop and implement innovative approaches to economic analysis that will address these shortcomings.

bring together many stakeholders to design smarter, more effective multimedia approaches to complex problems that defied satisfactory management through traditional statute-driven regulations. The role of the EPA on these situations will be as a leader, partner, and enabler, primarily acting as an enabler, focusing on capacity building and indirect support to the states through flexible grants, environmental information and monitoring systems, science, and technical assistance.

In April 1995, a report by the National Academy of Public Administration entitled "Setting Priorities, Getting Results: A New Direction for EPA," was released, recommending that the agency "hand more responsibility and decisionmaking authority over to the states and localities" and that a "new partnership needs to be formed, one based on 'accountable devolution' of national programs and on a reduction in EPA oversight when it is not needed." They also recommended that the agency begin work on a reorganization plan that would "break down the internal walls between the Agency's major media program offices for air, water, waste, and toxic substances."

The EPA offices had, in fact, already been instructed to examine whether they needed to reorganize in order to better meet the needs of their constituencies, and the offices submitted their reorganization plans by January 1996. However, implementation of these plans was delayed because of budgetary uncertainties. Despite such delays, the EPA by mid-1996 was still a much more flexible agency than it had been two years earlier, and it appears that the agency will continue evolving in the same direction.

Structure of the EPA. When the EPA was created, the agency was structured to bring regulatory authority over all forms of pollution control—research, standard setting, monitoring, enforcement, policy setting—within one federal body. This integrated management ideal, however, did not materialize, partly because of the agency's structure and partly because of its tremendous size. Basically, the EPA is headed by an administrator who is responsible for overall policy setting. The agency has a deputy administrator who helps the administrator. Under the administrator and deputy are six assistant administrators, three of whom are in charge of the "functional" missions of the EPA: research and development, planning and management, and enforcement, which apply to all EPA activities. The other three have "program" responsibilities and are responsible for each of the agency's regulatory programs. Unfortunately, there is little coordination among the various departments. Figure 3–3 diagrams the structure of the agency.

As with other agencies, an office of administrative law judges exists. These administrative law judges, like others in their profession, are fiercely independent and do not always side with the EPA's enforcement officers. The EPA is frequently represented before these justices by attorneys from the Department of Justice's Land and Natural Resources Division. Finally, the EPA has ten regional offices throughout the country (see table 3–4).

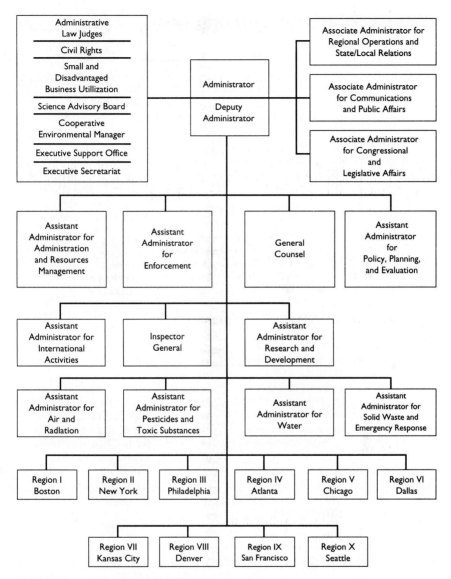

FIGURE 3–3 Environmental Protection Agency

Source: Environmental Protection Agency.

Interagency Cooperation

One of the ways the EPA can be more effective is to coordinate its enforcement efforts better, not just within the agency itself but with other agencies as well. A joint venture with OSHA proved to be fairly effective. During the spring of 1991, the two agencies jointly conducted surprise inspections at

TABLE 3–4 Environmental Protection Agency Regional Offices

Region		States Included
Region I	Boston, Massachusetts JFK Federal Building, 02203 (617) 565-3424	Connecticut, Massachusetts, Maine, New Hampshire, Rhode Island, Vermont
Region II	New York, New York 26 Federal Plaza, 10278 (212) 264-2515	New Jersey, New York, Puerto Rico, Virgin Islands
Region III	Philadelphia, Pennsylvania 841 Chestnut Street, 19107 (215) 597-9370	Delaware, Maryland, Pennsylvania, Virginia, West Virginia, District of Columbia
Region IV	Atlanta, Georgia 345 Courtland Street N.E., 30365 (404) 347-3004	Alabama, Florida, Georgia, Kentucky, Mississippi, North Carolina, South Carolina, Tennessee
Region V	Chicago, Illinois 230 S. Dearborn Street, 60604 (312) 353-2072	Illinois, Indiana, Michigan, Minnesota, Ohio, Wisconsin
Region VI	Dallas, Texas 1445 Ross Avenue, 75202 (214) 655-2200	Arkansas, Louisiana, New Mexico, Oklahoma, Texas
Region VII	Kansas City, Kansas 726 Minnesota Avenue, 66101 (913) 551-7003	Iowa, Kansas, Missouri, Nebraska
Region VIII	Denver, Colorado 999 18th Street, 80202 (303) 293-1692	Colorado, Montana, North Dakota, South Dakota, Utah, Wyoming
Region IX	San Francisco, California 1235 Mission Street, 94103 (415) 556-5145	Arizona, California, Hawaii, Nevada, American Samoa, Guam, Northern Mariana Islands
Region X	Seattle, Washington 1200 6th Avenue, 98101 (206) 442-1465	Alaska, Idaho, Oregon, Washington

twenty-nine of the nation's 140 hazardous waste incinerators run by some of the biggest corporations. As a result of the sweep, corporations were charged with 395 violations of federal standards. The EPA referred fifty-two violations to state authorities for enforcement actions, and OSHA assessed fines totaling $92,220 on incinerator operators. Perhaps fear of these new, coordinated sweeps may make plant operators a little more concerned about following federal health, safety, and environmental laws.

Such cooperative ventures are also being successfully undertaken with state agencies. For example, in December 1995, the cooperative efforts of the EPA's Criminal Task Force Investigation Division, the Texas Environmental Task Force, the Texas Parks and Wildlife Department, and the Texas Natural

Resource Conservation Commission led to the fifty-one-month incarceration of a violator of hazardous waste regulations. The violator, Reginald Gist, had been repeatedly notified by Dallas County Waste Control authorities that his business had been illegally dumping electroplating waste into the sewer system. He eventually abandoned the plant, leaving behind more than 70,000 gallons of hazardous waste, cleaned up by the EPA at a cost of more than $30,000. He opened a new facility in another Texas city, again illegally disposing of the waste in the sewage system and also by illegal dumping on other property he owned. When these violations were ultimately discovered, he pleaded guilty to two counts of violating the hazardous waste laws, leading to a jail sentence, a fine of $75,000, and his being prohibited from ever operating another plating business.

Many other federal agencies also aid in protecting the environment. Many of these agencies are housed within departments that also play significant roles in regulating the environment. The remainder of this chapter introduces some of these important agencies. Table 3–5, at the end of the next section, lists some additional agencies that also affect the environment.

The Department of the Interior and Its Agencies

Created as a cabinet-level department in 1845, the Department of the Interior is to natural resources what the EPA is to the regulation of pollution. It is responsible for seeking an optimally healthy balance between economic growth and the preservation of natural resources. As you might imagine, Interior is frequently a battleground between environmentalists and conservationists who want to preserve natural resources and those who want greater access to natural resources, such as those in the timber and cattle industries, mining operations, and sportspeople. State governments, especially in the West, also want to gain greater control of the public lands and natural resources within the department's control. Through its various agencies, the department is responsible for the management of more than 549 million acres of public land, administration of Native American lands and federal Native American programs, conservation and management of wetlands and estuaries, and protection and preservation of wildlife, including endangered species.

Bureau of Land Management.   Created in 1946, the Bureau of Land Management is the largest landholding entity in the United States and is responsible for the management of natural resources on about 15 percent of the country, more than 350 million acres. About half of the land managed by this agency is in Alaska, and most of the remaining lands are in the twelve westernmost states. Much of the land is designated for recreational use; some has been designated for conservation as wilderness. Natural resources include such items as timber, minerals, oil and gas, geothermal energy, wildlife habitats, endangered plants and animals, vegetation, and wild and scenic rivers.

TABLE 3–5   Federal Agencies That Play a Role in Environmental Regulation

Agency	*Primary Environmental Responsibility*
Army Corps of Engineers	Regulates construction projects on navigable waterways; regulates transportation and dumping of dredged materials into navigable waterways; and undertakes projects to prevent flooding, supply water for industrial and municipal use, create recreational areas, and protect wildlife and shorelines of oceans and lakes.
Consumer Products Safety Commission	Responsible for safety of consumer products, ensuring they do not contain carcinogens or toxic chemicals.
Federal Energy Regulatory Commission	Issues licenses for hydroelectric power; is responsible for the safe operation of dams.
Federal Maritime Commission	Certifies the financial responsibility of vessels that carry oil or other hazardous materials to cover costs of cleaning up their spills in navigable waters.
Food and Drug Administration	Ensures that foods and drugs are not adulterated or do not contain toxic substances.
Materials Transportation Bureau	Develops and enforces operating safety regulations for the transportation of all materials by pipeline; carries out inspection compliance and enforcement actions for transportation of all hazardous materials by air, water, highway, and rail.
National Institute for Occupational Safety and Health	Researches and develops occupational safety and health standards.
National Oceanic and Atmospheric Administration	Describes, monitors, and predicts conditions in the atmosphere, ocean, sun, and space environment; disseminates environmental data; and manages and conserves living marine resources and their habitats.
Nuclear Regulatory Commission	Licenses the construction and operation of nuclear facilities and the possession, use, transportation, handling, and disposal of nuclear materials.
Office of Conservation and Renewable Energy	Directs energy conservation programs and conducts studies.
Office of Surface Mining and Reclamation	Protects against adverse effects of coal mining; establishes standards for surface effects of coal mining; and promotes reclamation of previously mined lands.
Office of Water Research and Technology	Supervises and conducts research related to the nation's water quality.
Soil Conservation Service	Administers programs to develop and conserve soil and water resources.
U.S. Geological Survey	Maintains data center that conducts and sponsors research to apply data findings in mapping, geography, mineral and land resources, water resources, rangeland, and environmental monitoring.
Water and Power Resources Services	Develops and manages water and power resources in the western states.

U.S. Fish and Wildlife Service.   Probably most well known for its role in the "spotted owl controversy" in which the Fish and Wildlife Service listed the owl as endangered, this agency is responsible for safeguarding and improving wildlife and wildlife habitat in the National Wildlife Refuge System. Since 1983, this system has grown to 472 national wildlife refuges, waterfowl production areas in 166 counties, and 51 coordination areas. The agency is responsible for protecting migratory and game birds, fish, and endangered and threatened species. The agency also enforces regulations for hunters and preserves wetlands as natural habitats.

National Park Service.   This agency administers programs that conserve scenery, natural and historic objects, and wildlife in the national parks. It also is responsible for the management of 80 million acres of land.

The Department of Agriculture and Its Agencies

U.S. Forest Service.   This agency manages the nation's forests and grasslands. It is responsible for 33.6 million acres of wilderness areas. Like the Department of the Interior, this agency must confront competing interests of those who want to conserve and those who want to exploit our natural resources but focuses its energies on those resource uses that occur in the forest, such as lumbering, mining, farming, and grazing. The agency is currently embroiled in controversy for such actions as clearcutting, selling public timber below cost, and constructing roads for lumber companies in national forests.

The Department of Labor and Its Agencies

Occupational Safety and Health Administration.   OSHA is primarily responsible for promulgating and enforcing rules that affect the health and safety of the workplace. A sister agency, the National Institute for Occupational Safety and Health (NIOSH), is responsible for doing research related to occupational health and safety that may be used by OSHA and the EPA in setting health and safety standards.

Mine Safety and Health Administration.   This agency develops and promulgates health and safety standards for mines. It enforces standards, proposes penalties for violators, and investigates accidents. It works with states to help develop mine safety and health programs.

CONCLUDING REMARKS

Administrative agencies have enormous influence, given their authority to establish and enforce regulations. Remember, however, that their power is constrained by all of the traditional branches of government. Also, much of our environmental law is, in fact, administrative law, developed and enforced by agencies, especially the EPA.

One of the most significant aspects of administration law is the way in which administrative regulations are created. The three processes by which these regulations can be created all invite public participation, all begin by publication of the proposed rule in the *Federal Register,* and all conclude with publication of the final rule in the *Federal Register.* If these legally binding regulations are not created following the proper steps, they will be struck down by the courts.

Now that you understand how the administrative law system functions, you are ready to begin study of that specialized area of law on which this book focuses: environmental law.

QUESTIONS FOR REVIEW AND DISCUSSION

1. Distinguish formal from informal rule making.
2. Explain when rule making is exempt from public participation.
3. Explain the use of reg-neg.
4. Describe the grounds for which a rule made by an administrative agency can be overturned.
5. Trace the steps of adjudication that must be followed by an administrative agency.
6. Why should anyone in a heavily regulated industry be familiar with the *Federal Register*?
7. How do legislative, executive, and judicial branches each restrict the activities of administrative agencies?
8. Describe the structure of the EPA.

FOR FURTHER READING

ALFRED AMAN, ADMINISTRATIVE LAW IN A GLOBAL ERA (Ithaca, N.Y.: Cornell University Press, 1992).

ROBERT DURANT, WHEN GOVERNMENT REGULATES ITSELF: EPA, TVA AND POLLUTION CONTROL IN THE 1970'S (Knoxville: University of Tennessee Press, 1985).

ERNEST GELLHORN & RICHARD B. STEWART, ADMINISTRATIVE LAW AND PROCESS IN A NUTSHELL (St. Paul, Minn.: West Publishing Co., 1990).

ELLEN K. SILBERGELD, *The Risks of Comparing Risks,* 3 N.Y. U. ENVTL. L.J. 405 (1995).

ON THE INTERNET

http://www.fplc.edu/tfield/RiskIndx.htm
The RISK home page—Risk: Health, Safety, and the Environment

http://www.epa.gov/
EPA home page

http://www.nas.edu.edu/homepage/focus/ees.htm
National Academy of Sciences/National Academy of Engineering Institution home page

http://straylight.tamu.edu/bene/nbic/nbic.html
Home page for the National Biodiversity Information Center

NOTES

1. CEQ, Twentieth Annual Report, 1990, p. 204.
2. JEFFREY H. BIRNBAUM, *White House Competitiveness Council Provokes Sharp Anger among Democrats in Congress,* WALL S. J. B1 (July 8, 1991).
3. Ibid.
4. 401 U.S. 402 (1971).
5. 61 LW 2042 (1992).
6. DONALD J. REBOVICH, DANGEROUS GROUND: THE WORLD OF HAZARDOUS WASTE CRIME (New Brunswick, N.J.: Transaction Publishers, 1992).
7. PHILLIP DAVIS, *Browner Short on Specifics in Confirmation Hearing,* CONG. Q. WKLY. 127 (Jan. 16, 1993).

PART II

The Environmental Laws

The second part of this book provides the basics of the most influential environmental laws and introduces troublesome dilemmas arising from implementation of the laws. With the exception of chapter 4, which discusses the basics of environmental policy, each chapter first introduces the primary environmental problems the law must resolve, providing the scientific knowledge necessary for you to understand the problem. Later sections of each chapter then describe the laws themselves.

CHAPTER 4

An Introduction to Environmental Law and Policy

The area of law you are now beginning to study is one of extremely recent development. Twenty years ago there would not have been any law school, undergraduate, or MBA courses in environmental law, because there was no such cohesive body of law. Environmental regulation has evolved over that brief period from reliance on tort law to an emphasis on end-of-pipe controls through direct regulation and finally into an emphasis on pollution prevention.

Before the existence of a cohesive set of environmental laws, how, you may wonder, did we keep the ravages of pollution from degrading the quality of our water, air, and land? The answer is that we did not. Without protective legislation, lakes and rivers became unfit for fishing and swimming, the air in many cases became severely degraded, forests were destroyed, and valuable land was eroded. Today we are still paying the costs of cleaning up our mistakes from this era of minimal regulation.

In the first section of this chapter we examine the justifications that led to the adoption of the regulations designed to repair the ravaged environment and prevent its future degradation. We then examine alternate ways to provide that protection. The third section traces the evolution of environmental policy. Finally, the remaining two sections discuss the two major environmental policy statutes.

THE NEED FOR REGULATION

Some believe that we did not need to enact environmental protection laws because tort law would protect the environment to the extent that it needed protection. In fact, for a while, tort law was the way we feebly controlled pollution, and it was in a tort class where protection of the environment was discussed, if at all, in law school. But the dying streams and polluted skies made it evident that tort law was not working, and thus the adoption of environmental regulation was seen as necessary.

Tragedy of the Commons

Often when people seek to justify environmental regulation, they do so using a story told by Garrett Hardin entitled "The Tragedy of the Commons."[1] The tragedy develops this way: Picture a huge, lush pasture open to everyone. Many people survive by raising cattle; they take their cattle to the common pasture to graze. Each herdsman keeps as many cattle as possible. For a while, disease, famine, and tribal wars keep the number of cattle at a reasonable level. Eventually, however, the day of reckoning comes. There is just enough land to support all of the cattle.

The rational herdsman, however, asks himself, "What is the utility of adding one more animal to my herd?" Because the herdsman receives all the proceeds from the sale of the animal, he has powerful incentive to add to his herd. The negative effect of adding one more animal is the harm that results to the other herdsmen from resultant overgrazing. Because all herdsmen share in this negative effect, the negative consequences to the individual herdsman are minimal. Consequently, herdsmen tend to keep adding to their herds. As the same conclusion is reached by each herdsman, each continues to increase his herd without limit. But the space for the herd is limited. Herein lies the tragedy. They are locked into a system that guarantees the destruction of the commons and thus their own ruin. Hardin then concludes, "Ruin is the destination to which all men rush, each pursuing his own interest in a society that believes in the freedom of the commons. Freedom in a commons brings ruin to all."[2]

How, you may ask, is the tragedy of the commons related to environmental protection? Without environmental laws, the rational manufacturer finds that because the cost of a polluted river is borne by everyone, he pays only a fraction of the cost of dumping waste products into a stream. On the other hand, if he chooses to not pollute by properly treating his waste, he bears the whole cost of proper disposal. Therefore he will pollute. Because the calculations are the same for everyone, we are trapped in a system of destroying our environment as long as we behave only as independent, rational free enterprisers.

Just as with the tragedy of the commons, as long as there were few polluters relative to the size of the water and air, the absorptive capacities of these resources were not taxed and there were no problems. As population and industry increased, environmental tragedy emerged. Rivers became polluted, as did the air and the land. Nature's absorptive capacities were exceeded in many areas.

Free Rider Problem

Rather than using analogies like the tragedy of the commons, some people justify the need for environmental laws by pointing out that clean air and clean water are *public goods.* Public goods are goods that have the character-istic of *nonexclusiveness*—that is, once they are produced, others cannot be excluded from using them. Thus, when someone pays to produce the good, not only the payer but everyone else gets to use it. Those who do not pay become free riders. They get benefits paid for by others. No one, therefore, is going to pay for clean air and water, because every rational person would prefer to be a free rider. The problem is that as everyone seeks to become a free rider, no one but a few "irrational" saints will be willing to pay for clean air and water. Thus our environment will become degraded.

Pollution as an Externality

One common justification for any government intervention into the market is to eliminate negative externalities. Third parties have no impact on market prices; either government gives their interests a voice in production decisions or they have no voice. Thus, some argue that the government needs to step in to impose the costs of pollution on the polluting firm, so that it will have to increase the price of the product to reflect the true costs of producing the product. If the producer must pay to properly dispose of the hazardous waste created by the production of the product, citizens who would have otherwise been adversely affected by the improper waste disposal will not have to pay by incurring losses to their health. The important point here is that the marketplace by itself has no mechanism for achieving this objective of improved waste disposal.

An Environmental Ethic

Proponents of an environmentalist perspective believe that too often impor-tant decisions affecting the environment are made while taking into account only short-term impacts and economic factors, with little concern for the on-going maintenance and enhancement of the viability of ecosystems.

Environmentalists are heavily influenced by ecology, the study of the relationships of living organisms to their environments. In ecology, land is viewed as a biotic pyramid:

> Plants absorb energy from the sun. That energy flows through a circuit called the biota, which may be represented by a pyramid of layers. The bottom layer is the soil. A plant layer rests on the soil, an insect layer on the plants, a bird and rodent layer on the insects, and so on up through the various animal groups to the apex layer, which consists of larger carnivores. . . . Land, then, is not merely soil; it is a fountain of energy flowing through soils, plants and ani-mals. Food chains are the living channels which conduct energy upward; death and decay return the energy to the soil. The circuit is not closed. . . . [I]t is a sustained circuit, like a slowly revolving fund of life."[3]

When a change occurs in one part of the circuit, all other parts of the circuit must respond. Most changes that occur through evolution happen slowly, thus giving the circuit time to adapt. The more gradual and less violent the change, the more likely the successful readjustment in the pyramid.[4] The fear of ecologists is that humankind now has the capacity to make rapid changes in the circuit, and we do not know how the pyramid will respond. A substance we use to kill one harmful rodent may be absorbed into the food chain, causing death or mutation up the chain. When returned to the soil, that chemical may poison the soil, thus making plant growth impossible and resulting in a lack of food for insects, rodents, birds, and their predators in that area. Thus, the ecologists warn, we must think before we take steps that may interrupt ecological systems. The consequences of our actions may be graver than we had anticipated. The unregulated marketplace again has little incentive to heed these fears.

Some environmentalists point out that as the dominant species in the ecosystem, with all our knowledge and power, we have a duty or responsibility to care for that ecosystem, to preserve it for future generations. We have an ethical obligation to past and future generations to be careful stewards of the legacy we have inherited. Some also make a sort of environmental *noblesse oblige* argument. Because our species has gone beyond mere acquisition of food, clothing, and shelter, and we can understand the way ecosystems work, we have the special duty to preserve those systems. Finally, it is argued by many environmentalists, we must recognize that we are not the measure of all things. We are but a small part of the universe and have no right to destroy a significant portion of it to satisfy our own selfish desires.

As you read environmental cases, notice that while the courts attempt to focus purely on the law, there are times when they go beyond a strict interpretation of it. There are occasions when you will see the influence of the ecological perspective on a judge's decison making.

ALTERNATIVE WAYS TO CONTROL POLLUTION

Tort Law

As mentioned earlier, tort law was the first way we attempted to control pollution, and it still provides a limited means of control. However, a number of limitations make tort law unavailable in many cases and unsatisfactory as an overall means of pollution control.

Under tort law, the typical action brought to control pollution is a nuisance case. An action for *nuisance* can be brought whenever there is an *unreasonable interference with the use and enjoyment of another's land.* When someone interferes with a person's use of his or her land, the one interfering can be sued for nuisance. The person suing can receive an injunction requiring that the nuisance be stopped. Because pollution of the air and water is clearly an interference with others' use and enjoyment of their land, nuisance would seem an ideal solution. The person who has been harmed by pollution could bring an action seeking an *injunction,* a court order prohibiting the polluting behavior and/or providing *money damages* for the harm caused.

The case of *Boomer v. Atlantic Cement Company*[5] reflects some of the problems of using tort law. In *Boomer,* the defendants operated a large cement plant near Albany. They were sued by neighboring landowners who alleged injury to property from dirt, smoke, and vibrations emanating from the plant. The plaintiffs sought permanent injunctions and damages. During trial, a nuisance was found, and temporary damages were granted, but the request for an injunction was denied. The appellate court granted the injunction *unless* the defendants paid permanent damages of $185,000 to compensate for the plaintiff's economic loss. Given the relatively small amount of the monetary damages award, the injunction was essentially denied.

The ground for the denial of injunction, notwithstanding the findings that, first, there was a nuisance and, second, that plaintiffs had been damaged substantially, was "the large disparity in economic consequences of the nuisance and of the injunction." In denying the injunction on this ground, the court admitted that it was "overruling a doctrine which has been consistently reaffirmed in several leading cases in this court and which has never been disavowed here, namely that where a nuisance has been found and where there has been any substantial damage shown by the party complaining, an injunction will be granted." The rule in New York had previously been that such a nuisance would be enjoined even if a marked disparity had been shown in economic consequences between the effect of the injunction and the effect of the nuisance.

The court noted that the defendant's investment in the plant was in excess of $45 million and that it employed three hundred people. The court was convinced that the technology did not exist to enable the plant to operate without creating a nuisance—nor was the technology likely to be developed within the foreseeable future. The court made it clear that it was now going to balance the harm created by the nuisance with the costs of ceasing the nuisance. If the economic costs were great, no injunction would be granted. Thus, because pollution control is expensive, after *Boomer,* nuisance became an ineffective way to stop pollution. At best, tort law could be used to get damages to clean up some of the pollution's harm.

Problems with Using Tort Law. The major problem reflected in *Boomer* is the court's reluctance to grant injunctions, the only remedy that really controls pollution because what you really want to do is stop the pollution. However, courts will now balance the economic harm caused by the nuisance against the costs that would result from the injunction. If the harm from the injunction would be greater, then the courts will simply award *permanent damages.* The problem with this approach is that it allows the pollution to go on unabated. It leaves the injured party without a remedy for unforeseen future harms. And if the landowner sells the property to someone else, the courts could rule that the subsequent landowner can bring no action because permanent damages had already been awarded. Once the damages have been assessed, there is no motivation for the polluter to stop polluting.

Another problem is that of *standing*. Recall from chapter 2 that standing is the legal right to bring an action. Standing in a nuisance action is somewhat different from standing in most other cases. For purposes of standing, nuisance is classified as being either private or public. A *private* nuisance affects only a single or limited number of persons or affects one person in a unique way. When a nuisance is private, the affected individuals have standing to sue. If the nuisance affects a large number of persons, it is deemed a *public* nuisance. Only a public official can bring suit for a public nuisance. Herein lies the main problem with using nuisance law to control pollution: Most pollution is a public nuisance. Public officials, who are generally elected, may be very reluctant to bring a nuisance action against a major corporation in the town for several reasons. For one, the polluter means jobs, and public officials do not want to be accused of driving jobs out of town. Also, they do not want to anger a powerful constituent who may be responsible for sizable campaign contributions.

A third problem with using tort law is the difficulty of proving one's case. Remember that in a civil action the burden of proof is on the plaintiff. If there are multiple polluters, it is difficult to prove which one caused the damage. If seven factories are located along the stream that flows across your land, how do you demonstrate that the toxic chemical from the tire plant killed the fish?

Another difficulty is a comparative lack of resources. In the rare instance in which a nuisance is private, the plaintiff needs money to bring the action, and many do not have the money to do so. Finally, tort law is problematic in that it is reactive. The problem must exist before the law comes into effect. Ideally, the law should prevent the creation of the problem.

Subsidies, Emissions Charges, and Marketable Emissions Permits

Three alternate means of protecting the environment are subsidies, emissions charges, and marketable emissions permits. As we shift toward pollution prevention in the 1990s, we shall see the increasing use of these tools. *Subsidies* exist when the government pays, either directly by grants or indirectly by tax relief, to encourage pollution control. Subsidies are most likely to be effective when the polluter knows that eventually it is going to be forced to clean up the problem. So, if the company takes care of it now, the government will help pick up the tab. If it waits until the government chooses to impose a tighter standard, no subsidy will be available. Sometimes a firm that is able to control its emissions better because of technology installed with a subsidy may start to pressure the government to impose even stricter emissions limitations on that industry.

Traditionally subsidies have not fully covered the costs of reducing pollution, so businesses were likely not to use the subsidies because they did not wish to pay for pollution control when their competitors did not. In some respects this type of thinking is encouraged by a business climate in which managers are evaluated based on the bottom line at the end of the quarter or year. Our country's managers simply do not focus on the long-term calculations of benefit and cost.

Another alternative is to require *emissions charges.* In essence, we are saying that the air and water belong to the community, so if you want to use them, you must pay the owners, that is, the community. The larger the per unit fee, the more effective the charges are in reducing levels of emissions. The charges theoretically encourage development of pollution-control technology, because if a competitor could discharge less, it would lower costs and increase profits.

Emissions charges, however, are not without their problems. First, it is very difficult to monitor the emissions. Second, it is also hard to know how to set the fee. If the fees are too low, firms will simply continue to pollute, paying the price. If there are few firms in the industry, they may even tacitly agree simply to pass on the fees to consumers. If the fees are too high, and alternate technology to reduce emissions is extremely expensive or not available, only a few firms may be able to survive, thereby creating a monopoly. In such an event emissions charges can be a stimulus to concentrate economic power.

A related alternative is for the government to not only sell permits but let the polluters trade these permits among themselves, sometimes referred to as *emissions trading,* or *marketable emissions permits.* Governments would set overall emissions targets and then issue permits to meet those targets, thereby controlling the overall amount of pollution. Firms then possess incentives to reduce their emissions using low-cost methods so they can sell their permits. The total amount of pollution can be reduced by gradually reducing the number of permits issued. The major emissions trading program in the country today is the sulfur dioxide trading program described in chapter 5, and created by the 1990 Clean Air Act. Again, there are problems with this method. The government may find monitoring difficult. A second problem is that new entrants into an industry may be restricted by difficulty in obtaining a permit.

Green Taxes

A way to help control pollution that has not been attempted to any great extent in the United States is the use of green taxes. A *green tax* is a tax on polluting behaviors, the revenues from which may be funneled into environmental programs. Supporters of green taxes argue that these taxes correct the market's failure to value environmental services. They also seem to be somewhat effective in discouraging polluting behavior if they are set at a high enough level. In the United Kingdom, for example, a higher tax on leaded gasoline increased the market share of unleaded gas from 4 percent in April

1989 to 30 percent in March 1990. The United States is attempting to discourage the use of ozone-depleting chlorofluorocarbons (CFCs) with a tax it imposed in late 1989 of $3.02 per kilogram, increasing to $6.83 per kilogram by 1995 and to $10.80 per kilogram by 1999. A comprehensive set of green taxes could help shape our nation's behavior, while at the same time raising substantial revenues that could be used for environmental projects.

Direct Regulation

The primary means of protecting the environment is direct regulation, or command-and-control regulation. By *direct regulation,* we mean the setting of standards and mandating compliance through threat of fines for violations. Standards may be set in terms of levels of technology that must be used or total emissions allowed. The focus of the remaining chapters is primarily on direct regulation.

These regulations are often referred to as *end-of-pipe regulations* because they tend to concentrate on controlling pollutants toward the end of the manufacturing process. These direct regulations have been the focus of most environmental legislation. As the final section in this chapter reveals, however, we are beginning to shift away from the end-of-pipe regulations traditionally identified with direct regulation and toward ways of making it economically beneficial for firms to evaluate their entire production process in search of avenues whereby fewer pollutants would be created in the first place.

EVOLUTION OF OUR ENVIRONMENTAL POLICY

The Origins of Our Environmental Policy

When we think about our government, we generally do not think about our government's policies. We do not have national policies on many issues; our policy with respect to most issues has been laissez-faire, or "government hands off." Minimal government intervention, especially in business affairs, traditionally has been seen as desirable by those in power in this country. We are, for example, the only industrialized nation that does not have a coherent industrial policy. However, if there is any area in which our country seems to have adopted a national policy, it is with respect to the environment.

As noted earlier, before 1970, the United States did not really have any sort of environmental policy. To a large extent this absence of environmental regulation, as well as subsequent increases in regulation, reflected the state of scientific knowledge. We were not even aware of many environmental problems. Further, we did not have the ability to detect and measure low levels of chemical contaminants. For example, the ability to measure levels of many contaminants has gone from parts per thousand to parts per million.

We also did not have the computer technology available to do the types of modeling that today allow us to project the long-term impacts of certain levels of contaminants on the human environment. And even, in some cases, when we determined that a given level of pollution was harmful, we did not have the technology to immediately reduce emissions levels. Once the technology was developed, it was sometimes more costly than expected. Frequently, the cleaner the environment became, the more costly the technology for smaller and smaller reductions of emissions.

As mentioned in chapter 2, our system of government also helped to slow the evolution of environmental policy. Strong constituencies were needed to get the legislative and executive branches moving together toward protecting the environment. Once the laws were passed, they were still subject to the courts' interpretation. As we saw in chapter 2, the ideology of the majority of justices can change, and thus environmental policy as enforced by the courts may change.

Finally, our environmental policy is influenced by our values, the long-ingrained values of our culture, and the more temporary values that seem to change over time in response to economic conditions. Our independence has always encouraged a hands-off policy toward business, which may explain our lack of an earlier environmental policy. However, as our economy became stronger, other values, especially those reflecting a desire for an improved quality of life, became more dominant and encouraged the adoption of policies more favorable to the environment.

The Seventies: The Environmental Decade

The environmental movement of the early 1970s was inspired to a great extent by three books. Perhaps the most influential of these was Rachel Carson's *Silent Spring,* which made people aware of the effects of pesticides on birds and other wildlife. The other two were Paul Ehrlich's *The Population Bomb,* which alerted us to the potentially adverse impact that our rapidly increasing population could have on our natural resources, and Barry Commoner's *The Closing Circle,* which explained ecological principles in terms that laypeople could understand.

Also influential in generating public interest in preservation of the environment were a few cataclysmic events, such as the 1969 oil spill in Santa Barbara, California. On April 22, 1970, the first Earth Day was celebrated, and there were "teach-ins" about environmental problems across the nation. These events created the public pressure that caused policymakers in all branches of government to perceive environmental issues as politically emergent. Seeing almost unprecedented public support for a strong environmental policy, lawmakers set about adopting tough environmental regulations, often without fully considering the costs and technological feasibility of implementing such regulations.

In terms of institutionalizing an environmental policy that would have a long-term impact, two actions were probably the most significant. One was the creation of the EPA, to bring the coordination of environmental policy under the control of one agency. The other was passage of the National Environmental Policy Act (described later in this chapter), which requires every federal agency to consider the environmental impacts of every major activity it undertakes.

The years from 1969 through 1979 saw the passage of twenty-seven laws designed to protect the environment, as well as hundreds of administrative regulations. The decade of the 1970s, under this new environmental policy, witnessed vast improvements in the quality of the air, water, and land, even though many of the goals established by these laws had not been completely attained.

The Decade of the 1980s

By 1980, concern was growing over the costs of regulation in general. The economy was failing, and Reagan was elected under a banner of deregulation. As part of his general policy of "getting government off the back of business," Reagan appointed conservatives to head the EPA and the Interior Department, as well as to serve in key positions in these and other agencies that played significant roles in setting and enforcing environmental policy. Many of these newly appointed officials in fact came from businesses, legal foundations, or firms that had fought the regulations they were now supposed to enforce. Subsequently, many, with their deregulatory ideas, drove a number of senior executives and professionals out of the environmental agencies.[6]

Reagan also reduced the staffs of many agencies, in particular cutting EPA personnel by 20 percent.[7] Further reductions in enforcement were assured by cutting the EPA's budget by more than one-third, when adjusted for inflation, between 1981 and 1983.[8] Funding for conservation programs in the Interior Department, as well as for renewable energy programs, was also reduced. Reacting to less money and staff for enforcement, business soon recognized that there had been a shift in environmental policy and felt less constrained by environmental regulations.

At first, Congress went along with the administration's relaxation of environmental policies. After two years, the public, at the instigation of numerous environmental groups, began to make its dissatisfaction known. In March 1982, ten environmental and conservation groups issued an "indictment" of Reagan, alleging that he had "broken faith with the American people on environmental protection" by taking or proposing "scores of actions that veered radically away from the broad bipartisan consensus in support of environmental policy that has existed for many years" and citing 227 ways that the administration had subverted environmental policy.[9]

Congress, perhaps in response to a perception that the public disapproved of the administration's lax attitude toward the environment, began to oppose the administration's policies toward the environment by holding several oversight hearings on the EPA's handling of specific environmental matters. Congress also voted to strengthen a number of environmental laws that came up for renewal during the 1980s. In many instances the laws may have been stronger than they would have been with a more proenvironment president because of congressional belief that it needed to draft strong laws that could not be watered down by a weakened EPA.

Thus, the 1980s saw a reduction in funding for environmental programs and a relaxation in their enforcement, along with cutbacks in the budgets and staffs of agencies established to protect the environment. Much of the administrative burden associated with environmental policy was shifted to the states. However, by the end of the decade, there seemed to be a renewal of environmental vigor on the part of Congress.

The 1990s

As the 1990s approached, there was renewed interest in having a strong policy to protect the environment. "Green" products began cropping up all over. Major firms, such as McDonald's, started advertising that they were changing their products to become more environmentally friendly. Public opinion polls began to show more interest than ever in environmental protection. Further, enforcement at the EPA was given renewed attention. The years 1990 through 1994 produced record numbers of prosecutions and fines for environmental violations. Congress also seemed to be continuing its environmental support by passing a strong Clean Air Act.

Thus, there were many early indicators that the 1990s would see a strengthening of an environmental policy that had been weakening during the 1980s. Not all indicators were pointing in that direction, however. President Bush's appointee to head the EPA, William Reilly, though a disappointment to many environmentalists, was proving to be a bit more proenvironment and not quite probusiness enough for the president, so there were numerous conflicts within the executive branch.

Also, by the 1990s, many federal courts were dominated by conservative appointees. Early cases indicated that these new appointees were not necessarily going to be as willing as previous courts to take proenvironmental positions. And even the newly constituted U.S. Supreme Court indicated that it was going to give much less weight to preserving environmental values, even going so far as to overturn past precedents that it saw as having given too much protection to environmental concerns.

As the economy continued to slump during the early 1990s, people again became more concerned about the costs of environmental regulations. They also started to recognize that once the initial gains had been made in the 1970s and 1980s, future incremental gains were going to be much more costly; each incremental gain would also provide fewer visible benefits. These factors helped to create a shift in environmental policy away from the end-of-pipe regulation toward more pollution prevention and the use of more cost-effective ways to reduce pollution. As mentioned earlier, one of the factors that helped stimulate a concern for the environment during the late 1960s and early 1970s was that the economy was doing well; there was money available to be spent. At the beginning of the 1990s, the economy was not as strong.

An Increasing Use of Market Forces.   Part of this shift of environmental policy in the 1990s appears to be toward greater use of *market forces*. This term covers a broad range of strategies. Proponents of this trend are careful to point out that the term is not a code word for deregulation. Rather, they insist, it is a way of using the market forces to encourage pollution prevention.

One example of this type of market force incentive is the passage of "bottle bills," bills that require certain types of beverages to be sold in recyclable or reusable bottles. Consumers must pay a deposit for such bottles, which will be refunded when the bottles are returned. Consumers will be much more likely to recycle when there is a financial incentive to do so. At least nine states have such laws. Another example is what Seattle is doing in charging for refuse pickup based on poundage. If consumers pay by the pound to have their trash carted away, they will be motivated financially to reduce their trash. Pollution taxes and refundable deposits on hazardous materials are two other market-oriented incentives. What all these strategies have in common is that they make the polluter pay—and thus, theoretically, encourage reduction in pollution in order to avoid the costs.

Two of the more controversial strategies are pollution charges and marketable emissions permits, mentioned in an earlier section of this chapter. The former is an alternative to ordering plants to cut emissions by a specific amount. Instead, every unit of pollution discharged is taxed, thus giving an incentive to the firm to cut emissions. Critics, however, point out that for this scheme to work, the taxing agency would need detailed information about a company's costs in order to set fees at a level that would discourage pollution. The first major experiment in marketable emissions permits is taking place under the Clean Air Act of 1990. Described in detail in chapter 5, this policy is designed to alleviate one of the frequent criticisms of direct regulation: that the regulations do not take into account the differences among various competitors' compliance.

Voluntary Programs.   Another shift in environmental policy is toward more voluntary programs on the part of businesses to reduce pollution. One example of such a program is the 35/50 Project, a voluntary project in which more than six hundred companies were asked to reduce voluntarily their emissions of seventeen high-priority chemicals. The goal for the project is to achieve a one-third reduction of these emissions by 1992 and a 50 percent reduction by 1995. By April 1991, more than one hundred companies had expressed interest in the project.

Another example of such voluntary projects is the Green Lights Program. When a company agrees to participate in this voluntary project, it signs an agreement with the EPA committing itself to surveying all its facilities and installing new lighting systems that maximize energy savings as long as the new systems do not compromise lighting quality or profitability. In return, the EPA provides the company the information and technical support it needs to install the requisite lighting. By April 10, 1991, fifty corporations had become partners in the program, and approximately 75 percent of these were Fortune 500 firms.

It is difficult to project what environmental law developments will ultimately occur in the late 1990s. In 1992, democratic presidential and vice-presidential candidates who were characterized by their opponents as "environmental extremists" were elected. Vice President Gore had, in fact, written a book suggesting ways to improve environmental quality. When asked by an interviewer from the *Wall Street Journal* what recent event helped shape his vision of American society, Gore replied, "The UN Conference on Environment and Development conducted in Rio de Janeiro."[10]

Articles appearing soon after the election indicated that corporate environmental lawyers were taking the election of the new presidential team as a signal, at minimum, of renewed environmental enforcement. For example, in the *National Law Journal,* in an article entitled "Girding for a Change," the author opened by warning readers, "For the general counsels at the nation's corporations, the transition period between the last weeks of President Bush's tenure and the first months of a Clinton administration calls for a thorough re-examination of their companies' overall compliance program."[11] According to more than two dozen regulatory and compliance experts from private law firms, corporations, public interest groups, and law schools who were interviewed for the story, the new administration would bring new rules and an overall boost in enforcement. While enforcement in all regulatory areas was predicted to increase, the greatest increases were expected to come in the environmental area.[12]

While the use of criminal sanctions to punish and deter environmental violations continued to increase during the initial years of the Clinton administration, the Congressional elections of 1994, which gave control of the House of Representatives to the Republicans, brought in a new group of elected officials who were committed to regulatory reform. A major component of the reform was rolling back years of environmental regulation, which these new representatives believed had been hampering business and infringing on private property owners' rights. In fact, some of those new representatives had campaigned explicitly on a platform of protecting property rights and limiting government.

The newly elected Congress moved rapidly to attempt to fulfill their "Contract with America," a legislative plan that, if enacted, would significantly alter environmental regulation in the United States. Proposed and debated legislation would have dramatically cut the EPA's budget, exempted oil and gas production from toxic air pollutions standards and citizens' suits, weakened the Clean Water Act, ended federal jurisdiction over at least half of the wetlands currently protected, eliminated the National Biological Survey, placed a five-year moritorium on land acquisition by the Forest Service and Bureau of Land Management, allowed the leasing of the Arctic National Wildlife Refuge's coastal plain for the drilling of oil, reduced the protection given to endangered species, lifted the fourteen-year ban on drilling for oil along the outer continental shelf, and reduced by 10 percent the operating budgets of the Forest Service, the National Park Service, and the Fish and Wildlife Service. Riders were attached to various budget appropriations bills that would have prohibited the EPA from engaging in numerous regulatory functions, such as enforcing wetlands protection, issuing several drinking water standards, and enforcing Great Lakes water standards and several raw-sewage overflow controls. Clinton maintained that he would veto any bill undermining existing environmental protection.

Two proposals were of special concern to the environmental community. The first was the risk assessment bill. This bill would impose risk assessments on any rules that have an impact on the economy of at least $75 million per year. It would also provide for judicial review of such regulations. A complementary regulatory reform package in the House of Representatives would apply risk assessment, cost-benefit analysis, peer review, and prioritization standards to almost every new rule that would have an economic effect of at least $25 million. The second bill proposed to give Congress the authority to review and possibly veto virtually any new federal regulation.

Despite the furor generated by these reform proposals, or perhaps because of it, very few of these proposals became law by the end of 1995. Republicans did manage to place a rider on a defense department appropriations bill that prohibited the listing of new species as endangered until the end of 1995; that moratorium was then extended until September 30, 1996, or whenever the Endangered Species Act is reauthorized, whichever comes first. A budget rescission bill passed during the summer of 1995 contained a rider that opened up thousands of acres of Pacific Northwest forests for salvage logging. Neither the risk assessment bill nor the moratorium on new federal regulations managed to pass.

Some argue that the Republican Party misread the American people's intent, and that they are now coming to recognize that the public does in fact support the current system of environmental protection. An article appearing in the *New York Times* on January 26, 1996, reported that Republicans, increasingly concerned over political damage that might be caused by imposing deep cuts on the environment, were beginning to move away from confrontations on environmental issues; a Republican pollster disclosed that only 35 percent of the public would vote to reelect members of the House who voted to cut EPA funding. Perhaps in the closing years of the 1990s they may moderate their approach to regulatory reform and manage to make modifications in the present system. At minimum, there will probably continue to be debate over our current system of environmental protection.

NATIONAL ENVIRONMENTAL POLICY ACT

We begin our study of environmental regulations by examining the two major policy statutes: the National Environmental Policy Act (NEPA) of 1970 and the Pollution Prevention Act of 1990. Enacted twenty years apart, these acts, when contrasted, give a sense of the history and future direction of our environmental policies.

The National Environmental Policy Act was signed into law on January 1, 1970, and may be characterized as a planning statute. It does three things directly:

1. Establishes the Council on Environmental Quality (CEQ), the federal watchdog of environmental policy;

2. Requires federal agencies to take environmental consequences into account when they make certain decisions, which before NEPA, they could not do because consideration of such effects was rarely listed in agencies' enabling acts as a factor to be taken into account in agency decision making; and

3. Requires that an Environmental Impact Statement (EIS) be prepared for every major legislative proposal or other federal agency action having a significant impact on the quality of the human environment.

Council on Environmental Quality

The least controversial aspect of NEPA was its first mandate: the creation of the Council on Environmental Quality (CEQ). The CEQ was made up of three persons, one of whom was designated the chair. The role of the council was primarily advisory, mainly advising the president about environmental matters. For more than twenty years, the CEQ gathered and analyzed data, informed the president about the progress the nation was making toward cleaning the environment, and recommended legislation that needed to be passed and issues requiring attention. Every year the CEQ used the data it gathered to publish the *President's Annual Report on Environmental Quality*, which was available to the public.

The CEQ also helped federal agencies to meet their EIS requirements under NEPA by reviewing drafts of these statements. The CEQ established regulations pertaining to NEPA procedures.

The chair of the CEQ had additional duties. He or she attended meetings of the President's Domestic Policy Council when environmental matters were discussed, represented the president at international conferences, and drafted memos and executive orders related to the environment. The chair also coordinated federal agency activities involved with the World Commission on Environmental Development (WCED), an offshoot of the United Nations General Assembly that conducts research on environmental topics.

The CEQ was decimated during the 1980s. Adjusted for inflation, the CEQ's budget dropped from $4.1 million in 1975 to $700,000 by 1990, an 83 percent decline. Its staff fell from fifty-seven in 1977 to eleven by the late 1980s.[13] With such drastic cuts in budget and personnel, it became increasingly difficult for the CEQ even to produce its mandated annual report, which continued to diminish in size and fell several years behind schedule toward the end of the 1980s.[14] Many had hoped that the CEQ would return to its earlier form when Clinton was elected. But President Clinton surprised many by instead moving to abolish the CEQ in February 1993 and proposing a new Office of Environmental Policy, designed to have broader influence than the CEQ. The head of this new office would be a deputy assistant to the president; Kathleen McGinty, a former Senate staff aide to Albert Gore, was appointed to fill this new position. Among her tasks would be sitting in on meetings of the Domestic Policy Council, the National Security Council, and the Economic Policy Council.

While the Office of the Environment was established, and the major positions of the CEQ were left unfilled, the House refused to pass Clinton's bill. In August 1995, Clinton finally decided to rejuvenate the CEQ, merge the Office of Environmental Quality into the CEQ, and name Kathleen McGinty head of the CEQ. Many environmentalists were pleased with the revitalization of the CEQ because they believe it plays a unique role in oversight of NEPA.

Environmental Impact Statement

Far more controversial than the creation of the CEQ was the requirement of the Environmental Impact Statement (EIS). This requirement has a widespread impact on several government agencies, as well as on private firms seeking to do business under governmental agency contracts or licenses. Although the process has been criticized by many affected groups, most studies of NEPA's effectiveness have concluded that it has forced greater governmental awareness and more careful planning in many agencies. To get an idea of the impact of the EIS process, examine table 4–1, which lists the number of EISs filed by federal agencies during the years 1979 through 1992. Several major issues pervade an analysis of the EIS requirement, ranging from who must file the EIS and when, to disputes over what must be included in the statement, to whether the process is effective.

Threshold Considerations. Every time a federal agency undertakes an activity, it must decide whether to file an EIS. Filing an unnecessary EIS is a waste of time and money. Failure to file a necessary statement can be equally or more expensive if someone challenges the lack of an EIS and seeks an injunction in court. However, it is not always easy to know when an EIS is required. NEPA specifies three conditions that must be met for an EIS to be required. First, the activity must be *federal*. A federal activity is fairly broadly defined. If, for example, a private-sector construction firm wants to construct a building that requires a government license or if the project is going to be

TABLE 4–1 Environmental Impact Statements Filed by Federal Agencies, 1979–1992

Agency	1979	1980	1981	1982	1983	1984	1985	1986	1987	1988	1989	1990	1991	1992
Agriculture	172	104	102	89	59	65	117	118	75	68	89	138	145	129
Commerce	54	53	36	25	14	24	10	8	9	3	5	8	13	12
Defense	1	1	1	1	1	0	0	0	2	0	0	0	0	1
Air Force	8	3	7	4	6	5	7	8	9	6	11	19	20	19
Army	40	9	14	3	6	5	5	2	10	8	9	9	21	13
COE	182	150	186	127	119	116	106	91	76	69	40	48	45	56
Navy	11	9	10	6	4	9	8	13	9	6	4	19	9	6
Energy	28	45	21	24	19	14	4	13	11	9	6	11	2	15
EPA	84	71	96	63	67	42	16	18	19	23	25	31	16	4
GSA	13	11	13	8	1	0	4	0	1	3	0	4	3	15
HUD	170	140	140	93	42	13	15	18	6	2	7	5	7	2
Interior	126	131	107	127	146	115	105	98	110	117	61	68	64	79
Transportation	277	189	221	183	169	147	126	110	101	96	80	100	87	129
TVA	9	6	4	0	2	1	0	1	0	0	0	3	0	3
Other	98	44	76	55	22	21	26	15	17	20	23	18	24	29
TOTAL:	1273	966	1034	808	677	577	549	513	455	430	360	481	456	512

Source: Council on Environmental Quality

partly financed by a government loan, the licensing or lending agency is undertaking a federal activity.

Whether an EIS is required for a federal activity depends on whether the other two criteria are met. The federal activity must be *major;* however, there are no dollar guidelines as to what constitutes a major activity. The courts generally say that the activity requires a substantial commitment of resources, with resources being broadly defined to include both financial and human resources. A substantial commitment of either type of resource is sufficient.

The third criterion is that the proposed activity must have a *significant impact on the human environment.* The term "significant impact on the human environment" is so ambiguous that it initially generated substantial litigation. Then, in 1979, the CEQ tried to resolve some of the controversy by adopting a series of guidelines for the implementation of NEPA's procedural provisions. In these guidelines, the CEQ tried to define better what was meant by "significant impact." The CEQ stated that determining the significance of an impact necessitated examining both the context and the intensity of the action. Looking at the context was said to require consideration of both the short- and long-term effects of the activity and discovering the impact of the activity on the local area, the region, and society as a whole.

Examining the intensity of an activity was said to involve ten factors: (1) both beneficial and detrimental effects; (2) the degree to which the public health and safety may be affected; (3) unique characteristics of the geographic area that may be affected by the activity; (4) the degree to which the effects of the activity are likely to cause controversy; (5) the degree to which the effects on the human environment are highly uncertain or unique; (6) the degree to which the activity is likely to set a precedent for future actions; (7) whether insignificant effects from this activity, when combined with insignificant effects from other activities, will constitute significant effects; (8) the degree to which the act may affect places of scientific, historic, or cultural significance; (9) the degree to which an act may adversely affect an endangered species; and (10) whether the act threatens any law designed to protect the environment.[15]

Even with this "clarification" by the CEQ, it is still sometimes difficult to know whether an EIS is necessary. A demonstration of that difficulty can be made by examining two very similar cases. After reading the descriptions, try to decide whether the court in either case required an EIS.

Both cases involved the Department of Housing and Urban Development (HUD). In case 1, HUD was preparing to loan a developer $3.5 million to construct a high-rise in an area of Portland where there were no other high-rises.[16] In case 2, HUD was preparing to insure a developer's $3.7 million loan to construct a 272-unit apartment complex in Houston on a fifteen-acre lot.[17] Must HUD file EISs in both cases, either case, or neither case? The court in the first case required an EIS; the court in the second case did not.

There were two primary reasons for the different outcomes: First, the activity in case 1 was major, whereas the second was not. Though both involved millions of dollars, the actual transfer of money was likely to be much greater in the first case than in the second, because the former required the actual lending of money whereas the latter was only a guarantee of a loan.[18] The transfer of funds would occur only if the developer failed to pay the loan. Because of the careful screening of candidates for insured loans, failure of repayment did not appear likely. Second, the impact of the first activity was more significant. In the first case, the use was for a unique activity, whereas in Houston, where there was no zoning as the city developed, building a housing complex was not unique, regardless of where it was.[19] There was also the possibility that building one high-rise in Portland might set a dangerous precedent, leading to overcrowding in the area. Another factor, not mentioned in the statement of the case, was that there was organized opposition to the high-rise in Portland.

Some factors that may influence whether an EIS is required include the jurisdiction and the time.[20] Recall from your previous reading that most attorneys who do environmental work are quite aware that certain judges or courts tend to hand down more proenvironmentalist decisions than do others. In fact, in situations in which a corporation with operations in many states is being sued, and the company would fall within the jurisdiction of multiple courts, the plaintiff will carefully examine rulings of all those courts so that the case may be filed in the most environmentally friendly one.

Time may have an impact in three ways. First, though judges are supposed not to be influenced by the public, they would not be human if they were totally unaffected by public opinion. Thus, at a time when there is strong public sentiment in support of environmental protection, judges may be moved slightly toward requiring EISs in close cases. A second factor is that during a period when the federal courts are dominated by judges appointed by a strong environmentalist president, judges may be more likely to require EISs because appointees probably have political values similar to those of the president who made the appointments. Finally, the prevailing political climate may influence federal judges who are desirous of appointments to higher courts.

In any situation in which the need to file an EIS is questionable, some analysis of the significance of an activity's impact must obviously take place. If an agency decides that no EIS is necessary, although it believes others may disagree, the agency may try to protect itself by filing a Finding of No Significant Impact, or FONSI. This document states the reasons why the agency believes no EIS is necessary. The FONSI is usually accompanied by an environmental assessment that provides the evidence and analysis for the agency's decision.

Once the agency decides that it needs to file an EIS, certain procedural steps must be followed. These procedures are detailed in the following section.

Procedure under the EIS Requirement. One of the major criticisms of the EIS process is related to the time-consuming nature of the procedures necessary for preparing an EIS. Initially, the agency required to file the EIS will assemble a team of specialists to prepare a draft report. In many cases, this team will consist of outside consultants, many of whom may have a vested interest in preparing positive assessments so that they will be able to secure contracts from the agency in the future. Next, a draft version will be circulated within the agency, to be reviewed by several parties. There may frequently be disputes between those reviewers who are proagency or proindustry and those who are more environmentally concerned. The draft may be revised as a result of these initial comments.

Following the agency's completion of that draft, the document goes to the CEQ for review and comments. Then, in accordance with the Administrative Procedure Act's rules for informal rule making, the draft is published in the *Federal Register* for public comment. Many other agencies will submit comments at this time, as will citizens' groups and business interests.

After the public comments have been received, a similar process will be followed for the final draft. If a draft has been severely criticized, the agency is faced with the difficult decision of whether to try to "repair" the heavily criticized draft or draft an entirely new document. This type of dispute can tie up an agency for weeks or months. Preparing a new draft is time-consuming and costly, because all the steps have to be repeated with the new statement. However, proceeding with an inadequate EIS may lead to a successful legal challenge by parties opposed to the action. Once the agency is satisfied with its final draft, it publishes it in the *Federal Register.* For a routine EIS, this entire procedure may take from six to nine months. Court challenges may tie up this process for a year or longer.

After publication of the final draft, the sufficiency of the draft may be challenged in court. Also, the failure to file an EIS when required may also be challenged. This process of judicial review of the EIS has led to criticism by environmentalists. When reviewing the EIS, the court generally operates in an administrative law tradition, which means that the court will *not* substitute its judgment for the agency's. As long as the agency followed the proper procedures and included the requisite elements in the EIS, the court will allow the EIS to stand and the agency action to occur.

Even if the court finds that the EIS was inadequate, the only remedy is a temporary injunction of agency action until a proper EIS has been filed. This limited power of the courts has led many to argue that the filing of an EIS is a "toothless" requirement. You might think that given the limited remedy available under NEPA, few challenges would be filed. However, between 1974 and 1985, roughly 120 NEPA cases were filed each year.

The most frequent plaintiffs in challenges to EISs are citizens' groups and environmental groups. Table 4–2 lists the plaintiffs in NEPA lawsuits filed in 1990. The most frequent defendants tend to be the Department of

TABLE 4–2 Plaintiffs for NEPA Lawsuits, 1990

Plaintiffs	Number of Cases
Environmental groups	38
Individuals or citizens' groups	38
State governments	5
Local governments	9
Business groups	5
Property owners or residents	13
Indian tribes	2
Other	2
Total	112

Source: CEQ, Environmental Quality, 22nd Annual Report (1991).

Transportation, the Department of the Interior, the Army Corps of Engineers, and the Federal Energy Regulatory Commission.

Contents of the EIS. Whether an agency voluntarily prepares an EIS or is required to do so by the courts, certain elements must be contained in the document: (1) a statement of environmental impacts (positive and negative) of the proposed action; (2) any unavoidable adverse environmental impacts should the proposal be implemented; (3) alternatives to the proposal (including taking no action); (4) the relationship between short-term uses of the environment and enhancement of long-range productivity; and (5) any irreversible commitments of resources. The suggested format for the EIS is given in table 4–3.

POLLUTION PREVENTION ACT

The first environmental protection laws used a very directive approach. The EPA was to establish standards, and the other agencies and businesses were to meet those standards. Many of the early regulations, as you shall see when you read about specific laws in subsequent chapters, were "command and control" (dictated standards) or "end of pipe" (using technology to treat the waste or pollutant just before it was emitted). And, in fact, these are still the primary types of regulations today. The Pollution Prevention Act, however, recognizes that these end-of-pipe regulations may not be enough and focuses on the prevention of pollution.

Initially great gains were made using these strategies. Relatively minor investments led to dramatic decreases in pollutants. However, after twenty

TABLE 4-3 Format of Environmental Impact Statements

Item	Length	Contents Include
1. Cover sheet	Up to 1 page	Title and locations of proposed action; locale involved; agencies; names and addresses of persons who can supply further information; relevant dates; one-paragraph abstract of statement.
2. Summary	Up to 15 pages	Summary of statement stressing major conclusions, areas of controversy, and issues to be resolved.
3. Table of contents		
4. Purpose and need for action		
5. Alternatives, including proposed action		Heart of the statement. Rigorous evaluation of all alternatives, including why some were eliminated from consideration; including alternative of no action; identifying agencies' preferred action; and including appropriate mitigation actions.
6. Affected environment	No longer than necessary	Succinct description.
7. Environmental consequences		Discussions of direct and indirect effects and their significance; energy requirements; possible conflicts with land-use plans of other governmental bodies; depletable resource requirements and conservation potential of alternatives; urban quality; historical and cultural resources; and means to initiate impacts if not already discussed.
8. List of preparers	Not to exceed 2 pages	Names and qualifications.
9. List of agencies, organizations, and persons to whom copies are to be sent		
10. Index		
11. Appendixes (if any)		Material prepared in connection with the EIS that is analytical and relevant to any decisions to be made and substantiates any analysis fundamental to the EIS.

years of implementation of these end-of-pipe controls, it became increasingly costly to get increasingly smaller reductions of pollutants. It was apparent to Congress that a new approach was necessary. That new approach was embodied in the Pollution Prevention Act of 1990, passed by Congress on October 27, 1990. In its findings, presented in Section 2 of the act, Congress stated:

(1) There are significant opportunities for industry to reduce or prevent pollution at the source through cost-effective changes in production, operation, and raw materials use. Such changes offer industry substantial savings in reduced raw material, pollution control, and liability costs as well as help protect the environment and reduce risks to worker health and safety.

(2) The opportunities for source reduction are often not realized because existing regulations, and the industrial resources they require for compliance, focus upon treatment and disposal, rather than source reduction; existing regulations do not emphasize multi-media management of pollution; and businesses need information and technical assistance to overcome institutional barriers to the adoption of source reductions practices.

(3) Source reduction is fundamentally different and more desirable than waste management and pollution control. The Environmental Protection Agency needs to address the historical lack of attention to source reduction.

The wisdom of these findings is supported by an article in the *Wall Street Journal.* According to the article, chemical companies, traditionally a group with an oft-criticized record on the environment, are making a major shift and beginning to see waste as avoidable and inefficient. The more unusable by-products a process creates, the less efficient it may be. For example, at one Du Pont plant, which generated 110 million pounds of waste annually, engineers adjusted their production process to use less of one raw material and slashed the plant's waste by two-thirds. The resulting savings from the change in process amounted to $1 million a year.[21]

As a result of its findings, Congress established the following policy: "Pollution should be prevented or reduced at the source whenever feasible; pollution that cannot be prevented should be recycled in an environmentally safe manner, whenever feasible; pollution that cannot be prevented or recycled should be treated in an environmentally safe manner whenever feasible; and disposal or other release into the environment should be employed only as a last resort and should be conducted in an environmentally safe manner." To implement this new policy, the administrator of the EPA is required to establish a separate office within the agency to serve as administrator under the act.

The act also authorizes the provision of matching grants to states for programs to promote the use of source reduction techniques by business. Between 1989 and December 1995, more than $36 million in such grants have been awarded to support state and tribal pollution prevention programs. To collect, compile, and disseminate information generated by the grants, the administrator is authorized to establish a clearinghouse to serve as a center for source reduction technology transfer.

Finally, certain biennial reports are required of the administrator of the act. These reports are to include such information as analysis of grant results, identification of industries and pollutants that require priority assistance in multimedia source reduction, and evaluation of data gaps and duplication of data collected under federal environmental protection acts.

Because this act is relatively new, we cannot yet assess its effectiveness. It is clear, however, that many industries are already beginning to move in the direction of pollution prevention. As you shall see later in this book, while we have set forth this policy of pollution prevention and are increasing the use of incentives to prevent creation of pollutants, our primary mode of protecting the environment is still the command-and-control approach.

CONCLUDING REMARKS

The primary justifications for environmental protection range from the analogy of the tragedy of the commons to economic justifications to arguments from an environmental ethos. Taken together, these justifications seem to provide strong support for many of the regulatory programs you are going to be studying.

You have been introduced to various strategies that are adopted to protect the environment, such as tort law, emissions charges, marketable emissions permits, subsidies, and green taxes. In addition, the 1990 Pollution Prevention Act encourages initial prevention and voluntary actions. However, our main approach to environmental problems continues to be direct regulation, which is the focus of the remainder of the book. Chapter 5 examines our approach to controlling air quality. We concentrate on air quality first because the Clean Air Act was the first major end-of-pipe pollution-control law, and subsequent acts for other protected resources were modeled loosely on it.

QUESTIONS FOR REVIEW AND DISCUSSION

1. Explain the relationship between the tragedy of the commons and the need to control pollution.
2. Explain what a *free rider* is and how that concept is related to environmental law.
3. Why is tort law alone an ineffective way to control pollution?
4. Explain the advantages and disadvantages of using emissions charges and subsidies to control pollution.
5. What factors influence the development of environmental policies?
6. Explain when an Environmental Impact Statement must be filed.
7. What must be contained in an EIS?
8. What is the purpose of the 1990 Pollution Prevention Control Act?

FOR FURTHER READING

RICHARD O. BROOKS, *A New Agenda for Environmental Law*, 6 J.L. & LITIG. 1 (1991).

DINAH BEAR, *Using the National Environmental Policy Act to Protect Biological Diversity,* 8 TUL. ENVTL. L.J. 77 (1994).

Comment, *NEPA's Role in Protecting the World Environment,* 131 U. Pa. L. REV. 353 (1982).

Comment, *NEPA Violations and Equitable Discretion,* 64 OR. L. REV. 497 (1986).

KEITH HAWKINS, ENVIRONMENT AND ENFORCEMENT: REGULATION AND THE SOCIAL DEFINITION OF POLLUTION (New York: Clarendon Press, 1984).

FRANK MULLER & J. ANDREW HOERNER, *Greening State Energy Taxes: Carbon Taxes for Revenue and the Environment,* 12 PACE ENVTL. L.J. 5 (1994).

Note, *Legal Institutions and Pollution: Some Intersections between Law and History,* 15 NAT. RESOURCES J. 423 (1975).

EDWARD W. ORTS, *Toward Reflexive Environmental Law,* 89 NW. U. L. REV. 1227 (1995).

PETER YEAGER, THE LIMITS OF THE LAW: THE PUBLIC REGULATION OF PRIVATE POLLUTION (New York: Cambridge University Press, 1991).

ON THE INTERNET

http://www.panda.org/
News and information on all aspects of conservation, the environment, and sustainable development

http://www.os.kcp.com/home/catalog/polprepro.html
Provides background information about pollution prevention

http://ingis.acn.purdue.edu:9999/cttpp/
Home page of the Center for Technology Transfer and Pollution Prevention, Region 5

http://www.webcom.com/~staber/press_releases
Contains press releases issued by the EPA

NOTES

1. GARRETT HARDIN, *The Tragedy of the Commons,* 162 SCI. 1243 (1968).
2. Ibid.
3. ALDO LEOPOLD, A SAND COUNTY ALMANAC, 214–220 (New York: Oxford University Press, 1968).
4. Ibid.

5. 287 N.Y.S 2d. 112 (1967).

6. NORMAN VIG, *Presidential Leadership: From the Reagan to the Bush Administration,* in ENVIRONMENTAL POLICY IN THE 1990'S: TOWARD A NEW AGENDA (NORMAN VIG & MICHAEL KRAFT, eds., Washington, D.C.: Congressional Quarterly Press, 1990).

7. Ibid.

8. Ibid.

9. Ibid.

10. *Getting Personal,* WALL ST. J. R3 (Jan. 20, 1993).

11. MARGARET C. FISK, *Girding for a Change,* NATL. L.J. S1 (Dec. 14, 1992).

12. Ibid.

13. MICHAEL KRAFT & NORMAN VIG, *Environmental Policies from the Seventies to the Nineties,* in ENVIRONMENTAL POLICY IN THE 1990'S: TOWARD A NEW AGENDA (NORMAN VIG & MICHAEL KRAFT, eds., Washington, D.C.: Congressional Quarterly Press, 1990).

14. Ibid.

15. 40 C.F.R. § 1508.27.

16. Goose Hollow Foothills League v. Romney, 334 F. Supp. 877 (1971).

17. Hiram Clarke Civic Club v. Lynn, 47 F.2d 421 (1973).

18. DAVID FIRESTONE & FRANK REED, ENVIRONMENTAL LAW FOR NONLAWYERS (South Royalton, VT: Soro Press, 1983).

19. Ibid.

20. Ibid.

21. SCOTT MCMURRAY, *Chemical Firms Find That It Pays to Reduce Pollution at the Source,* WALL ST. J. A1, col. 6 (June 11, 1991).

CHAPTER 5

Air Quality Control

W hen people think about air quality problems, they often think of bumper-to-bumper traffic spewing exhaust on a freeway or steel mills with smokestacks blackening the air with soot. The first major air pollution control act, the Clean Air Act of 1970, was designed to remedy such problems. This act was passed because people no longer considered visible pollution to be evidence of economic progress but rather as a problem in need of a regulatory solution. Although this first major statutory response significantly improved air quality, air pollution is still one of the most serious environmental problems in the United States. As recently as 1990, the EPA estimated that more than 100 million Americans lived in areas where air pollution levels exceed federal ambient air quality standards.[1]

To understand the current approach to air quality control, we first need to understand which pollutants we are trying to restrict, and why we need to control them. The first section provides this information. Whereas these "criteria pollutants" have been the initial focus of regulation, other air quality problems must be remedied, and these are introduced in the second and third sections. A fourth section explains the early and unsuccessful approach initially adopted to protect the air. Finally, the last section explains the current approach.

THE MAJOR AIR POLLUTANTS

Every minute of the day, vast quantities of pollutants are pouring into the atmosphere. These pollutants come from both natural and human sources and are normally cycled and destroyed through natural processes. However, the quantity of human-made pollutants has begun to overload the atmosphere's self-cleansing processes, causing damage to the environment and health problems. Although we shall discuss the primary harm caused by each individual pollutant, you should be aware that much damage also comes from the interactions of these pollutants.

The first six air pollutants we will discuss are currently regulated by Congress under the Clean Air Act. They are referred to under the act as criteria pollutants. It is these criteria pollutants that were initially perceived as the major air quality problem, and so were the initial focus of governmental ef-

TABLE 5–1 Problems Associated with Criteria Air Pollutants

Pollutant	Problems
Sulfur dioxide	Causes lung and respiratory tract damage and contributes to acid rain, which damages trees, buildings, vegetation, and aquatic life.
Nitrogen oxides	Causes lung and respiratory tract damage and contributes to acid rain and smog.
Carbon monoxide	Replaces oxygen in bloodstream, causing angina, impaired vision, poor coordination, and lack of alertness. Contributes to formation of ozone.
Ozone	Irritates eyes, reduces lung function, increases nasal congestion, and reduces resistance to infection.
Particulates	Reduces resistance to infection, irritates the eyes, ears, and throat, and causes temporary or permanent lung damage.
Lead	Damages neurological systems and kidneys.

forts to improve the quality of our air. Many people still regard the regulation of these pollutants through the establishment of ambient air quality standards to be the heart of air pollution control in the United States. A brief summary of the problems caused by these pollutants is presented in table 5–1.

Sulfur Dioxide

Sulfur dioxide (SO_2) is a highly corrosive gas that can be transported long distances in the atmosphere because it bonds to particles of dust, smoke, or aerosols. Volcanic emissions are the largest natural source of atmospheric sulfur dioxide, although decaying organic matter and sea spray are also important. However, slightly more than half the approximately 170 million tons of SO_2 emitted globally each year come from human-made sources. The major human source of sulfur dioxide is the burning of fossil fuels to generate electricity. The United States relies on these fuels for 90 percent of its energy needs.

Since 1900, the global output of sulfur dioxide has increased sixfold.[2] However, between 1974 and 1987, most industrial nations lowered their SO_2 emissions in urban areas through direct regulation and also by a shift away from heavy manufacturing toward burning lower-sulfur coal.

The primary health danger from SO_2 is damage to the lungs and respiratory tract. In combination with nitrous oxide, SO_2 also contributes to the creation of acid rain, which causes harm to vegetation and buildings. Acid rain is discussed in greater detail later in this chapter.

Nitrogen Oxides

Nitrogen oxide (NO_x) refers to two harmful gases: nitric oxide (NO) and nitrogen dioxide (NO_2). Nitric oxide, almost immediately upon release, is converted into nitrogen dioxide. On a global basis, about half the approximately 150 million tons of NO_x emitted annually comes from natural sources, predominantly lightening and decomposing organic matter. The other half comes from human activities, with motor vehicles the largest source. Power plants and industrial emissions also make substantial contributions. Though industrialization and development have led to substantial NO_x emissions in the United States, new technology has resulted in a decrease from peak discharge levels.

The primary negative health effects from NO_x mirror those of SO_2: damage to the lungs and respiratory tract. In combination with other air pollutants, NO_x contributes to depletion of the ozone layer, acid deposition, and smog.

Carbon Monoxide

A third harmful gas is carbon monoxide (CO). Unlike most air pollutants, an estimated 60 percent of CO comes from natural sources. The major human-made source is the incomplete burning of fuels by motor vehicles in some urban areas. Other human sources of CO include wood stoves, incinerators, and industrial processes. Over the past fifteen years, the United States, Japan, and Germany have reduced their CO emission. In the United States, 98.7 million metric tons of CO were emitted during 1970; that amount steadily declined year after year, primarily as a result of automobile emission controls. Emissions fell to 61.4 million metric tons during 1987.[3] Yet by 1992, carbon monoxide levels still exceeded the Federal Air Quality standard in twenty U.S. cities, thereby affecting more than 14 million people.

Carbon monoxide traditionally has been perceived as the least harmful of the criteria pollutants in terms of its effect on human health, but increasing evidence suggests that it presents a serious health risk. When carbon monoxide is inhaled, it replaces oxygen in the bloodstream, causing angina, impaired vision, poor coordination, and lack of alertness. It may temporarily reduce one's attention span and problem-solving abilities. CO has been implicated in some accidents caused by decreased attention and reduced sensory ability. The health effects are especially severe for people who have heart and lung problems. Some animal studies have also indicated that CO can damage the central nervous system of offspring who had chronic prenatal exposure to the pollutant. Carbon monoxide contributes to the greenhouse effect and to the formation of ozone, itself an air pollutant.

Ozone

Some people argue that ozone is the most intractable and widespread pollution problem. Ozone, as a pollutant at low altitudes—not to be confused with the ozone layer of the atmosphere, which actually protects life on earth—is not directly emitted into the air as are most of the other pollutants with which the Clean Air Act is concerned. Rather, ozone is a gas formed when nitrogen oxides react with oxygen in the presence of sunlight, a reaction that can be enhanced by the presence of reactive hydrocarbons and other pollutants commonly found in urban environments. Chemically, ozone is a form of oxygen that has three oxygen atoms instead of two.

We cannot measure emissions of ozone, so we examine the concentration of ozone in the air. The EPA considers the maximal safe level to be 0.12 ppm (parts per million). During 1988, ninety-six U.S. regions exceeded this standard on some days. Concentrations vary significantly from region to region, however, and even from day to day in the same place, depending on such factors as weather and the amount of industrial activity.

Ozone causes eye irritation, nasal congestion, asthma, reduced lung function, possible damage to lung tissue, and reduced resistance to infection. Ozone harms vegetation by damaging plant tissue, inhibiting photosynthesis, and increasing a plant's susceptibility to disease and drought.

Particulates

A fifth criterion pollutant is particulates. Particulates as a pollutant refers to solid and liquid materials, varying in size from aerosol to large grit and suspended in the air. The primary human-made sources of particulates are steel mills, power plants, cotton gins, smelters, cement plants, and diesel engines. Other sources include grain elevators, demolition sites, industrial roadwork, construction work, and wood-burning stoves and fireplaces. Natural sources include soil erosion and pollen. Emissions controls have drastically reduced the amount of suspended particulates emitted into the atmosphere from human-made sources in the United States.[4]

The health impacts of particulates vary, depending on the particulates' size, shape, and chemistry. Fine particles pose a much greater risk to human health than do those with a diameter greater than ten micrometers. The larger particles can be filtered out by the body's defense mechanisms, whereas the finer ones may pass through the defense mechanisms and travel into the lungs where they may become embedded. Once in the lungs, the particulates may lead to respiratory illness or lung or other systemic damage. Evidence for this contention is available in a demonstrated statistical correlation between high levels of particulate matter in the lungs and hospital admissions for pneumonia, bronchitis, and asthma.[5] Some particulates are carcinogenic; others may merely irritate the eyes and throat.

Lead

The first five air pollutants were regulated as criteria pollutants under the Clean Air Act of 1970. Lead is the only pollutant to be added to the initial list of criteria pollutants. Lead emissions result primarily from burning leaded gasoline. It is also present in paints and leaded pipes.

We can see the greatest impact of regulation on pollution levels when we look at lead emissions. In 1970, 203.8 thousand metric tons spewed forth from human sources in the United States. By 1987, this amount had fallen to

8.1 thousand metric tons.[6] These dramatic reductions resulted primarily from a prohibition of leaded gas.

Lead is of concern because it can harm the neurological system and kidneys of humans and animals. It can also inhibit respiration and photosynthesis in plants and block the decomposition of microorganisms.

AIRBORNE TOXINS

Another substantial group of pollutants causes both long- and short-term harm when emitted in small concentrations. Generally refered to as airborne toxins or toxic air pollutants, this group is large and not well defined, and we know relatively little about their effects on health. Most of what we do know about their toxicity comes from studies of industrial workplaces, where these pollutants may be present in elevated concentrations, and from animal studies.

It is estimated that at least 189 toxic air pollutants are currently, or will be by 1999, regulated under the most recent Clean Air Act amendments. Some toxic pollutants of high concern are benzene, primarily from chemical and plastics plants; vinyl chloride, from similar sources as benzene; chlorinated dioxins, from sources such as chemical processes and high-temperature burning of plastics in incinerators; asbestos; beryllium; mercury; arsenic; radionuclides; and coke oven emissions. These were the only toxic air pollutants regulated before the passage of the 1990 Clean Air Act amendments.

SOME SIGNIFICANT AIR QUALITY PROBLEMS

In recent years attention has shifted somewhat away from questioning how to control conventional and toxic pollutants to more global air quality problems. These international issues are the concern of this section.

Acid Deposition

The existence of acid deposition or acid precipitation has been known for years. Only recently, however, has acid deposition been recognized as a problem. Acid deposition is a process that begins with the emission of sulfur dioxide or nitrogen oxides. These pollutants interact with sunlight and water vapor in the upper atmosphere to form sulfuric and nitric acids, which fall to earth as acid snow or acid rain. Sometimes the compounds may dust other airborne dry particles and fall as *dry deposition.*

Acidity is measured on a pH scale that ranges from 0 to 14, with 7 being neutral, higher levels being basic, and lower levels indicating acidity. "Pure" rain, uncontaminated by human or natural sulfates, has a pH of about 5.6. Figure 5–1 depicts a pH scale and shows where various substances would fall on such a scale. Most rain is slightly acidic. Acid precipitation be-

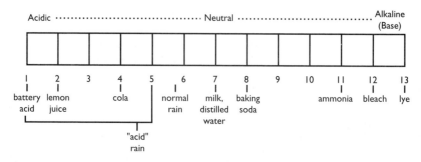

FIGURE 5–1 Measuring the Acidity of Various Substances

gins to become a problem when the pH levels fall below 5. Rainfall with a pH level as low as 4.3 has been measured in parts of Canada and the United States.

As noted, a primary cause of acid precipitation is sulfur dioxide emissions. According to the National Commission on Air Quality, between 75 and 90 percent of the sulfate concentration of rain falling on any state in the eastern half of the United States is attributable to sources outside those states. This export of acid gases has resulted from the use of tall smokestacks (more than five hundred feet high), which use smelters and electric utilities to disperse their emissions into the upper reaches of the atmosphere. Unfortunately, the result has simply been to spread the acidic deposition over greater areas. Ohio, Indiana, Illinois, and Kentucky alone are responsible for nearly one-fourth of the SO_2 production in the United States, primarily from the burning of coal to generate electricity.

The extent of harm caused by acid rain depends on the amount of acid deposition in an area and its sensitivity. The Midwest has heavily alkaline soils that can buffer the effects of acid rain. Lakes that lie on limestone, sandstone, or other alkaline foundations, primarily those located in the western and midwestern regions of the nation, are likewise resistant to damage from acid deposition. Regions where lakes and soils lie on granite or thin glacial tills have much lower buffering capacity and thus are more susceptible to damage.

Considerable debate exists over exactly how acid deposition causes harm. The primary harm attributed to acid rain is damage to aquatic life, including the elimination of several species of fish and invertebrates in acidified regions. (When the pH of a lake falls below 5.0, most of its fish cannot survive.) Some fish taken from acidified lakes have high concentrations of mercury and other heavy metals that have been leached from the underlying soils, which makes them unfit for human consumption. Furthermore, acid precipitation erodes stone buildings and monuments.

Depletion of the Ozone Layer

We have previously discussed how ozone is a pollutant in the air we breathe. However, in an upper layer of the atmosphere, the stratosphere, between nine and thirty miles above the surface of the earth, ozone acts as a filter to help prevent ultraviolet (UV) radiation from reaching the earth. Ultraviolet radiation is known to cause skin cancer in humans, be harmful to plant life, and potentially cause severe disruptions to the ecosystem.

There is growing and alarming evidence that the ozone layer is being depleted in several areas. Originally the major concern was about the "hole" developing in the atmosphere over Antarctica; during the past twenty years, ozone levels over Antarctica dropped by more than 50 percent. The "hole" is clearly visible by satellite measurement. Greater concern, however, was aroused by a 1988 study that showed a 2 percent decline in the ozone layer worldwide since 1969. The decline has been as much as 3 percent over some urban areas in North America and Europe, and greater than 3 percent over some parts of Australia, South America, and New Zealand.

The primary causal factor for the decline in the ozone layer is chlorofluorocarbons (CFCs), substances for which emissions increased 28 percent from 1970 to 1985. CFCs are compounds made of chlorine, fluorine, and carbon that have been used as aerosol propellants, coolants, sterilizers, solvents, and blowing agents in foam production since their development in the 1920s. These compounds do not break down in the lower levels of the atmosphere. Instead, they rise up to the stratosphere where they are broken down by ultraviolet light. When broken down, the chlorine reacts with ozone (O_3) to convert it back into molecular oxygen (O_2), thus destroying the ozone layer. What is even worse is that the chlorine molecule acts as a catalyst and moves on to destroy ozone molecule after ozone molecule. A chlorine atom from a single fluorocarbon molecule can destroy as many as twenty thousand ozone molecules. Seventy-five percent of the world's production of this hazardous compound is in the United States and Europe.

A second human-made compound contributing to the depletion of the ozone layer is halon. Halons are used primarily in fire-extinguishing foams. Halons contain bromine, which also acts as a catalyst to deplete the ozone layer. There is some evidence from laboratory tests that nitrogen oxides may also remove ozone from the stratosphere. As you may recall, nitrogen oxides are released primarily by the burning of fossil fuels. They also come from the use of nitrogen-rich fertilizers.

The Greenhouse Effect

Probably the most controversial air quality problem is the greenhouse effect. Everyone basically agrees on the definition of the greenhouse effect; the controversy centers on whether such an effect is occurring, and if so, at what rate and with what consequences.

The greenhouse effect occurs when carbon dioxide, methane, CFCs, nitrous oxide, and traces of a few other gases act in a manner analogous to the glass in a greenhouse. Visible light passes through the layer of gas to the earth's surface, heating it. The warmed surface then radiates energy back out toward space, but the greenhouse gases capture some of this heat, which warms the atmosphere. A certain amount of greenhouse effect is necessary because without it, Earth would be a frozen planet like Mars, with an average temperature of about 0°F. The question scientists are grappling with is whether increases in the amount of carbon dioxide in the atmosphere (primarily from the burning of fossil fuels and the destruction of rain forests) have created a warming trend that may cause an increase of 6°C over the next century.

The evidence is not clear. A recent study in the United States (2 percent of the earth's surface) found that temperatures had not increased during the past one hundred years. However, the global average air temperature at the earth's surface has increased 0.5°C over the past century. Also, between 1982 and 1988, ocean surface temperatures, as monitored by satellite, increased by approximately 0.1°C per year.

Possible Effects of Rising Temperatures.   A 1988 study by the American Association for the Advancement of Science predicted that an "equivalent doubling" of CO_2 will raise the average global temperature 2 to 5°C, with the middle and upper latitudes (including North America, Europe, and Asia) warming at twice the global average.[7] The warming could have an effect on precipitation. Some areas in the higher latitudes, such as the Soviet Union and Canada, could receive more rain and snow. Some wet tropical areas could receive more rainfall. The midwestern United States could become hotter and drier. There could also be an increase in the frequency and severity of hurricanes and other tropical storms because of increased ocean temperatures.

According to the EPA, sea levels could rise seven feet (2.2 meters) by the year 2100 as a result of the expansion of water as it warms, perhaps exacerbated by the melting of polar ice. This rise in sea levels could displace populations in some coastal areas, such as in Egypt and Louisiana. Some low-lying river deltas and floodplains where rice is currently grown would be inundated with water and lost. Global warming could have an impact on forests because trees are sensitive to climate variation.

Agriculture might also be affected. Precipitation patterns could change, and much of the midwestern United States could experience long, dry summers with insufficient rain to raise traditional crops of corn and wheat. Irrigational practices might help mitigate these changes but would increase costs and disrupt current farming practices.

Indoor Pollution

Indoor pollution has only recently received much attention. This type of pollution occurs when airborne toxins, irritants, and other air pollutants become trapped inside buildings; this problem has been exacerbated by the construction of energy-efficient buildings. The EPA has estimated that as many as 30 percent of new and remodeled buildings have indoor air quality problems.

Poorly ventilated buildings trap airborne pathogens, such as bacteria, fungi, and viruses; radioactive gases, such as radon; a wide range of inorganic compounds including lead and mercury; and organic compounds such as formaldehyde and chloroform. Many of these harmful pollutants are caused by indoor smoking, the use of wood stoves and space heaters, chemicals on furniture finishings, and the use of cleaning solvents, wood finishing products, and air fresheners. Figure 5–2 illustrates some of these sources of indoor pollution.

FIGURE 5–2 Air Pollution in the Home

Source: EPA, *Environmental Progress and Challenges: EPA's Update* (Washington, D.C., U.S. Government Printing Office, 1988), p. 32.

In the short run, these pollutants can cause "sick building syndrome," which is associated with runny noses; headaches; eye, nose, and throat irritations; fatigue; lethargy; irritability, dizziness; and nausea. In the long run, they may lead to impairment of the nervous system and cancer.

One indoor pollutant discovered in the 1960s that presents a special problem because it is naturally occurring is radon. Radon is a gas emitted as a result of the radioactive decay of radium-226, found in a wide variety of rocks and soil. Radon enters homes through cracks in the foundation and structure and is trapped in buildings with poor ventilation. Research by the EPA in thirty-four states revealed that one in five homes had excessive levels of radon. When radon is inhaled, the particles release radiation that can damage lung tissue and cause cancer. The EPA estimates that radon may be responsible for between five thousand and twenty thousand lung cancer deaths per year.

THE INITIAL APPROACH TO AIR QUALITY CONTROL

Now that we understand some of the air quality problems, we shall examine how the United States has attempted to address those issues. The central legislation, and the law we shall focus on, is the Clean Air Act and its amendments. Although we often think of the Clean Air Act of 1970 as the first piece of air quality regulation, there actually have been small amounts of regulatory activity in this area since the late 1800s. No legislation was very effective, however, until the Clean Air Act.

Air Pollution Control Act of 1955.   The main function of the first piece of federal clean air regulation was simply to provide federal money for research into air pollution control. It authorized the surgeon general to investigate complaints of pollution problems brought by state or local governments.

Motor Vehicle Control Act of 1960.   In 1960, Congress recognized that automobiles were causing air quality problems. Motor vehicle emissions of carbon monoxide, hydrocarbons, and nitrogen oxides were blamed for 60 percent of all air pollution. Congress passed the Motor Vehicle Act of 1960, which authorized research into the air pollution effects of motor vehicles.

Clean Air Act of 1963.   The first national air quality act was the Clean Air Act of 1963, which did not mandate any reduction of pollution. There were four major features to this act.

First, it authorized the surgeon general to conduct investigations into specific or local pollution problems at the request of any state or local government, and it permitted the secretary of HEW to make such investigations on his own initiative if the pollution affected a state other than the state that was the source of the pollution. However, any recommendations following the investigations were advisory only; the states could ignore them.

Second, the act expanded the research and technical assistance programs established under the Motor Vehicle Act of 1955, and provided grants to state and local governments to aid them in developing and improving their control programs.

Third, it provided for the development of air quality criteria by the secretary of HEW. These criteria were to reflect scientific knowledge of the effects of various pollution concentrations. Again, the criteria were advisory only.

Finally, the 1963 act provided for federal abatement of action in cases in which the health and welfare of citizens was being endangered by air pollution. The secretary of HEW could convene a conference on his own initiative when the pollution was interstate; it could be convened at the request of the governor for intrastate problems. The conference would issue a technical report on the problem, and the secretary would recommend an enforcement action by state or local authorities. These conferences and their enforcement practices were cumbersome, time-consuming, and largely ineffective. From 1963 to 1970, fewer than twelve conferences were held, and only one enforcement action was brought in court.

If you take just a minute to examine the major provisions of this act, you can probably tell what the primary criticisms were. Two obvious problems were the failure of the act's standards to be mandated and its ineffective enforcement. In addition, the act did not define air pollution, stating only that the statute's purpose was to prevent and control air pollution. Also, the act's limited enforcement was hampered by a requirement that the courts take into consideration the practicality and economic and physical feasibility of stopping pollution.

Such a requirement is seen by many as defeating the purpose of the law. They argue that effective statutes must be "technology forcing"; that is, they must require polluters to develop the necessary technology if it does not presently exist.

Motor Vehicle Air Pollution Control Act of 1965. This act authorized the secretary of HEW to prescribe "standards applicable to any class or classes of new motor vehicles or new motor vehicle engines." There was no express prohibition of state controls, but there was stress on the need for uniformity. This act was not particularly effective because it required that consideration be given to economic and technological feasibility of obtaining the standards. Industry could reasonably, if inaccurately, argue that current practices were already selected on the basis of economic and technological practicalities.

1967 Air Quality Act. The 1967 amendments to the Clean Air Act of 1963 (1967 Air Quality Act) provided the first comprehensive federal scheme of air pollution control. This was the first act to establish an orderly procedure for adoption and achievement by states of ambient air quality standards. Under this act, HEW was to designate broad "atmospheric regions" in which meteorology, topology, and other factors influencing air pollutant concentrations were similar (ten regions covering the entire nation were so designated). Next, HEW was to designate "air quality" regions based on jurisdictional boundaries, urban-industrial concentrations, and other factors, including atmospheric areas necessary to provide adequate implementation of air quality standards. The purpose of the act was to create regions within which pollution could be regulated with an integrated set of controls.

Once HEW made the appropriate designations, states were required to adopt ambient air quality standards for the air quality regions, defining permissible concentrations of pollutants. If states failed to establish adequate standards, HEW could promulgate standards after a process of consultation and a public hearing. Finally, states were to adopt, subject to HEW approval, state implementation plans designed to ensure that the state's air would meet the ambient standards. The plan would designate sufficient limitations to be imposed on the sources of air pollution within each region to ensure that the permissible atmospheric concentrations of pollutants were not exceeded. The means for enforcement was the conference. Under this act, federal auto emissions controls were made preemptive of state's controls. In other words, states could not meet the standards by imposing more restrictive limits on auto emissions.

The 1967 Air Quality Act was a significant improvement over previous legislation. To some degree it reflected growing awareness that purely local regulation could not control the pollution problem. Unfortunately, the act was relatively ineffective in achieving rapid and effective control of air pollution. Some attribute the failure to the emphasis on air quality regions, which cut across established state and jurisdictional lines; consequently, it was difficult to obtain agreement on standards or implementation plans.

There were also numerous delays in implementing the steps of the act, such as delays by the federal government in designating regions and issuing criteria documents. States delayed adoption of plans because of a lack of personnel, information, and political will. Another reason for the act's ineffectiveness was that, like previous air quality regulations, this act failed to define air pollution. Reductions in pollution were less likely because the act imposed economic and technological feasibility conditions on the standards. And finally, the legislation left extensive discretion to the states.

THE CURRENT APPROACH TO AIR QUALITY CONTROL

After years of ineffective legislation, the Clean Air Act of 1970 was passed. Arguably, several factors led to the development and passage of this law. First, congressional dissatisfaction with the lack of progress was high. Despite an increasing federal role and rising public concern, most indices showed more emissions and a decline in ambient air quality. Second, state governments responsible for enforcement of pollution-control policies were perceived as weak and vulnerable to industry "blackmail." A related concern was the fact that strict regulations in some states but not in others could put some firms at a competitive disadvantage.

Further, the HEW division responsible for federal air pollution programs was seen as lacking in zeal. Finally, political considerations may have played a role. A democratic Congress could blame failures on the Nixon administration.

This act created a new partnership between state and federal governments, giving the states primary responsibility for directly monitoring, controlling, and preventing pollution while assigning responsibility to the federal EPA for establishing the standards the states must enforce, conducting research, and providing financial and technical assistance to the states. When necessary, the federal EPA steps in to aid the states in implementation and enforcement of regulations. This act, as amended in 1976 and 1990, governs air quality today.

It is easiest to examine the act and its amendments by dividing it into five sections: national ambient air quality standards, new source performance standards, no significant deterioration policy, mobile source emissions standards, and hazardous air toxins standards.

National Ambient Air Quality Standards

Central to the Clean Air Act are the national ambient air quality standards (NAAQSs). Under the 1970 act, the administrator of the EPA is required to determine which pollutants emanating from numerous and diverse mobile and stationary sources have an adverse impact on human health and welfare and to establish ambient air quality standards for these pollutants. The term *ambient air quality* refers to the quality of air representatively sampled from an area. In order to make it easier to measure and monitor air quality, the EPA divided the United States into 247 air quality regions, each having common pollution sources and characteristic weather.

The EPA initially determined that carbon monoxide, sulfur dioxide, hydrocarbons, total suspended particulates, nitrogen dioxide, and ozone required regulation. The hydrocarbon standard was subsequently dropped and lead added. Before setting standards, the EPA prepares a criteria document for each pollutant that contains the scientific evidence of the negative health effects of each pollutant and the methods for controlling the emissions of them. For each of these criteria pollutants, the administrator must set two standards: primary and secondary ambient air quality standards. Primary standards are necessary to protect human health. Human health is interpreted to include the health of the most sensitive individuals, such as children and older adults. Secondary standards are sufficient to protect public welfare. Public welfare includes visibility, plant life, and animal life. Every five years the evidence for the standards must be reviewed and new data analyzed to ensure that the standards are still valid.

State Implementation Plans.   Once the federal EPA issues the standards, in accordance with APA rule-making procedures, responsibility then passes to the states. The EPA, in coordination with the states, established air quality regions, with each state representing at least one region. The states are required to develop state implementation plans (SIPs) that provide means for attaining the NAAQSs within the air quality regions in the state. The states are essentially free to use any types of restriction they desire.

At least in theory, there are strict guidelines for the SIPs. An SIP for a criteria pollutant is to be submitted to the federal EPA for approval within nine months of the date that the NAAQS is promulgated. (This deadline can be extended up to eighteen months for a plan to meet the secondary standard.) The EPA must approve or reject the plan within four months. If an inadequate or incomplete SIP is submitted, the EPA must promulgate a plan, or part thereof, for the state. Or the EPA can cut off funding for highways within the state or ban construction in nonattainment areas.

As noted, SIPs are to provide for attainment of an NAAQS within three years of the date of its promulgation. A two-year extension upon request of the governor is possible if the technology for certain sources is unavailable.

The Problem of Nonattainment.   For the criteria pollutants described, after extensions, the deadline for attainment under the 1977 amendments was January 1, 1987. One month after that deadline, the EPA estimated that 80 million people were living in areas that did not have air that met the NAAQSs. An air quality region is defined as not in compliance when the second-highest one-hour average concentration per day exceeds the NAAQS. Figure 5–3 demonstrates how the emissions of criteria pollutants have declined as the states attempt to meet the NAAQSs. By 1987, the emissions of all of the criteria pollutants had been significantly reduced from the amount emitted in 1977. Unfortunately, during 1988 and 1989, levels of ozone and particulates had started increasing once more, and nitrate oxide emissions had leveled. In 1989, eighty-one cities were still unable to meet all of the NAAQSs[8] and suffered no consequences for their failure to do so. In 1996, the EPA estimated that 90 million people still lived in areas where at least one NAAQS was violated.[9]

The greatest successes were attained in meeting the NAAQSs for lead and nitrogen oxides. The most difficult problem remaining is attainment of ozone standards. Most urban areas in the United States are said to be in nonattainment.

The 1990 amendments to the Clean Air Act address the problem of ozone nonattainment. Ozone nonattainment areas are divided into five classes, depending on the degree to which the pollutant is exceeding the standard: marginal, moderate, serious, severe, and extreme. Each class has a deadline for attainment, ranging from three years for the marginal class to twenty years for the extreme class. Interim goals have been set for all classes except marginal. How the nonattainment areas will meet these goals has not

Sulfur Dioxide Emissions

Particulate Matter

Nitrogen Oxide Emissions

Volatile Organic Compounds

Carbon Monoxide Emissions

Lead Emissions

Amounts measured in thousand short tons

FIGURE 5–3   U.S. Air Pollution Trends

Source: OAR Publication: Emission Trends Report, 1900–1949 (1995).

yet been determined, because the states will have to set forth the means of attainment in their revised SIPs. One certainty, at least according to most commentators, is that to meet the standards tens of thousands of never before regulated small and mid-sized businesses are going to have to be regulated.

Permit Program.   One of the ways these smaller firms may be regulated is by the permit system added by the 1990 amendments. This permit system, one of the big changes imposed by the 1990 Clean Air Act Amendments, is modeled after the one imposed by the Clean Water Act of 1972 for water pollutants. Under the 1990 amendments, all large, and many small, sources of air pollution are required to obtain five-year permits that spell out limits on the pollutants they emit.

Challenges to permits themselves must be made in hearings before the issuance of the permits. Once it is issued, a "permit shield" arises. As long as a plant is operating in accordance with its permit, it cannot be in violation of the Clean Air Act.

Automobile Inspection and Maintenance Program.   Urban areas with populations of two hundred thousand or more that were classified as moderate, serious, severe, or extreme are required to have vehicle inspection and maintenance programs that meet EPA guidelines. Such programs must include annual emissions testing and enforcement through vehicle registration. Additional programs discussed later under Mobile Source Performance Standards also help nonattainment areas move toward attainment.

No Significant Deterioration (NSD).   Focusing on nonattainment areas sometimes causes us to overlook the fact that some air quality regions already met or were cleaner than the NAAQS. The existence of these clean regions presented Congress with a problem. Should the air quality in these areas be prevented from deteriorating at all? Such a policy would maximize the preservation of a clean environment for future generations. Many living in clean areas, however, opposed such a policy, arguing that it would, in effect, be punishing them for not polluting. A no-degradation policy might prohibit them from bringing in substantial new industries.

Congress reached a compromise with the NSD policy. All "clean" air quality regions were to be designated Class I, II, or III. Class I air was the most pristine, and there would be only minimal increases in ambient concentrations permitted. Class II air would be allowed a moderate amount of degradation, consonant with moderate, well-controlled growth, and remain significantly cleaner than required under the NAAQSs. Class III areas would be allowed slightly more deterioration from new sources, and in some cases allowed to degrade to the level of the secondary standards.

Originally, all clean air quality regions were designated Class II. The state, once it had conducted a public hearing on the matter, could petition the EPA for reclassification. The EPA generally approved requests for reclassification as long as there was no evidence that the state acted capriciously or arbitrarily. The 1977 amendments required mandatory Class I designation for all international parks; natural wilderness areas and national memorial parks exceeding five thousand acres; national parks exceeding six thousand acres; and all areas designated Class I under the 1970 act. Such areas cannot be reclassified by the EPA.

New Source Performance Standards

While each state decides how it will meet the NAAQSs, there is one matter over which the states really have no control: the new source performance standards (NSPSs). These standards are said to be "technology forcing" because they require industry to use a certain level of technology that may or may not be in use at the time the standard is promulgated.

Under the Clean Air Act, Section III, the EPA is directed to set forth technology-based new source performance standards for categories and classes of new sources of air pollutants. New sources include both newly constructed plants and older plants that have been modified after the date of the effective regulation. The standard of performance is defined by the act as a standard for the emission of air pollutants that reflects the degree of emissions limitation achievable through the application of the best system of emissions reduction that (taking into account the cost of achieving such reduction) the administrator determines has been adequately demonstrated.

Thus, for every category of stationary sources, the EPA must establish NSPSs for the various criteria pollutants. Obviously, this task is difficult. The standard "adequately demonstrated" is certainly ambiguous. Another issue is how to define each category.

Whenever there is obvious ambiguity in a statute, that law invites litigation. Owners of plants subject to NSPSs have not been reluctant to challenge NSPSs and have met with varying degrees of success. An early case that addressed the issue of adequate demonstration was *Portland Cement Association v. Ruckelshaus.*[10] This case, referred to as Portland Cement I, arose when the EPA was promulgating new source performance standards for the cement industry. The cement manufacturers' association argued that EPA's proposed standards were too stringent because the technology demanded had not been "adequately demonstrated."

The association believed that "adequate demonstration" implied that it would be possible for any cement factory currently in existence to meet the new standards. The court rejected this argument, stating that Section II "looks toward what may clearly be projected for the regulated future, rather than the state of the art at the present, since it is addressed to standards for the new plants—old stationary source pollution being controlled through other regulatory standards."

In justifying its decision, the court explained that the issue was really one of the performance level that was "achievable." The justices noted that the senate report drafted in conjunction with passage of this Clean Air Act provision made it clear that it did not require the technology actually to be in "routine use" at a plant when the standard was promulgated but must be available for installation in new plants.

Seven years later, in *National Lime Association v. Environmental Protection Agency*,[11] the court gave further guidance as to what constituted "adequately demonstrated" technology. In rejecting standards the EPA had promulgated for lime manufacturing plants, the court reasoned as follows:

> Our review has led us to conclude that the record does not support the "achievability" of the promulgated standards for the industry as a whole. This conclusion is a cumulative one, resulting from our assessment of the many points raised by the industry at the administrative level and in this court; no one point made is so cogent that remand would necessarily have followed on that basis alone. . . . The Agency's failure to consider the representativeness—along various relevant parameters—of the data relied upon is the primary reason for our remand. The locus of administrative burdens of going forward or of persuasion may shift in the course of a rulemaking proceeding, but we think an initial burden of promulgating and explaining a nonarbitrary, non-capricious rule rests with the Agency and we think that by failing to explain how that standard proposed is achievable under the range of relevant conditions which may affect the emissions to be regulated, the Agency has not satisfied this initial burden.
>
> Bearing this initial burden will involve first, identifying and verifying as relevant or irrelevant specific variable conditions that may contribute substantially to the amount of emissions, or otherwise affect the efficiency of the emissions control systems considered. And second, where test results are relied upon, it should involve the selection or use of test results in a manner which provides some assurance of the achievability of the standard for the industry as a whole, given the range of variable factors found relevant to the standards' achievability.

The court went on to say that the EPA should have included its rationale for why it believed the standard was attainable, and remanded the case for a more adequate explanation or, if necessary, for supplementary data to justify the standard in terms of the "representativeness" of the sources tested. The court held that test results were not necessarily required, but the agency's assumptions should be stated, and where possible, test data used to verify the assumptions. Comparing the two opinions, one gets the distinct impression that today the courts are willing to give the EPA much less discretion with respect to determining the feasibility of attaining a standard.

Mobile Source Performance Standards

One of the most successful aspects of the Clean Air Act, and probably the most controversial, is the *mobile source performance standards,* also referred to as the *auto emissions standards.* The mobile source performance standards are primarily designed to reduce the emissions of hydrocarbons, carbon monoxide, and nitrous oxides. The reductions are controlled primarily through the Federal Motor Vehicle Control Program. Under this program, the EPA sets national emission standards for fuel evaporation, CO, NO_x, VOC, and particulates. Car manufacturers must design cars to meet the standards. Since the first standards were set, there has been a running battle between the manufacturers and the EPA over whether standards are too stiff. The manufacturers have generally succeeded in getting deadline extensions, but then eventually meet the once allegedly "unattainable" reductions.

One of the greatest successes of the EPA's regulation of mobile sources was the mandated reduction of lead content in gasoline. Beginning in 1975, the EPA started requiring the use of lead-free gasoline in new cars. By 1985, the EPA required a reduction of lead content in gasoline from an average of 1.0 gram per gallon to 0.5 gram per gallon and to 0.1 gram per gallon in 1986. Today, more than 70 percent of the gasoline sold is lead free.

Title II of the 1990 Clean Air Act amendments contains new tailpipe emissions standards, rules requiring the reformulation of gasoline, and provisions to force automakers to design and manufacture cars that can run on alternate fuels.[12] Other sections of these amendments require additional controls to reduce vehicle-related smog. By 1998, manufacturers must have reduced all new vehicles' exhaust emissions of nitrogen oxide by 60 percent of 1990 levels; emissions levels of other pollutants must be reduced by 35 percent. To ensure that manufacturers meet these standards, the EPA will certify a prototype of each new model that has emissions controls effective up to fifty thousand miles. Additional measures under the 1990 amendments include the requirement for vapor recovery equipment on gasoline pump nozzles and mandatory auto inspection and maintenance.[13]

The EPA, in June 1991, took one of its first steps toward implementing this act by proposing rules to mandate the sale of cleaner gasoline in the most severely polluted cities. Under these rules, oxygenated gasoline (gasoline blended with an oxygenate such as ethanol) was being sold during the winter in thirty-one cities that had carbon monoxide problems by November 1992. Table 5–2 lists the cities participating in the program as of January 1, 1996.

The rules also mandated that by January 1995, gasoline reformulated to reduce the emission of ozone-forming hydrocarbons be available for sale in the nine smoggiest cities. These cities—Baltimore, Chicago, Hartford, Houston, Los Angeles, Milwaukee, New York, Philadelphia, and San Diego—account for almost 25 percent of the country's gasoline consumption. Seventeen additional areas also opted to join the program in an attempt to meet Clean Air Act goals.

Prompted by consumer complaints, many of which are shared by participants in the winter oxygenated fuel program, a number of areas that voluntarily complied are changing their minds. Consumers complained about the additional cost of the fuel—generally from three to seven cents more per gallon, but sometimes as high as seventeen cents more.[14] Others complained about a drop in mileage of as much as 15 percent, and were afraid that the

TABLE 5–2 Cities Participating in Wintertime Oxygenated Fuels Program on January 22, 1996

Albuquerque, NM	New York-New Jersey-Long Island, NY-NJ
Baltimore, MD	
Chico, CA	Philadelphia-Wilmington-Trenton, PA-DE-NJ
Colorado Springs, CO	
Denver-Boulder, CO	Phoenix, AZ
El Paso, TX	Portland-Vancouver, OR-WA
Fort Collins-Loveland, CO	Provo-Orem, UT
Fresno, CA	Raleigh-Durham, NC
Grants Pass, OR	Reno, NV
Greensboro-Winston Salem-High Point, NC	Sacramento, CA
Klamath County, OR	Salt Lake City, UT
Las Vegas, NV	San Diego, CA
Los Angeles-Anaheim-Riverside, CA	San Francisco-Oakland-San Jose, CA
Medford, OR	Seattle-Tacoma, WA
Minneapolis-St. Paul, MN	Spokane, WA
Missoula, MT	Stockton, CA
Modesto, CA	Washington, DC

fuel was damaging their engines. Finally, some motorists complained of headaches and nausea from the new fuels. The largest number of complaints seemed to come from the Milwaukee area, and when EPA officials called a special meeting about the program at a downtown hotel, more than three hundred angry motorists jammed the session, heckling the officials and demanding that regular gas be returned to the pumps.[15]

Despite the complaints, officials from the reformulated fuels industry and the American Automobile Association believe that reformulated gasoline is one of the most cost-effective ways to reduce pollution.[16] Industry officials, as well as representatives from the EPA, maintain that there is no evidence linking reformulated fuel to health problems. They also say that tests have shown a decrease of only 1 to 2 percent of miles per gallon, and that the fuel is not harmful to engines.[17]

1990 Air Toxics Program

The sections of the Clean Air Act that we have discussed so far are directed primarily toward reduction of conventional air pollutants. Toxic, or hazardous, pollutants, substances that in low concentrations can cause serious long- and short-term damage to human health and the environment, are also regulated under the act. Table 5–3 lists the effects of some of these toxic pollutants.

Under the Clean Air Act of 1970, the EPA was given the authority to issue national emissions standards for hazardous or toxic pollutants. Unfortu-

TABLE 5–3 Health Effects of Regulated Hazardous or Toxic Air Pollutants

Pollutants	Health Effects
Asbestos	A variety of lung diseases, especially lung cancer
Benzene	Leukemia
Vinyl chloride	Lung and liver cancer
Beryllium	Primarily lung disease; also damage to liver, spleen, kidneys, and lymph glands
Mercury	Damage to the brain, kidneys, and bowels
Radionuclides	Cancer
Arsenic	Cancer
Coke oven emissions	Respiratory diseases, cancer

Source: Adapted from EPA, *Environmental Progress and Challenges: EPA's Update* (Washington, D.C., 1988), p.13.

nately, while Congress had directed the EPA to regulate toxic pollutants, of an estimated two hundred air pollutants that the agency had deemed hazardous, only eight had been regulated by 1989.[18]

Frustrated by the EPA's limited regulation of air toxins, Congress included a strict new air toxins program in Title III of the 1990 amendments. The program is designed to force both large and small industrial plants to reduce significantly their emissions of 189 pollutants listed as hazardous by the EPA. The law imposes strict deadlines on the EPA, forcing the agency to issue at least twenty-five new rules for reducing hazardous pollutants from new and existing sources.

One of EPA's first tasks under the new law was to designate categories and subcategories of the sources that emitted these pollutants, which the agency published on July 16, 1992, along with a schedule for the issuance of standards for each category and subcategory.

For major sources—those that emit or have the capacity to emit either ten tons per year of a toxic air pollutant or twenty-five tons of a combination of toxic pollutants—the EPA will determine the standard of maximum achievable control technology (MACT) for each toxic pollutant emitted. For existing facilities, MACT is defined as the emissions reduction that the best performing 12 percent of similar facilities have attained, assuming there are at least thirty such facilities. (If fewer than thirty facilities exist, the EPA will use the five best facilities.) For new facilities, MACT is the best emissions control any facility in that category or subcategory is achieving. For area sources, those emitting fewer pollutants than the major sources, the EPA has the discretion to order lower standards. EPA may require area sources to meet generally achievable control technologies (GACT) or management practices.

By November 18, 2000, the EPA must have promulgated standards for all categories and subcategories. Incremental deadlines must also be met prior to this final date. By November 1996, the EPA must have evaluated the risk to the public from air toxins that will remain after MACT controls are in place. Based on its evaluation, it is to make recommendations to Congress for further regulation.[18]

One final mandate under the air toxins program was that by November 15, 1992, the EPA had to have completed an accident-prevention program including release prevention, detection, and correction requirements such as monitoring, training, and record keeping.[19]

THE 1990 CLEAN AIR ACT AMENDMENTS

Though many provisions of the 1990 Clean Air Act amendments are detailed in the preceding sections, other aspects are not. The reason for this omission is that many of the regulations that will result from this act are not yet written. Until the passage of the Clean Air Act amendments of 1990, the EPA would generally issue seven or eight regulations a year for all environmental matters. As a result of this act, however, within two years the agency was required to issue fifty major regulations and thirty minor ones, a massive undertaking, especially in light of the fact that, in the past, approximately 80 percent of the EPA's regulations were challenged in court.

To attempt to prevent such litigation and implement the amendments as soon as possible, the EPA is trying a somewhat different approach to rule making under the amendments. It is using reg-neg (see chapter 4), whereby it tries to meet formally and informally with industry and environmental groups affected by the law during the early stages of drafting the rules in an attempt to gain some early consensus.

Acid Rain Control Program

One of the more noteworthy aspects of the Clean Air Act amendments of 1990 is the acid rain control program. Accepting scientific evidence that the way to control acid rain is to reduce sulfur dioxide emissions, Congress imposed a program of controls that would cut these emissions in half by the year 2000. To accomplish these reductions, a limited number of allowances were created under Title IV of the amendments. Each allowance authorizes its holder to emit one ton of sulfur dioxide per year. The allowances are issued by the EPA using a formula specified in the statute. The first phase of reductions began January 1, 1995, and affected 110 of the highest-emitting electricity generating plants. The second, more stringent phase of the program, goes into effect January 1, 2000, and affects a much larger number of plants. After that date, the EPA will not be allowed to issue more than 8.95 million allowances annually. This limitation in the sulfur dioxide emissions will be cut in half by then.

Once an allowance is "used up," the allowance is surrendered to the EPA and no longer exists. If a plant emits less sulfur dioxide than is permitted by its allowances, the plant may sell or transfer its unneeded allowances, or may "bank" them for the next year. If a plant's emissions exceed its allowance for a given year, the plant owners must secure additional allowances or face fines of up to $2,000 per ton of excess emissions, plus possible civil and criminal penalties. Violators will also face a reduction of their next year's allowances.

On December 3, 1991, the EPA issued proposed rules for the trading program that required more than three hundred pages in small type in the *Federal Register.* The first auction was held by the Chicago Board of Trade, on behalf of the EPA, in March 1993. Allowances to emit 150,010 tons of sulfur dioxide were sold to bidders for prices ranging from $122 to $450 per ton. Buyers were primarily electrical generating plants, but also present among the bidders were environmental groups who were buying the allowances simply to retire them, and thereby make a small contribution to cleaning up the air a little more quickly.

By 1995, after three years of the program's operation, there was almost uniform surprise over the lack of trading going on and the low prices of the allowancess. In 1995, the price fell to less than $140 per ton. Given the low price of allowances, it would have been cheaper for a significant number of plants to buy extra allowances, yet these plants have instead chosen to opt for the more expensive route of installing costly pollution-control equipment or switching to less-polluting fuel.

Some believe that the utilities may be stockpiling the allowances for January 1, 2000, when the number of allowances is cut back. At that time, their value is predicted to rise. An employee of the EPA pointed out that the number of trades and prices of the emissions was really not important. What mattered was whether the program was reducing emissions at the lowest possible cost, and from his perspective, it was. And even though the program has been in place for only a few years, it has become the model for about a dozen emission trading programs across the United States and is being examined worldwide as a possible method of pollution control.

Enforcement of the 1990 Act

Whether, and to what degree, the Clean Air Act of 1990 is successful depends to a great extent on how the states implement and enforce the act. Many critics say that the states failed to attain the goals established by the SIPs largely because, first, the states were so slow to develop and approve the plans, and second, there was much confusion about what was required from each specific source. Under the new act, whereby each source will ultimately need a permit that will specify all the regulations applicable to that source, as well as emissions limits, monitoring requirements, and maintenance procedures, there will be less confusion as to what requirements each source must meet.

Enforcement may also be strengthened because most criminal violations under the new act are now felonies; violations under the previous act were generally considered misdemeanors, and were, therefore, not of much interest to the Justice Department. Under the 1990 Act, the EPA may file a civil action in a federal district court against any owner or operator of a stationary source who "knowingly violates any requirement or prohibition" in an applicable SIP or permit or violates any provision of the act. The EPA may seek a permanent or temporary injunction to obtain compliance with the SIP, permit, or law or civil damages of up to $25,000 per day per violation. The EPA may also seek criminal penalties of fines or prison terms of up to five years against violators of the act. The agency may also issue an administrative order and impose a civil penalty of up to $25,000 per day of violation if it acts within one year of the violation. Administrative penalties are sometimes viewed as a superior alternative simply because they are easier to obtain.

To help the EPA in its enforcement efforts, the act grants the agency the authority to award up to $10,000 to any person (excluding a government official acting in an official capacity) who "furnishes information or services which lead to a criminal conviction or judicial or administrative civil penalty"[20] for any violation of the act.

Finally, the 1990 amendments contain citizen suit provisions. Any person can bring an action in a federal district court against state and federal officials who fail to take an action required under the law and against any source believed to be in violation of the act, a regulation, or its permit. The court may order the EPA to perform its duties and impose civil penalties; emissions standards may be enforced. Costs of litigation may be awarded to the initiator of the citizens' suit when deemed appropriate by the court.

SOLUTIONS BEYOND THE CLEAN AIR ACT

Some pollution-control problems are addressed by the Clean Air Act and its amendments, but others are not. Two problems that could not be addressed nationally because they are global problems requiring international solutions are depletion of the ozone layer and global warming. Both are in fact being resolved on an international level through treaties (see chapter 10), which will result in substantially reducing, if not eliminating, emissions that cause these problems by the year 2000.

Problems of indoor pollution likewise require a different type of solution than traditional regulation. A nontraditional approach was attempted through the 1986 Radon Gas and Indoor Air Quality Act, which directed the EPA to implement a public information and technical assistance program. Under this act, the EPA is conducting research to try and identify and rank the risks posed by various indoor pollutants and to discover better ways to diagnose building-related diseases and correct their causes. The agency's current emphasis is on education, and it has prepared several documents offering guidance on construction of new homes and rehabilitation of old ones to reduce the risks from indoor pollution. A campaign to encourage the public to test for and repair radon problems has begun. Meanwhile, the EPA is still exploring strategies to reduce the risk from radon and other indoor pollutants.

CONCLUDING REMARKS

Conventional air pollution, indoor air pollution, toxic emissions, acid rain, the greenhouse effect, and depletion of the ozone layer are the primary air quality problems facing the nation today. We began to address these pollution problems seriously with the 1970 Clean Air Act. This act, which has been amended twice, still provides the basic structure for attempts to improve air quality. Over the course of the past twenty-five years, some major improvements have been made in air quality, although there is still a long way to go. But with the passage of the 1990 Clean Air Act amendments, which bring more sources under regulation, take more stringent steps toward controlling acid rain and air toxins, provide compliance deadlines that appear to be more reasonable than some imposed by the earlier Clean Air Act, and strengthen enforcement provisions, we can be hopeful that air quality will continue to improve.

    Now that you understand the basic scheme for regulation of air quality, you are ready to move on to water quality. As you examine the way we protect water, try to compare and constrast approaches to the two different mediums.

QUESTIONS FOR REVIEW AND DISCUSSION

1. List and describe the harmful effects of the six conventional air pollutants.
2. Explain the difference between a conventional air pollutant and a toxic air pollutant.
3. What is acid deposition?
4. Why is the thinning of the ozone layer a problem?
5. Conceptually, how did the regulation of air quality from 1970 to the present differ from air quality legislation before 1970?
6. How is the treatment of existing air pollution sources different from the treatment of new sources of air pollution?
7. What is the significance of an area being designated a Class I air quality control region?

8. How does the 1990 air toxins program differ from the program for controlling air toxins established under the previous Clean Air Act?

FOR FURTHER READING

BRUCE ACKERMAN & WILLIAM HASSLER, CLEAN COAL AND DIRTY AIR: OR HOW THE CLEAN AIR ACT BECAME A MULTIBILLION DOLLAR BAIL-OUT FOR HIGH SULFUR COAL PRODUCERS AND WHAT SHOULD BE DONE ABOUT IT (New Haven: Yale University Press, 1981).

ANDREW BROWNLOW & JIM FALK, THE GREENHOUSE CHALLENGE: WHAT'S TO BE DONE? (New York: Viking Penguin, 1989).

JUTTA BRUNHEE, ACID RAIN AND OZONE LAYER DEPLETION (Dobbs Ferry, N.Y.: Transnational Publishers, 1988).

GARY C. BRYNER, BLUE SKIES, GREEN POLITICS (Washington, D.C.: Congressional Quarterly Press, 1993).

DAVID DURENBERGER, *Air Toxics: The Problem,* EPA J. 30 (Feb. 1991).

DAVID FISHER, FIRE AND ICE: THE GREENHOUSE EFFECT, OZONE DEPLETION, AND NUCLEAR WINTER (New York: Harper Collins, 1990).

RICHARD LIROFF, REFORMING AIR POLLUTION REGULATION: THE TOIL AND TROUBLE OF EPA'S BUBBLE (Washington, D.C.: World Wildlife Fund, 1986).

ALAN WELBURN, AIR POLLUTION AND ACID RAIN: THE BIOLOGICAL IMPACT. (New York: Wiley, 1988).

ON THE INTERNET

http://www.epa.gov/oar/oagps/airtox/fsindex.html
Explains the EPA rules and regulations that apply to air toxins in thirty categories

http://www.epa.gov/OMSWWW/13-fuels.htm
Provides information about the oxygenated fuel program

http://www.rahl.net/sufive/enviro/cleanAir/cleanFuelVeh.html
Provides information about clean fueled vehicles

http://www.iclei.org/kioski.html
Provides information about climate change

http://www.epo.gov/doc.s/acidrain/ardhome.html
Provides information about the acid rain program

NOTES

1. GARY BRYNER, CLEAN AIR ACT OF 1990 (Washington, D.C.: Congressional Quarterly Press, 1993).
2. CEQ, Environmental Quality, 20th annual report, 1991, p. 470.
3. Ibid., p. 472.
4. Ibid., p. 471.
5. C. ARDEN POPE III, *Respiratory Disease Associated with Community Air Pollution and a Steel Mill, Utah Valley,* AM. J. PUB. HEALTH 623 (May 1, 1989).
6. CEQ, note 2, p. 470.
7. PAUL C. WAGGONER, ed. CLIMATE AND WATER: REPORT OF THE AMERICAN ASSOCIATION FOR THE ADVANCEMENT OF SCIENCE PANEL ON CLIMATIC VARIABILITY, CLIMATE CHANGE, AND THE PLANNING AND MANAGEMENT OF U.S. WATER RESOURCES (Washington, D.C.: AAAS, 1988).
8. Pope, note 7, p. 471.
9. EPA, Office of Air Quality Planning and Standards, THE PLAIN ENGLISH GUIDE TO THE CLEAN AIR ACT, 3 (Jan. 22, 1996).
10. 486 F.2d 375 (D.C. Cir. 1973).
11. 627 F.2d 416 (D.C. Cir. 1980).
12. BRUCE INGERSOLL, *EPA Proposes Rules on Sale of Cleaner Gas,* WALL ST. J. 3 (June 12, 1991).
13. Ibid.
14. GARY LEE, *EPA Allows Regular Gasoline as Alternative in Milwaukee,* A2 WASH. POST (Feb. 25, 1995).
15. Ibid.
16. DAVID SOUTHERLAND, *Gas Prices Fall But Clean Fuels Issue Burns Hot,* B9 WASH. POST (Dec. 22, 1994).
17. Ibid.
18. DAVID WOLLIN, *Air Toxins Laws Force Industries to Plan Ahead,* NAT'L. L.J. May 13, 1991, p. 256.
19. Ibid.
20. Ibid.

CHAPTER 6

Water Quality Control

Controlling water quality means different things to different people. For instance, it includes providing good quality drinking water—knowing that when you turn on your tap the water is safe to use for cooking, washing, and drinking without taking any special precautions. It means that local streams, lakes, ponds, rivers, and ocean beaches are places where you can safely swim, boat, and fish. It means that fish and other aquatic organisms are healthy. To the farmer, it means that water used for irrigation does not have excess amounts of salts or residuals of pesticides or pathogens. Increasingly, protecting water quality also means protecting underground aquifers, sources of groundwater vital to much of the population. To meet the need for protecting water for so many uses, a variety of complex laws and regulations have been developed.

To understand water *quality* control, we must also understand water *quantity* control. Many parts of the world have plenty of water available but face critical shortages in obtaining water of adequate quality. Technology exists to desalinate ocean water but is not economically or environmentally feasible to produce enough freshwater from the oceans to contribute substantially to the water supply.

In this chapter, we first examine the basic measures of water quality and the significance of various pollutants. With that background, we turn to discussion of how water supply is controlled, focusing on the differences between the two major water laws. Finally, we examine the two important federal laws, the Water Pollution Control Act and the Safe Drinking Water Act, that provide the basis of the system used in the United States to protect this vital resource.

THE MAJOR WATER POLLUTANTS

Any system for classifying pollutants must be somewhat arbitrary, particularly when concerned with water quality from a number of perspectives. Critical water quality parameters may be very different for people and for fish, for industries and for ecosystems. By organizing pollutants into some kind of a system, enough understanding can be gained of their potential effects to see the need for a regulatory program.

148

Pathogens

Throughout the United States, there has been little worry that drinking tap water or being near surface water will lead to disease. Yet, the World Health Organization reports that almost one-fourth of the world's population suffers from one of four water-related diseases: gastroenteritis, malaria, river blindness (onchocerciasis), or schistosomiasis.[1] Some estimate that waterborne diseases are responsible for about 25 million deaths annually in the underdeveloped regions of the world.[2] In contrast, only 564 waterborne disease outbreaks, affecting approximately 140,000 people, were reported between 1971 and 1988 in the United States. However, the number of reported diseases is rising dramatically, although it is unclear whether morbidity or just the reporting of disease is increasing.[3] The EPA reports that 30 million Americans were served by drinking water systems in 1994 that failed to meet all public health standards.[4] A single outbreak in Milwaukee in 1993 from the pathogen *Cryptosporidium* resulted in more than four hundred thousand infected individuals and approximately one hundred deaths.

The kind of pathogens responsible for waterborne disease include bacteria, viruses, protozoa, and parasitic worms. Bacteria are microorganisms that are ubiquitous in the environment, and the human body harbors hosts of bacteria, particularly in the gastrointestinal tract. Although many bacteria are useful to our bodily functions, some are incompatible with good health. Because of the great diversity of organisms potentially found in water, it is impractical to directly monitor for each specific type of pathogen. Thus, groups of bacteria called *coliform* or *fecal coliform* are routinely monitored to indicate potential contamination.

Cholera, typhoid fever, shigellosis, and bacterial gastroenteritis are among the more important waterborne bacterial diseases; they are transmitted through contact with water contaminated by wastes from infected individuals. These diseases, characterized by severe diarrhea, can result in death (particularly in weaker individuals, such as the very young and old, or those suffering from other stresses such as malnutrition).

Viruses are simpler organisms than bacteria. Unlike bacteria, viruses are not normally flora of the human system; only infected individuals are carriers. Viruses usually are more difficult to detect and destroy than bacteria. Infectious hepatitis and viral gastroenteritis are the primary viral-caused waterborne diseases. These diseases may occur from drinking water that standard tests indicate is safe from bacterial contamination; no routine tests are currently available to search directly for the presence of viruses.

Protozoa and parasitic worms are more complex organisms than bacteria and viruses. Backpackers have probably heard about the protozoan *Giardia lamblia* and how contracting giardiasis from drinking visually pure water from apparently pristine locations can result in severe and prolonged diarrhea. A major outbreak of the protozoan *Cryptosporidium* in Milwaukee resulted from the city changing its water treatment protocols to try to improve water quality.

Schistosomiasis is an extremely debilitating disease in which parasitic worm larvae invade the body, develop into adults, and cause chronic inflammation and pain. It is seldom fatal itself, but can so weaken victims as to make them susceptible to other diseases. Parasitic worms are not a major problem in the United States, but massive infections are common throughout large sections of the developing world.

Conventional Organics

Other pollutants from organic sources can adversely affect water quality without being directly responsible for disease. Wastes resulting from such operations as food processing, petroleum refining, and municipal wastewater treatment can result in serious disruption of aquatic ecosystems. These wastes often have relatively large amounts of residual organic matter that can be used for energy by aquatic bacteria and other microorganisms, but to use this material, dissolved oxygen is taken from the water. If the amount of food exceeds the supply of dissolved oxygen, the water turns anoxic killing organisms such as fish. Large amounts of organic material may support greater populations of nuisance organisms, such as filamentous bacteria (e.g., *Sphaerotilus natans*), that can clog water supply screens and that look and smell objectionable.

This type of organic pollution is typically quantified through a measure of the amount of oxygen needed for all of the organic material to be decomposed as it is used as food. The most common of these measures are biochemical oxygen demand (BOD) and chemical oxygen demand (COD). The higher these demands, the more conventional organics exist in the water. If the oxygen demands are known and the rate of oxygen entering the water can be measured or calculated, accurate predictions can be made of the resultant oxygen content.

Oil and grease is frequently used as a measure of a group of organic materials that share similar analytical properties and includes a large variety of materials, from extremely toxic materials like benzene to benign plant waxes. Nevertheless, it is a useful measurement because of the simplicity of analysis and its use in indicating the gross level of organic pollution.

Toxic Organics

Some organic compounds are extremely toxic, presenting problems at very low concentrations; common examples are polychlorinated biphenyls (PCBs), dioxins, and many solvents and pesticides. Most of the toxic organics of greatest concern in water are not naturally occurring but are products of chemical synthesis from industrial operations.

Many trace organic toxins are slow to degrade, remaining stable in the environment for extended periods. Some become concentrated in plants and animals as they move up through the food chain; low levels in water lead to medium levels in aquatic plants and relatively high levels in aquatic animals. Furthermore, the effects of contamination often are only expressed after considerable time. These characteristics greatly complicate efforts to relate exposure to effects and to understand the relationship between a given dose and a probable outcome.

The effects of trace organics on human health are variable. Many organics are thought to be carcinogens, and regulatory decisions are often made based on this risk. However, other effects may include mutagenesis, teratogenesis, nervous system damage, and damage to the liver and other internal organ systems. Ecological health effects may be even more variable and difficult to detect.

Nutrients

Unfavorable conditions caused by excess plant growth can result from organic material developing in situ, as well as brought in as waste. If excess fertilization occurs in a water body, photosynthesis of such organisms as algae and rooted aquatic vegetation can proceed rapidly. As the vegetation becomes increasingly luxuriant, it can become more of a problem. When vegetation dies (or at night when photosynthesis cannot occur), oxygen may be used faster than it can be replenished. Ensuing anoxic conditions destroy favorable life forms, result in objectionable tastes and odors, and encourage undesirable species.

Excessive fertilization can occur when nutrients are added to a system. The nutrients most often effective in stimulating growth are nitrogen and phosphorous. Too much pollution from nutrients, causing overfertilization and too much vegetative growth, results in a condition called *cultural eutrophication.* This condition can be caused by water running off well-fertilized agricultural fields, water containing high levels of phosphorous-based detergents, or a variety of industrial processes.

In addition to damaging ecosystems, nitrogen can directly affect public health. Excessive levels of nitrate, the form of nitrogen usually found in surface and groundwater (unless subject to gross contamination), can cause methylmeglobenemia, or blue baby disease. In infants, excessive nitrate in the diet reduces the capacity of blood to transport oxygen (turning the blood a bluish color), which disrupts normal central nervous system development and functioning.

Heavy Metals

Another important group of toxic water pollutants are heavy metals. Substances such as mercury, cadmium, and lead are inherent in our industrialized society yet are extremely hazardous if not controlled properly. Similar to toxic organics, metals can present significant problems at extremely low concentrations.

While some waters naturally have relatively high concentrations of a metal or metals, most problems with high concentrations result from discharge from industrial waste waters or other anthropogenic sources. Heavy metals are usually found in the environment at levels below that causing any adverse effects. To make heavy metals useful, they are mined, concentrated, and refined; residuals from this process, and from the subsequent use of the refined material, can result in elevated concentrations that are harmful or toxic.

Other Measures

A variety of other properties are used to characterize water and determine its most suitable uses. Mineral content is an important attribute with regard to the suitability of a water supply for agricultural use, as well as for potability. One common measure of minerals is water hardness, the sum of the dissolved calcium and magnesium. Another common measure is alkalinity, which indicates the stability of water to changes resulting from addition of acids (e.g., acid rain).

The gross level of materials in water can also be determined in terms of solid content. *Total dissolved solids* refers to the material that cannot be easily filtered out of water. Conversely, *suspended solids* refers to contaminants that can readily be removed through filtration. An alternate measure is turbidity, which indicates the amount of material in water that scatters light.

The pH of water is an important measure of water quality used in a number of applications. Either a very low pH (indicating acidic conditions) or a very high pH (indicating basic conditions) is unfavorable to most life. However, a neutral condition of pH 7 (neither acid nor base) is not synonymous with normal or good quality either. For example, noncontaminated rainwater is slightly acid, with a pH around 5.6. Treated domestic supplies are commonly released from the treatment plant with a pH greater than 8.

SOME SIGNIFICANT WATER QUALITY PROBLEMS

Degradation of water quality can adversely affect both human health and ecosystems. Regulatory attention recently has been directed to both areas, although much more focus is given to pollutants that have a direct link with human health risk.

Trace Organics

The threat of pathogens in drinking water supplies is an important issue in the United States; however, more media attention is given to chemical contamination. In particular, the relationship between chemicals used to destroy pathogens and the risk associated with the residual chemicals and their by-products remains of high concern.

Chlorine has been widely used since before the turn of the century to destroy pathogens in drinking water and is responsible for a large reduction in morbidity and mortality caused by waterborne disease. Chlorine continues to be the disinfectant of choice for domestic supplies, although it is clear that by-products of disinfection may have harmful effects. These disinfection by-products, or DBPs, result from the reaction between dissolved organic compounds and chlorine or other disinfectants. Trihalomethanes (THMs) are the most well known of the DBPs. In 1979, the EPA promulgated rules restricting THM concentrations in drinking water. Standards were based on the carcinogenicity of chloroform, the THM found in most waters. As research proceeded on THMs, information also was obtained on other disinfection by-products that form when water is chlorinated or alternate disinfectants are used. A dilemma has emerged: disinfection remains vital to water treatment as a method of destroying pathogens but also may result in increased risk of cancer and other diseases caused by chemical exposure. Clearly it is not a viable alternative to stop using disinfectants in drinking water supplies and risk massive outbreaks of cholera, typhoid fever, and other waterborne diseases. Thus, researchers are actively looking for alternate disinfectants and treatment techniques that adequately destroy pathogens (for a reasonable cost) without leaving residual chemicals that might damage human health.

Researchers are actively investigaing and regulating a variety of other organics that may be toxic at trace levels in water. For example, organic solvents have been found to contaminate important groundwater aquifers serving hundreds of thousands of people in Long Island, New York, and the San Gabriel Valley, California, among other areas. This type of pollution is generally undetectable by human senses, with adverse health effects occurring long after initial exposure.

Perhaps even more difficult to understand is the significance of trace levels of organics in waters not used for drinking. PCBs and other toxic organics are frequently found in sediments from drainages of many industrialized areas; it is unclear what this means to the ecosystems. In fact, there is substantial controversy over whether it is better to leave contaminated sediments in place or to dredge and remove the sediments (and potentially resuspend the toxic chemicals).

Lead

Lead has been the focus of much attention as a contaminant of water. In fact, as the major sources of airborne lead are being controlled (leaded gasoline and lead-based paints—see chapter 5), the relative contribution of lead exposure from water may be increasing.

Lead in a domestic water supply has two primary origins: the source water and the plumbing system. The EPA has assessed the prevalence of lead in raw (untreated) water supplies and found that about 250 surface water systems and 600 groundwater systems had water leaving the treatment plants with lead concentrations greater than five micrograms per liter. This means that less than 1 percent of the public water supplies in the United States, serving a population of less than 3 percent of the 226 million people using public systems, have potential lead contamination from these sources. More concern is expressed over lead leaching into water from plumbing systems. Lead solders and fluxes used to connect copper pipes can contain up to 50 percent lead; brass and bronze alloys used in faucets and other fixtures can also contain large amounts of lead. The EPA estimates that there are about 10 million lead service lines in use in the United States and about 20 percent of all public water systems have at least some lead service connections or lines within their distribution systems.

Considerable debate has raged about how to control lead in drinking water systems. Most control strategies focus on ensuring that water quality is adequate as it leaves the treatment plant, which assumes that significant deterioration will not occur before its use. However, lead content can change considerably during the delivery process, depending on the specific plumbing system (both in the public system and in the individual building).

Radon and Other Radionucleotides

Interest in possible contamination by radiation has increased considerably over the last several years. Driving this interest are the disaster at Chernobyl, media attention on development of low-level radioactive waste disposal sites, and renewed efforts to develop nuclear power plants. An important additional factor is a new awareness of radon, an invisible, odorless radioactive gas that is almost ubiquitous in its distribution. The threat to humans from radon is predominantly from airborne exposure (see table 6–1). In fact, water containing elevated radon concentrations presents a threat largely from the radon gas released when the water is exposed to the atmosphere (e.g., showering) rather than from direct consumption.

Natural surface water supplies generally carry little threat of human radiation contamination because radon volatilizes into the atmosphere. However, groundwater can have high concentrations of radon because of sustained association with naturally occurring radon-emitting rock (uranium and radium), with little chance for removal through volatilization. Even though relatively little information links adverse health effects to radon in water, radon limitation has become the focus of major new activities designed to protect drinking water quality.

PROTECTING WATER THROUGH GOVERNMENT ACTIONS

A number of federal laws relate to water quality; however, the Federal Water Pollution Control Act (FWPCA) and the Safe Drinking Water Act (SDWA)

TABLE 6–1 Public Exposure to Radon

Exposure Pathway	Cancer Fatalities per Year in U.S. Due to Radon Exposure		
	Lower Estimate	Most Likely Estimate	Upper Estimate
Inhalation of Radon Gas Released from Water to Indoor Air	—	6	—
Inhalation of Radon* Progeny Derived from Waterborne Gas	40	86	408
Ingestion of Radon* in Drinking Water	11	100	212
Inhalation from Outdoor Air	280	520	1,500
Inhalation from Indoor Air	6,740	13,600	30,600

* Caused by exposure through community water supplies only

Source: Report to the United States Congress on Radon in Drinking Water: Multimedia Risk and Cost Assessment of Radon, EPA 811-R-94-011 [March 1994].

provide most of the structure for managing water quality. They deal primarily with, respectively, ensuring the quality of surface waters and ensuring the quality of domestic supplies. To properly focus on water quality issues, it is also important to understand how rights to use water are obtained in the United States.

Water Rights

Water rights is traditionally a state issue, with only limited involvement on the federal level. Specific policies governing rights to water reflect the tradition brought into the state by its founders and the nature of the state's water resources. Federal activity largely involves situations in which water flows or is located between more than one state or country.

Two fundamental doctrines govern the right to use water. In eastern and some western states, the right to use water depends on a physical link between the water source and the user, meaning that the owner of property on the bank of a stream, river, or lake can make reasonable use of that water. This is called a *riparian right*. In many western states, where water is scarce, rights can be claimed for beneficial uses both adjacent to and away from water sources. Rights are prioritized with respect to time; if supply is limited, the first to acquire the right can have all the supply. Only after an earlier right has been exhausted can later rights be met. This is called an *appropriated right*.

Riparian Rights. Riparian rights are derived from the English tradition, which in turn comes from Roman law. Each owner of riparian land is entitled to receive water undiminished in quality or quantity by upstream users. This entitlement puts an obligation on each riparian landowner not to degrade the water source.

Riparian landowners in all states (including those with appropriative water laws) generally have rights to use their adjoining surface waters for such nonconsumptive uses as fishing and recreation. Within states using a riparian system to control consumptive uses, water diversion by a riparian landowner historically was restricted to domestic use. Upstream landowners could not divert water to irrigate fields, to use in mining or industry, or for any other use in which the quality or quantity of downstream supply would be reduced.

This limitation to domestic supply prevents water-based development. To allow growth, this historic restriction has been replaced in most states by one limiting diversions to those needed for reasonable use. Under this doctrine, a riparian landowner may divert water if the use does not interfere with the legitimate use of the water by other holders of riparian rights. States individually determine reasonable use, based on such factors as the following:[5]

- purpose of the use,
- suitability of the use to the watercourse,
- economic value of the use,
- social value of the use,
- harm associated with the use,
- practicality of avoiding the harm,
- practicality of adjusting the quantity of water use,
- protection of existing values of the water and associated land, and
- equity between the water user and any injured parties.

Specific preferred uses depend on state policy, but use has generally been granted for agriculture, mining, and (historically) milling. During times of limited supply, allocation of water depends on reasonableness of competing uses.

In states with riparian rights systems, eminent domain may be used to acquire water rights by nonriparian water companies or municipalities, which can then provide a domestic water supply. Alternately, if a nonriparian landowner uses a water supply for a sustained and continuous period (fifteen years in many states), a prescriptive right may be established that allows for the continued use of that supply. Furthermore, many states with riparian right systems also have administrative permit systems for water diversion and allocation. These administrative permits allow for diversion of water for beneficial uses to nonriparian landowners and to ensure that riparian landowners' use of water is reasonable.

Riparian rights reflect historic development patterns in wet climates, where water was usually abundant. In areas where water is scarce, riparian rights are not easily adapted to ensure that water is used to maximal benefit.

Moreover, riparian rights disadvantage nonriparian land that could be productively developed if a secure water supply were available.

Appropriative Rights.   Most of the western United States is drier than the East, and water supply is much more limited. For development to occur, water must be available and long-term rights secured. The system of appropriative water rights provides a mechanism for obtaining water rights as a function of water use. By making use of water (such as diverting it from a stream for agriculture or industry), a right is developed to that water supply. Earliest water users have priority for using the water supply if the supply is limited; subsequent water users have inferior rights.

Water is appropriated, and rights established, through the actual consumptive use of water. Diverting water and returning some portion to the waterway (such as returning power plant cooling water), only establishes a right to the net amount removed. If water is not used where an appropriative right exists, that right can be lost. Appropriative rights are established because of demonstrated needs; without this need the legal right for future use is superseded by the rights of current users.

An appropriative right is not dependent on landownership but on diverting and consumptively using water for a beneficial use. Most states with appropriative systems also have statutes that govern how much water can be taken and specify beneficial uses (only Colorado maintains a pure appropriative system in which rights depend only on using water).[6] Typically, agricultural, industrial, and domestic uses are all accepted as rights that may be secured.

Appropriated rights are complicated by the varying availability of water. In a wet year, all rights may be satisfied; in a dry year many users may have unmet needs. Further complicating this issue is the need for water to maintain healthy aquatic ecosystems. Is it right for appropriated users to take all a stream's available water for human consumptive use and degrade or destroy the natural ecosystem? In other words, do fish have rights?

A key case demonstrating an interest in protecting quality of waterways by limiting appropriative rights was *National Audubon Society v. Superior Court (Mono Lake),* decided by the California Supreme Court in 1983. In 1940, the City of Los Angeles had appropriated for its domestic supply most of the flow of four streams draining into Mono Lake. The Audubon Society filed suit in superior court to stop diversions because of environmental damages resulting from loss of supply to the lake. Mono Lake, the second largest lake in California, is located at the base of the Sierra Nevada mountain range (east of Yosemite National Park) and receives most of its water supply from Sierra snowmelt. Because of the hot, arid climate causing rapid evaporation (leaving salts behind to concentrate), the lake is saline. Fish do not live in the lake, but many waterfowl thrive (most feeding on the abundant population of brine shrimp). By diverting flow away from the lake, the surface elevation has dropped. In addition to reducing the area of the lake, previously submerged bridges have transformed islands into peninsulas. Where island rookeries were once protected, coyotes and other predators now have access to nesting sites and young birds. Continued or increased diversion of feeder streams clearly would cause deterioration of the lake ecosystem, including a large reduction in the waterfowl population.

At issue in the case was whether appropriated rights (even those given some time ago) must consider the public trust doctrine (requiring government protection of important natural resources). The court ruled that the public trust doctrine and appropriative rights are "parts of an integrated system of water law" so both must be considered in determining appropriate use of water. This decision allows legal challenges, based on natural resource values, to state administrative decisions for water appropriation. It forces administrative decisions to include considerations of long-term resource impairment, as well as economic development.

A few other states have integrated natural resource values more directly into their systems for appropriating water. For example, Montana has a statutory program that allows water to be appropriated for future uses. These future uses can include maintaining minimal flows needed to protect in-stream water quality. State agencies can establish an appropriated right for water that never is *used* in the traditional sense of being removed from the stream channel.

Protecting Waters of the Nation

Protecting water quality was not a major concern of the federal government until relatively recently. Historically, federal involvement was largely defined by three acts: the Rivers and Harbors Act of 1899 protected navigable water through restrictions on discharge; the Public Health Service Act of 1912 provided for federal investigation of water pollution affecting public health; and the Oil Pollution Act of 1924 prohibited discharge of oil into coastal waters. These acts were not broadly interpreted or widely enforced so had little impact on water quality.

With a growing population and increasing rate of waterborne disease, the need for a more active federal role became evident. During the 1930s and 1940s, federal money was used to help states and cities construct wastewater treatment plants. In 1948, the Federal Water Pollution Control Act was passed, formalizing government obligations for water pollution control. State governments maintained primary responsibility, with the federal role focusing on providing financial assistance and research support through the U.S. Public Health Service.

The 1956 and 1965 amendments to this act strengthened the role of the federal government but left primary responsibility with the states. Increasing funding granted by the federal government for construction of local wastewater treatment plants was important. The 1965 amendments (also known as the Water Quality Act) moved federal responsibility from the Public Health

Service to the newly created Federal Water Pollution Control Administration. The 1965 amendments also represented a compromise in the face of clearly deteriorating water quality throughout the nation. Industry opposed federal standard setting as an obstacle to business, and states opposed an increased federal presence in an area traditionally left to them. Yet, something had to be done. These amendments permitted the federal government to establish water quality standards if states refused to establish their own. However, an effective and enforced set of standards was not developed, and water quality continued to diminish.

During the late 1960s, a series of events turned public attention toward the deteriorating environment and led to a public demand for action. Two of the most dramatic incidents occurred on opposite sides of the continent, in Ohio and California. In June, 1969, the Cuyahoga River near Cleveland, caught fire. Clearly, this river was little more than an industrial sewer, with oily waste concentrating sufficiently to turn a major waterway into a fire hazard. Soon thereafter, more than 250 million gallons of crude oil leaked from an oil drilling operation offshore of Santa Barbara, California. The media gave substantial coverage to both events, and pictures of dead, oil-coated waterfowl, sea otters, and other wildlife crowded the front pages of newspapers. The public was ready to support major changes.

In response, Congress passed the Federal Water Pollution Control Act (FWPCA) of 1972 (over the veto of President Nixon). It mandated major changes in the way water quality would be controlled in the United States and provided the basis for water quality programs used today. Three subsequent acts made substantial amendments to the FWPCA: the Clean Water Act of 1977 (CWA), the Water Quality Act of 1987 (WQA), and the Oil Pollution Act of 1990. These amendments followed the basic principles established in the 1972 act and have resulted in a complex and comprehensive system of water pollution control.

A strong federal role is now integral to our system of water quality protection. Ambitious water quality objectives are clearly established for the nation: "The objective of this Act is to restore and maintain the chemical, physical and biological integrity of the Nation's waters." Note that water quality goals include more than maintaining a safe drinking water supply. Specific reference is made to providing for "the protection and propagation of fish, shellfish and wildlife, and . . . recreation in and on the water." Thus, *all* waters of the nation are required to be fit for fishing and swimming.

To protect water quality, either restrictions can be set on pollutant dischargers (assuming that if sufficient restrictions are applied, the water body will be protected), or ambient quality standards can be established (with restrictions imposed to control pollutant sources or other conditions if these standards are not met). This act uses both approaches. All discrete point sources of discharge into surface water, such as factories, pulp and paper mills, food processing plants, and wastewater treatment plants, are required to obtain a discharge permit. These permits are administered through the National Pollution Discharge Elimination System (NPDES) process, so dischargers must follow specifications of their NPDES permits. Effluent limitations are dependent on the type of pollutant and type of discharger. In setting these limitations, three broad categories of pollutants are identified: conventional, nonconventional, and toxic. The level of required discharge control depends on the category of pollutant. Requirements also vary depending on whether the discharge is a new or existing source. Furthermore, municipal wastewater treatment plants must meet somewhat different standards than those required for other dischargers.

The least stringent level of control is imposed on existing dischargers of conventional pollutants, requiring only that best conventional pollutant control technology (BCT) standards are met. Only five conventional pollutants are specified; biochemical oxygen demand (BOD), suspended solids, pH, and fecal coliform were established in the 1977 amendments and the EPA subsequently added oil and grease.

In setting BCT standards, the EPA is required to consider the relationship between the costs of pollution control and the derived benefits; these costs must then be compared to the cost of compliance at wastewater treatment plants. Additionally, the EPA is required to consider "the age of equipment and facilities involved, the process employed, the engineering aspects of the application of various types of control techniques, process changes, non-water quality environmental impact (including energy requirements), and such other factors as the Administrator [of the EPA] deems appropriate."[7]

Toxic and nonconventional pollutants must be controlled using best available technology economically achievable (BAT), a more rigorous standard than BCT. A list of more than sixty toxic chemicals, known as priority pollutants, has been developed by the EPA.[8] Nonconventional pollutants are anything not included in these other two categories, that still may pose a threat (such as thermal pollution).

BCT standards "shall include consideration of the reasonableness of the relationship between the costs of attaining a reduction in effluents and the effluent reduction benefits derived," while BAT standards require only that standard determination "shall take into account . . . the cost of achieving such effluent reduction." This reduced requirement for cost assessment has resulted in EPA establishing BAT standards primarily on health-based criteria. The 1977 amendments to the act specify that effluent standards for toxic pollutants consider "the toxicity of the pollutant, its persistence, degradability, the usual or potential presence of the affected organisms in any waters, the importance of the affected organisms and the nature and extent of the effect of the toxic pollutant on such organisms, and the extent to which effective control is being or may be achieved under other regulatory authority."[9]

The FWPCA and its subsequent amendments do not specifically identify a system for setting standards. The EPA established standards for existing industry based on industrial classifications, assuming that plants performing similar functions should have similar effluent limitations. However, this approach was challenged. E. I. Du Pont Nemours & Co. claimed that the EPA was required to uniquely establish effluent standards on each plant, responsive to plant-specific conditions. The U.S. Supreme Court decided that it would be impractical to do so (estimating that there were more than forty-two thousand dischargers), and that the legislative intent of the act would best be upheld by allowing for control based on industry class. However, standard setting must include sufficient flexibility to allow for some variation for individual plants.[10]

New sources are subject to more rigorous effluent limits than existing sources, based on the belief that it is cheaper to minimize effluent pollutants if environmental controls are considered during plant design than it is to retrofit existing facilities. New sources include major modifications to existing facilities, as well as new construction. Effluent limits for new sources are based on consideration of an entire process rather than the BAT and BCT approach requiring pollution controls to be imposed following waste generation (commonly known as *end-of-pipe* treatment). As specified in the FWPCA, standards must consider "control of the discharge of pollutants which reflects the greatest degree of effluent reduction which the Administrator determines to be achievable through application of the best available demonstrated control technology, *processes, operating methods, or other alternative* [emphasis added] including, where practicable, a standard permitting no discharge of pollutants." Congress listed twenty-seven pollution sources in the FWPCA for which the EPA was required to develop performance standards. The EPA was also given the authority to add to this list; forty sources were consequently identified in the NPDES Primary Industry Categories list.[11] The EPA is required to periodically review new source requirements and make amendments reflecting changes in technology and economic conditions.

The system for controlling effluent from public wastewater treatment plants (called *publicly owned treatment works,* or POTWs) differs slightly from that of other dischargers. POTWs must meet effluent standards characterized by waste receiving "secondary treatment." EPA initially defined secondary treatment to effectively limit compliance to those communities using activated sludge technology meeting rigorous performance standards. This requirement was subsequently viewed as excessive in many situations, particularly where small POTWs were discharged into waters capable of rapidly assimilating the wastewater. Moreover, it was viewed as economically impractical and ecologically unnecessary for many small communities. Thus, these requirements were modified.

A system also is in place to control discharges of pollutants into municipal sewage. The EPA's guidance is rather broad but prohibits discharges that do the following:

- create a fire or explosion hazard in the sewers or treatment works,
- are corrosive (with a pH lower than 5.0),

- obstruct flow because of solids or viscous materials,
- upset the treatment processes, and
- increase the temperature of wastewater entering the treatment plant to more than 104°F (40°C).

These regulations also are intended to ensure that the hazardous waste management system is not circumvented through the use of municipal sewers.

Categorical standards have been promulgated for twenty-five industry types (table 6–2). For each, standards have been adopted specifying limits on pollutants characteristic of that industry. Industries not identified in a category must meet general requirements intended to prevent the discharge of any pollutant detrimental to the treatment system.

Most of the regulatory burden for the pretreatment program is on local POTWs. Each POTW is required to identify all industrial sources and the volume and characteristics of industrial discharge in its waste shed. Using this information, limits on problem dischargers are imposed that protect the POTW; this program requires the POTWs to expend considerable resources (in industrialized communities) to ensure that pretreatment requirements are met.

TABLE 6–2   Industrial Categories Subject to National Categorical Pretreatment Standards

Aluminum forming	Meat processing
Asbestos manufacturing	Metal finishing
Battery manufacturing	Metal molding and casting
Builder's paper	Nonferrous metals forming
Carbon black	Nonferrous metals manufacturing
Cement manufacturing	Paint formulating
Coil coating	Paving and roofing
Copper forming	Pesticides
Dairy products processing	Petroleum refining
Electrical and electronic components	Pharmaceutical
Electroplating	Phosphate manufacturing
Feedlots	Plastics molding and forming
Ferroalloy manufacturing	Porcelain enameling
Fertilizer manufacturing	Pulp and paper manufacturing
Fruits and vegetables processing	Rubber processing
Glass manufacturing	Seafood processing
Grain mill manufacturing	Soaps and detergents manufacturing
Ink formulating	Steam electric manufacturing
Inorganic chemicals	Sugar processing
Iron and steel manufacturing	Timber products manufacturing
Leather tanning and finishing	Textile mills

Source: 40 C.F.R. Pt. 403 App. C.

In contrast to the pretreatment program, other aspects of the water quality regulatory system are largely controlled at the state and federal levels. The NPDES system is administered through the EPA; however, similar to many environmental statutes, most states have assumed active management responsibilities, while the EPA maintains only an oversight role.

In addition to a nationally based system of discharge controls based on industry types, a second regulatory strategy is based on ambient water quality. Subject to federal review, states are required to establish water quality standards for intrastate waters. If discharge standards are not sufficient to meet these ambient regulations, additional discharge standards must be imposed.

This system of water quality control has resulted in substantial improvements in water quality. *Point sources* of pollution have been controlled to such an extent that much of the remaining pollution comes from *nonpoint sources*. Nonpoint pollution originates from a variety of small sources that in combination may result in significant pollution; examples are agricultural storm water runoff carrying fertilizers and pesticides and oil dripping from cars and trucks. Recent EPA estimates indicate that between 50 and 70 percent of impaired or threatened surface waters are affected by nonpoint source runoff from agriculture, with urban runoff responsible for another 5 to 15 percent.

Nonpoint source pollution from urban areas is being addressed by regulations governing municipal and industrial storm water discharges. The WQA required implementation of a comprehensive two-phased approach for addressing storm water discharge. Under Phase I, permits are required for large (population greater than 250,000) and medium (population 100,000 to 250,000) municipal areas; this currently applies to 173 municipal areas. Each regional office of the EPA has considerable latitude regarding appropriate permit requirements for individual municipalities. Furthermore, industries identified by class by the EPA or by the NPDES permitting agency also must obtain a permit governing storm water discharge.

Phase II of the storm water control program is only now being implemented. In addition to providing those controls identified in Phase I, the EPA is required to issue regulations needed to control additional storm water discharges. On April 7, 1995, EPA promulgated a rule establishing a system to provide this protection. The NPDES permitting authority (usually a state agency or a Native American tribe) will identify those Phase II dischargers that are contributing to water quality impairment or significant pollution. These dischargers will need to apply for a permit within 180 days of notice. All other Phase II dischargers (those entities discharging only storm water, except for those dischargers classified as Phase I) have six years to apply for a permit if the EPA has a program in place requiring a permit at the time that they are due. This approach was developed to deal with those dischargers presenting the most severe threat to water quality first and to allow flexibility in developing appropriate limitations on other dischargers based on water quality impact.

Civil and administrative penalties (some quite severe) may be assessed against violators of FWPCA regulations (and subsequent amendments). "Knowing endangerment," whereby someone places another person in imminent danger, carries a maximum penalty of fifteen years imprisonment and a $250,000 fine ($1 million for organizations). "Negligent violations" carry a maximum penalty of $25,000 a day; continued operation of a process not meeting standards could quickly become expensive. The EPA also may seek civil penalties, including injunctive relief and fines. The EPA may issue administrative orders directly but will pay a fine if these orders are not followed.

Citizen suits are authorized for anyone adversely affected by a discharger. Provisions are included that allow payment of the plaintiff's attorney fees, making it more practical for individuals or local groups to seek relief against major companies. Citizen suits provide individuals the opportunity to seek civil remedies against dischargers or to force the EPA to take action against dischargers or otherwise meet its legal responsibilities for protecting water quality. Remedies can include fines and adoption of compliance schedules.

Protecting Drinking Water

Traditionally, drinking water protection has been the responsibility of individual states, not the federal government. Drinking water quality was governed by local and state boards of health, or was not governed at all. The role of the federal government was limited largely to providing research grants, loans for development of treatment works, and technical assistance, and to being involved in interstate and international quality issues.

In 1974, the Safe Drinking Water Act (SDWA) was passed in response to growing concern over contamination of domestic supplies with synthetic organic chemicals and other pollutants. The statute required the development of national domestic water quality standards. It also provided for protection of groundwater supplies, the source of domestic water for about 50 percent of the U.S. population.

This act was intended to protect public water supply systems and to ensure that they supply potable water free from biological, chemical, or physical contamination. Public water systems are defined as systems that have at least fifteen service connections or serve twenty-five or more people for at least sixty days annually. Consequently, homes and businesses served by individual wells (common in rural areas) are not regulated. Public water supply systems are further separated into community and noncommunity systems, serving resident and nonresident populations, respectively. Furthermore, specific standards or compliance schedules are often based on the size of the community system.

The EPA was charged in the SDWA with developing National Interim Primary Drinking Water Regulations to protect human health and "secondary standards" to protect the aesthetic quality of drinking water. Interim standards were required to be proposed by March 1975, with final standards adopted by September 1977. The EPA could not meet this ambitious schedule and by 1986 had adopted interim standards on only twenty-three contaminants.

Amendments to the SDWA made in 1986 provided a new timetable for establishing water quality standards and expanded the number of contaminants to be considered. For contaminants that may have an adverse effect on human health, the EPA is responsible for developing (concurrently) maximum contaminant level goals (MCLGs) and maximum contaminant levels (MCLs). MCLGs are nonenforceable health goals established at levels for which no adverse health effects should occur. MCLs are enforceable standards set as close to MCLGs as possible, but they take into account the feasibility of achieving standards based on available technology and the costs of treatment. Congress requires that the eighty-three contaminants listed in the Advanced Notice for Proposed Rule Makings of March 4, 1982, and October 5, 1983, have MCLGs and MCLs established. Seven substitutes to this list are allowed, and the EPA has exchanged seven of the original chemicals with seven organic contaminants suspected as carcinogens.

In addition to the contaminants specified by Congress in the SDWA amendments, the EPA is required to develop a list of contaminants that need regulation to protect drinking water quality. This "drinking water priority list" (DWPL), contains an additional seventy-seven substances or groups of substances for which MCLs and MCLGs need to be developed.

A number of chemicals that have been identified as needing to be regulated in drinking water, a complex process for establishing specific standards, and strict deadlines for implementation (most of which have already passed) have emerged from this deluge of statutory requirements and rule making. Not all of the chemicals initially controlled through interim regulations have had final MCLs established, and so the interim regulations continue to be enforced. Yet, final standards have been promulgated for other chemicals more recently identified as potentially hazardous in drinking water. To stay current on the status of particular chemical standards, resources must be consulted such as the *Federal Register,* and the *Code of Federal Regulations,* or the EPA's Office of Ground Water and Drinking Water.

Rather than trying to develop standards independently, the EPA has been involving directly the regulated community (and other individuals with interest and expertise) in the rule-making process. This process of *negotiated rule making* is viewed as the most practical approach to this complex regulatory issue. For example, regulating DBPs requires consideration not only of the health effects of residual chemicals but also those associated with alternate disinfection practices and the costs to the community of new forms of water treatment. Between 1992 and 1993, the EPA conducted a formal negotiation to develop a consensus-based standard. The standard was proposed on July 29, 1994, and is expected to be promulgated soon. In addition to setting standards for DBPs (in particular, THMs and haloacetic acids), it requires changes to treatment processes of many systems independent of DBP levels in plant effluent. These treatment requirements are included to reduce DBP formation downstream of the water treatment plant in the community distribution system.

Examples of national primary drinking water standards currently in effect are shown in appendix A of this chapter. In some cases, rather than meeting specific water quality standards determined by monitoring, an assumption is made that specific standards will be met if the appropriate treatment technology is used.

Compliance and enforcement responsibility is intended for the state level, an approach common to most federal environmental programs. State programs must be at least as stringent as the federal specifications. Community systems are monitored by the water utilities, following a plan approved by the state (or the federal EPA if the state does not have primacy). Monthly monitoring requirements are based on the system size, with larger systems taking more samples. Noncommunity systems can be monitored quarterly, although local conditions may necessitate additional sampling.

The rapidly expanding requirements for drinking water control are imposing an enormous burden on water purveyors. In addition to the expense of monitoring, water systems may have to be modified to meet new requirements. The EPA is authorized by the SDWA to enforce regulations by administrative orders and to collect administrative penalties for noncompliance. However, this authorization does not deal with the fundamental question of identifying financial resources needed to meet these new requirements.

Individuals may sue public water systems in federal court for failure to meet required standards. Individuals will learn of failures because administrators of water systems are required to notify their service communities of MCL violations. Following the traditional requirements for citizens' suits, individuals must first give sixty days notice to the EPA, state, and alleged violators before pursuing court action. Notification must come after the event has occurred, thus this requirement is not directly useful as a preventive tool; however, repeated notification should effectively demonstrate a pattern of failure. Individuals can then respond by pursuing legal remedies, working through the political system to upgrade services, or personally seeking alternate supplies.

CONCLUDING REMARKS

Our system governing the use and quality of water is more mature than most other areas of environmental law and regulation. Water is one of the basic needs of life, so we have a history of concern coincident with the development of population centers and large pollution sources.

We experienced a period when many important water systems were substantially degraded. Now, gross contamination of surface water has been virtually eliminated throughout the United States. We can have confidence almost anywhere in the country that tap water from a public system has met rigorous quality requirements, although we still need to be aware that questions remain regarding the long-term effects of trace levels of chemicals allowed (both as trace levels of contamination and as residuals of water treatment). We still are just beginning to respond to difficult questions regarding how to manage nonpoint sources of pollution and toxic materials that are difficult to detect. We also are facing a situation in which water is becoming an increasingly expensive commodity, both because of costs involved in treatment and increased demand. We are consuming groundwater at a faster rate than it is being replenished, which is resulting in a diminishing supply, increased costs of use, and water quality problems. While perhaps not having the notoriety of such environmental issues as hazardous waste management (see chapter 8), water law and regulation remains an active and vital issue.

QUESTIONS FOR REVIEW AND DISCUSSION

1. Why is cultural eutrophication a problem?
2. Describe the difference between conventional and toxic organics. How do the relative allowed concentrations of each compare?
3. Why are disinfection by-products (DBPs) allowed by law to be present in water, even though they may be carcinogens?
4. What is the difference between riparian and appropriative water rights? Under what conditions are each of these most suited?
5. Is the federal water quality control program designed to focus on protection of public health or environmental quality?
6. How does the regulatory burden differ for a discharger into a sanitary sewer compared to a discharger into natural water?
7. What is the primary source of contamination to surface water in the United States? What regulatory program has been implemented in response to this problem?
8. What are drinking water *secondary standards?*
9. Why are technology-based standards sometimes used instead of specific (concentration) standards?

FOR FURTHER READING

Marc Resiner, Cadillac Desert: The American West and Its Disappearing Water (New York: Viking, 1986).

J. L. Sax & R. H. Abrams, Legal Control of Water Resources (St. Paul, Minn.: West Publishing Co., 1986).

1–7 Waters and Water Rights (R. E. Clark, ed. Allen Smith Co., 1967–1978).

ON THE INTERNET

http:www.bna.com/hub/bna/envirld.AWPC.html
Monthly updates and weekly reports on water pollution control

http:www.hpcc.gov/blue94/section.4.9.html
Information about EPA's Grand Challenges in Water pollution management

http:/www.cais.com/tne/neis/water.html
National Environmental Information Services' most requested water documents

http://epa.gov/docs/Region4Wet/overview.html
Overview of Section 4 of Clean Water Act

http://www.voyagepub.com/publish/stories/wat.html
News on water quality issues related to lakes

http://www.upx.net/user/richp/sdwa__cba.html
Analysis of a congressional Budget Office study of the SDWA

http://www.epa.org/In__The__Drink/Health__Effects.html
Information about health effects of common drinking water contaminants

NOTES

1. AMERICAN PUBLIC HEALTH ASSOCIATION, THE NATION'S HEALTH (Washington, D.C., March 1979).
2. THE GLOBAL TOMORROW COALITION, THE GLOBAL ECOLOGY HANDBOOK (Boston: Beacon Press, 1990).
3. DEPARTMENT OF HEALTH AND HUMAN SERVICES, HEALTHY PEOPLE 2000, NATIONAL HEALTH PROMOTION AND DISEASE PREVENTION OBJECTIVES, U.S. Department of Health and Human Services, Public Health Service, DHHS Publication No. (PHS) 91–50212 (Sept. 1990).
4. U.S EPA, STRENGTHENING THE SAFETY OF OUR DRINKING WATER: A REPORT ON PROGRESS AND CHALLENGES AND AN AGENDA FOR ACTION, U.S. EPA Office of Water (4601) EPA 810-R-95–011 (March 1995).
5. D. H. GETCHES, WATER LAW IN A NUTSHELL, 58 (St. Paul, Minn.: West Publishing Co., 1984).
6. L. RICE & M. D. WHITE, ENGINEERING ASPECTS OF WATER LAW, 25–26 (New York: Wiley, 1987).
7. Federal Water Pollution Control Act, § 304 (b)(4)(B) (1972).
8. 40 C.F.R. § 401.15.
9. Federal Water Pollution Control Act § 307(a)(3)(2) (1972).
10. E. I. Du Pont Nemours & Co. v. Train, 430 U.S. 112 (1977).
11. 40 C.F.R. § 122 App. A.

CHAPTER 7

Controlling Toxic Substances

In 1948, Swiss chemist Paul Muller received the Nobel Prize in medicine for discovering the insecticidal properties of DDT. Through its use to control mosquito populations, DDT saved untold lives from malaria. But within ten years, this insecticide had produced so many adverse effects that it had been banned or its use severely restricted in several parts of the world.[1]

The experience with DDT is just one example of the potential risks and benefits of the chemical age in which we live. The legal system's main problem, therefore, is finding a way to encourage the development and use of helpful chemicals while preventing inadvertent, widespread use of chemicals with toxic effects. This chapter and chapter 8 explore the regulatory schemes that have been developed to help identify toxic substances and manage their use and disposal.

This chapter begins with a discussion of toxicity. Then federal regulation of toxic substances under the Toxic Substances Control Act; the Federal Insecticide, Fungicide, and Rodenticide Act; and the Federal Food, Drug, and Cosmetics Act is explained. The last section discusses the use of tort law to control toxic substances.

IDENTIFICATION OF POTENTIALLY TOXIC SUBSTANCES

Toxic substances are regulated by a wide variety of environmental laws, as table 7–1 illustrates. In chapters 5 and 6, on air pollution and water pollution, you were introduced to some of these regulations. This chapter focuses on the two main laws that regulate potentially toxic substances used in commerce. Before we examine these specific laws, however, we need to ask what is meant by the term *toxic substance*. Generally, *toxic* refers to something that is directly poisonous to humans. However, nowhere in the Toxic Substances Control Act does Congress specifically define the term; in fact, none of the acts that regulate potentially toxic substances define the term. Instead, some acts list certain substances that must be regulated as toxins; other

TABLE 7-1 Environmental Laws Regulating Toxic Substances	
Statute	*Regulated Substances*
Asbestos Hazard Emergency Response Act	Asbestos
Clean Air Act	Hazardous air pollutants
Clean Water Act	Hazardous water pollutants
Comprehensive Environmental Response, Compensation, and Liability Act	Hazardous waste
Federal Food, Drug, and Cosmetics Act	Pesticide residues
Federal Insecticide, Fungicide, and Rodentcide Act	Pesticides
Marine Protection Research and Sanctuaries Act	Toxic waste
Occupational Safety and Health Act	Toxic substances in the workplace
Resource Conservation and Recovery Act	Hazardous waste
Safe Drinking Water Act	Pesticides and other hazardous substances
Toxic Substances Control Act	Toxic substances used in commerce

statutes focus on the risk of harm imposed by certain substances that makes them subject to regulation as toxins.

Many substances regulated as toxins have certain characteristics that make their regulation especially urgent. For example, extremely low doses of a potentially toxic substance can produce adverse effects in humans, animals, or plants. A conventional pollutant may be harmful in parts per million, whereas a toxic pollutant may be harmful in parts per trillion. Also, the harmful effects of a toxic substance may not show up for decades after the exposure. Further, potentially toxic substances may bioaccumulate. If, for example, the toxin is in the water, that substance may accumulate in the bodies of fish so that it would be much more heavily concentrated in the fish than it would be in the surrounding water. Another, and closely related, characteristic is that toxic substances often persist, that is, they fail to break down biologically for a long time. When they do break down, their degradation may produce toxic by-products.

Scientific Uncertainty

One of the biggest problems with environmental regulation, and especially the regulation of toxic substances, is that of scientific uncertainty. We can see the smog hanging over the skyline and feel it burning our eyes, but we can neither see nor taste the DDT bioaccumulating in the fish we just ate. And while there are ways to determine when a chemical in a set dosage is harmful, there is no test that can prove beyond a doubt that a chemical will not cause any harm to human health or the environment.

So how is a regulatory agency to determine whether a chemical is "safe"? Although they regularly struggle with this issue, the courts have not come to a definitive conclusion. They have not specified precisely what degree of evidence of harm is necessary for a substance to be banned or regulated, but they have said that assessing risk and determining how to regulate involve not only factual evidence but also policy considerations. In *Ethyl Corp. v. EPA,*[2] a case involving regulation of a conventional pollutant under the Clean Air Act, the court said:

> Undoubtably certainty is a scientific ideal—to the extent that even science can be certain of its truth. But certainty in the complexities of environmental medicine may be achievable only after the fact, when scientists have the opportunity for leisurely and isolated scrutiny of an entire mechanism. Awaiting certainty will often allow for only reactive, not preventative regulation. Petitioners suggest that anything less than certainty, that any speculation, is irresponsible. But when statutes seek to avoid environmental catastrophe, can preventative, albeit uncertain decisions legitimately be so labeled?

Thus, the courts have tended not to hold the EPA to a rigorous standard of proof when determining when a substance can be regulated.

The District of Columbia Circuit Court, in *Lead Industries Association, Inc. v. EPA,*[3] even went so far as to say that "feasibility and cost" were irrelevant when the EPA was determining a reasonable margin of safety to protect the public health. However, in *NRDC v. United States EPA,*[4] the same court, in considering the regulation of a hazardous air pollutant, stated that an "ample margin of safety to protect human health" does not have to mean "risk free"; there can be an "acceptable" risk to health.

Still, despite the courts' lack of assistance, agencies such as the EPA and OSHA must determine acceptable risk. They generally do so by using the processes of risk assessment and risk management.

Risk Assessment

Risk assessment is generally defined as the process of characterizing the potentially adverse consequences of human exposure to an environmental hazard. Risk assessment is a necessary preliminary state before risk management, the process by which policy choices are made once the risks have been determined. To understand the process that agencies go through to make these assessments, we can examine the scientific basis for risk assessment.

As noted earlier, one of the risks a potentially toxic substance may pose is that of carcinogenicity. In deciding whether to regulate a chemical in a manner that would sustain judicial scrutiny, an agency may undertake risk assessment. The four-step process detailed in the following sections would be typical of such an assessment. This process was first described and recommended in 1983 by a committee of the National Research Council.[5]

Hazard Identification. Four types of information are generally used at the hazard identification stage of risk assessment: comparisons of molecular structures (there is almost unanimous acceptance of this approach within the scientific community), short-term studies, animal bioassay data, and epidemiological studies.

An initial step that may lead to further identification of a potential carcinogen is the comparison of a substance's physical and chemical properties with those of a known carcinogen. These comparisons are primarily useful in setting priorities concerning which substances most urgently need further investigation. Short-term studies of the effects of the substance on single-cell animals may be the next step. If exposure causes mutation, this result is generally an indicator that a substance is likely to be carcinogenic, and thus further studies are warranted. Because these short-term studies are quick and relatively inexpensive, they provide a good screening device.

The most commonly used data to support regulation of a substance as a carcinogen are obtained from animal bioassays. To support a finding of carcinogenicity, scientists usually look for consistently positive results in both genders and in several strains and species. Higher incidences at higher doses are also considered important. Although animal bioassays are important, they are viewed cautiously. There are several fundamental biological similarities among all mammals, and so we can expect similarities in response to chemical toxicity. Usually, in cases in which human and animal responses can be compared, these similarities are borne out. Thus far, all human carcinogens (except possibly arsenic) have also been shown capable of causing cancer in some (but not all) animal species. Usually, but not always, the same sites of the bodies of both humans and animals are most vulnerable to the carcinogen. Benzidine, for example, is most strongly linked to bladder cancer in dogs and humans, but to liver cancer in rats. So we rely on animals tests, but cautiously.

Another question with respect to animal bioassays is whether it is ethical to use animals to test for carcinogenicity. Increasingly, people are organizing to protest the use of animals in research.

Epidemiological data that show a positive association between exposure to an agent and disease is considered the most convincing evidence about human risk. This evidence, however, is generally very difficult to obtain because the number of people exposed to any particular hazard may be low, exposures may be confounded by exposures to other substances, and the latency period may be uncertain. Even if these problems did not exist, we still would not want to risk waiting to regulate until people had been exposed to the potentially hazardous substance.

Dose-Response Assessment. Once the hazardous substance has been identified, the next step is to determine the response of humans to various levels of exposure. In a very limited number of cases, sufficient epidemiological data are available to allow extrapolations from the exposures observed in the studies. A problem with such extrapolations, however, is that the general population may contain some people, such as children and older adults, who are more sensitive than the people in the studies.

Because epidemiological data are not generally available for most substances that are being assessed, dose-response assessment usually requires assessments of animal studies. One problem with these studies is that the amount to which the animals are exposed in the tests for hazard identification is much higher than the doses to which humans would generally be exposed. Scientists have developed a number of mathematical models that they use to predict risks to humans exposed to lower doses. Adjustments must also be made to account for differences in size and metabolic rates.

Exposure Assessment. The third step in the process is to determine which populations would be exposed to the chemical and in what dosages. Although in rare cases, especially more structured sites such as workplaces, exposures may be directly measured, more typically, exposure data must be estimated.

When a community's exposure is being assessed, the ambient concentrations of chemicals to which people are exposed are calculated on the basis of emission rates, assuming that transport and conversion processes are known. For some chemicals no data are available, and estimates of exposures must be made. When chemicals are present in food or absorbed when a consumer product is used, the exposure assessment is even more complicated because of people's different dietary and personal habits. Part of the exposure assessment process also involves ascertaining which groups would be exposed to the substances. Some groups, such as children or pregnant women, might be especially susceptible. Exposure of a group to a mixture of potential carcinogens is also a factor requiring consideration, although such calculations are nearly impossible to make.

Risk Characterization. The final step, the estimate of the magnitude of the public health problem, requires no further scientific knowledge or concepts. At this stage, the value judgments of the assessors are most likely to come into play. Because of the general deference the courts give agency decision making, following such a procedure as the one just described would give the agency's rule a strong chance of being upheld. Remember, the courts tend to look most carefully at the procedures that agency decision makers follow.

FEDERAL REGULATION OF TOXIC SUBSTANCES

Since the 1950s, global economic activity has quadrupled,[6] and manufacture of synthetic organic chemicals has grown dramatically from a tiny, specialty enterprise to a huge, powerful industry. Organic compounds or chemicals, by definition, are those containing carbon, which bonds easily with itself and other elements. Scientists have learned to take advantage of carbon's unique properties to create hundreds of thousands of new chemical compounds and thus new consumer goods. Between 1945 and 1985, there was a fifteenfold increase in the production of synthetic organic chemicals, from 6.7 million to 102 million tons per year.[7] Worldwide, more than 70,000 chemicals are in everyday use,[8] and between five hundred and one thousand new ones are added every year.[9]

Creation of this plethora of synthetic organic substances is, unfortunately, not without risk. As we know all too well, the toxic effects of a chemical may not become known until several years after people are exposed to the substance. This long latency period, during which hundreds of thousands of people may be exposed, is one of the main problems of some toxic substances.

Pesticides, substances designed to eradicate pests such as rodents, insects, fungi, and weeds, are a special category of toxic substances. Undoubtedly, their use has increased crop yields worldwide. However, there are also a number of problems associated with these substances. First of all, because they are toxic, they have the capacity to harm not only targeted pests but also humans and wildlife. A related problem is that only a small percentage of the pesticide actually reaches the target pests; the rest may contaminate the soil and drinking water.

Another problem associated with pesticide use is that a given pesticide does not retain its effectiveness for a long time. Although a pesticide may be highly effective at first, some of the targeted pests, the strongest ones, will survive and breed. Through natural selection, a newer, stronger strain of the pest that is resistant to the pesticide will evolve, resulting in lower crop yields again until some new, stronger pesticide is developed, one that is potentially more dangerous not only to the pests but to the environment in general.

The remaining sections of this chapter discuss how some of the problems created by potentially toxic substances are addressed, through federal regulation and state common law.

Toxic Substances Control Act

The primary federal law designed to regulate toxic substances is the Toxic Substances Control Act (TSCA). Three significant policies are set forth at the beginning of this act:

1. Data on environmental effects of chemicals must be developed by industry.

2. Government must have adequate authority to prevent unreasonable risk of injury to health or the environment, particularly imminent hazards.

3. Government authority must be exercised so as to not "impede unduly or create unnecessary barriers to technology while fulfilling the primary purpose of the Act."

The policy statement may sound attractive; in fact, it contains language that both environmentalists and laissez-faire businesspersons may embrace. Unfortunately, it is a policy statement full of ambiguity, promoting the often conflicting goals of ensuring environmental safety and encouraging technological development. As you read the following sections on how the act regulates both new and existing chemicals, ask yourself whether the law performs a good balancing act.

Treatment of Old Chemicals.   When we examine the structure of the act, we see that TSCA can be divided into two parts: treatment of old chemicals and treatment of new chemicals. By 1979, the EPA had compiled an inventory of all chemicals commercially used or produced in the United States between January 1975 and July 1979, as required by TSCA.

Once the inventory was completed, the Interagency Testing Committee had to categorize all chemicals as high priority or not. High priority goes to those chemicals suspected of causing cancer, mutation, or birth defects. Putting a chemical on the high priority list means that the chemical is subject to further investigation and testing.

Under TSCA, no more than fifty chemicals can be listed as high priority within a twelve-month period. Every six months the list is revised. Once the EPA has placed a chemical on the list, the agency has twelve months to assess the risk of the chemical or issue testing rules if it has insufficient data to assess risk. Using a hybrid form of rule making, the EPA must publish these testing rules within reasonable time limits. The publication must include the purpose of the tests and the methodologies to be used. Test results must be published in the *Federal Register.*

Unfortunately, according to the U.S. National Research Council, the EPA currently has more than forty-eight thousand chemicals on its inventory of toxic substances and has no information on the toxic effects of 79 percent of them. Fewer than one-fifth have been tested for acute effects, and fewer than one-tenth for chronic (e.g., carcinogenic), reproductive, or mutagenic effects.

Treatment of New Chemicals.   The centerpiece of the EPA's regulation of new chemicals is the *premanufacturing notice* (PMN), sometimes referred to as a "section 5 notice." The PMN must be submitted ninety days before the manufacture or import of any new chemical for sale or use in commerce. This notice must contain a significant amount of information about the chemical, including its chemical name; chemical identity; molecular structure; trade names or synonyms; by-products resulting from its manufacture, processing, use, or disposal; intended categories of use by function and application; and the estimated maximum quantity to be manufactured or imported during the first year of production and for any twelve-month period during the first three years. Details about the manufacture of the product that must be contained in the notice include the site where the chemical will be manufactured, processed, or used by the manufacturer, as well as information with respect to worker exposure and releases to the environment. Perhaps the most important information in the notice, however, are the test data. The notice must contain all available test data related to the impact of the new chemical on human health and the environment, including effects resulting not only from use of the substance but also from its manufacture, processing, distribution, and disposal. If some of the data was obtained from scientific journals, citations to the journal articles must be included. Any new data gathered or generated subsequent to submission of the PMN must be given to the EPA.

Within five days of receipt of the PMN, the EPA must publish a notice in the *Federal Register* containing the name of the new chemical, its intended use, and the test data submitted by the manufacturer to demonstrate that the chemical does not present an unreasonable risk of harm to health or the human environment. Within forty-five days, the EPA must act to limit the amount to be produced, sold, or processed; prohibit the sale or manufacture of the chemical; or require further testing and temporarily enjoin the manufacture or sale until the data are provided. In taking action, the EPA must select the "least burdensome control." If no action is taken, the manufacturer is free to use the new chemical after the ninety-day period has transpired.

Environmentalists are highly displeased with the PMN program, for several reasons. First, by 1983, stop or limit orders had been issued for only 13 of 2,300 chemicals. It is highly unlikely that only 13 chemicals had insufficient testing done to ensure their safety. Of course, those who quote that statistic often ignore the fact that several hundred chemicals were actually withdrawn by the manufacturer rather than risk EPA disapproval. Second, the statute is considered weak because it requires only *known* data to be reported; there is no requirement for testing. Some argue that this requirement discourages thorough testing. If a firm is fearful of a certain side effect, it may simply not test for it. Of course, firms reject this criticism, arguing that fear of civil liability to persons harmed from a toxic substance provides them with the incentive to perform the necessary tests.

A 1983 Office of Technology Assessment study of 740 PMNs showed that 47 percent had no toxicity data; the other 53 percent had only limited data. Where were the EPA temporary injunctions for insufficient testing? Further, only 17 percent had any test data about carcinogenic effects, birth defects, or mutations.

But it is not just environmentalists who criticize the PMN process. Chemical firms are also critical. They say the procedure is expensive, requiring unnecessary red tape. After all, the firms argue, they would not produce unsafe chemicals, because if they did, they would be liable in tort for negligence. These situations are not like water or air pollution, they claim, where causation is difficult to prove. There will not be the potential anonymity created by 50 dumpers; only *one* manufacturer made the product that caused the injury. And because chemicals affect so many people, the liability would be enormous.

Federal Insecticide, Fungicide, and Rodenticide Act

Not all potentially toxic chemicals are regulated primarily under TSCA. The first toxic substances to arouse public concern (herbicides, insecticides, fungicides, and rodenticides) are all commonly referred to as pesticides and are regulated primarily under the Federal Insecticide, Fungicide, and Rodenticide Act (FIFRA).

Registration under FIFRA. For purposes of FIFRA, an item's being labeled an "economic poison" means that it must be registered and properly labeled before it can be distributed in the United States. As of March 1990, approximately 24,000 such products had been registered by the EPA.[10]

When a pesticide is to be registered, data showing its impact are submitted to the EPA. The EPA will register the pesticide when four factors exist:

1. The pesticide's composition is such as to warrant the proposed claims for it;
2. its labeling complies with the act;
3. the pesticide will perform its intended function without unreasonable risks to people and the environment (taking into account economic, social, and environmental costs and benefits of the pesticide); and
4. when used in accordance with commonly used practice, the pesticide will not cause unreasonable risk to the environment.

The obvious question that arises with respect to these factors is: What is *unreasonable risk?* Originally, risk referred primarily to carcinogenicity. Today, however, the EPA also examines reproductive, immunological, and neurological effects of the pesticide, as well as its impact on groundwater and on the growth and reproduction of wildlife and fish. The EPA, when determining unreasonable risk, engages in a weighing of the economic, social, and environmental costs and benefits of the pesticide. In other words, if there are few or no substitutes available to do the same job, a greater risk to human health might be considered more reasonable than if there were numerous alternatives available. Some people criticize this standard as being insufficiently protective of health and the environment, noting that most other risk-based environmental standards are lessened only because of a lack of technology.

A second question arises with respect to what constitutes a *proper label.* This requirement dates back to the original Federal Environmental Pesticide Control Act of 1947, which was simply a labeling act. Today, a proper label is one that contains the warnings necessary to prevent injuries to persons and the environment.

A pesticide can be registered for general or restricted use. General use is by far the most desired form of registration. In essence, a general-use pesticide meets the standards set by the EPA and can be sold to anyone in any quantity. Restricted-use pesticides have the potential to have unreasonable impact. However, these unreasonable effects can be mitigated or prevented if the use and/or sale of the pesticide is restricted in some manner—hence the term *restricted use.*

The most common restriction is to limit use to certified applicators who take a test. *Use* is defined by the statute as application of the pesticide *by* or *under supervision of* a certified applicator. Other possible restrictions include a limit to the frequency of use of the pesticide or to locations in which the substance can be sold or applied. The pests that may be targeted and the amount used per application can also be limited.

Under the 1988 amendments to FIFRA, the EPA is required to expedite its review of applications for pesticides that meet one of two criteria. The first standard is when the pesticide is identical or substantially similar in composition and labeling to a currently registered pesticide (often referred to as a "me-too" application). Alternately, the pesticide may be one that differs in composition and labeling from a currently registered pesticide only in ways that would not significantly increase the risk of adverse environmental effects.

Registration lasts five years. If the EPA receives no request for renewal within thirty days before the end of registration, notice of impending cancellation is published in the *Federal Register.* The manufacturer has thirty days within which to protest the cancellation, or the registration terminates.

The EPA does not always grant registration for five years. Sometimes it grants only *conditional* registration. Conditional registration is given when certain required data are not submitted and two conditions exist:

1. The pesticide and proposed use are substantially similar to a currently used pesticide (i.e., they have similar active ingredients) or differ in ways that would not substantially harm the environment; and

2. no significant harm or risk of unreasonable adverse effects would result from the pesticide's use.

If the active ingredient of the pesticide is not currently being used, conditional registration can be granted for the time needed to generate and submit the required data, not to exceed one year. Again, there must be no unreasonable risk (considering costs and benefits), and the granting of the conditional registration must be in the public interest.

If registration is denied, the EPA notifies the applicant of the reasons for denial. The applicant has thirty days to correct the condition that led to the denial. If no correction is made, the notice of denial will be published in the *Federal Register,* along with the reasons for denial. Within thirty days, the applicant may seek an EPA hearing and administrative review of the denial.

Cancellation of Registration.   As noted, if a pesticide manufacturer does not request renewal of the registration before the end of the five-year period, the process for termination of registration automatically begins. Sometimes, however, the EPA may move to cancel a registration earlier. This action for cancellation will occur whenever the EPA obtains information that an existing pesticide may present an unreasonable risk. The EPA will then undertake an intensive review of the pesticide. If it believes the risk is unreasonable, the agency will issue a notice of intent to cancel registration. Table 7–2 identifies some pesticides that have been removed from the market through this process.

Interested parties, generally users and manufacturers, then have thirty days to contest the cancellation by requesting a hearing. If no such request is made, cancellation is effective. If the cancellation is challenged, there must be a hearing to determine whether the registration should be cancelled.

There have been a whole series of opinions resulting from litigation between the EPA and the Environmental Defense Fund concerning the issue of who should have the burden of proof in cancellation hearings. The resultant case law has established that once the EPA issues a notice of cancellation, a presumption arises in favor of cancellation. Issuance of the notice is presumed to mean that a substantial question of safety exists that requires suspension in the absence of proof by the manufacturer that the risk is minimal or that the countervailing benefits outweigh the risks. Once the EPA has obtained evidence that one mode of exposure is hazardous, the presumption also arises that all modes of exposure are hazardous.

If a manufacturer contests a cancellation, the hearing process can be extremely time-consuming, often taking up to two years. During this time, the pesticide will continue to be sold. Many believe that in light of the presumption in favor of cancellation, it seems irrational to allow the continued production and sale of the pesticide until the final outcome of the cancellation proceedings has been determined.

There is an important exception to this time-consuming process. Suspension can be immediate if the continued use of the pesticide presents an imminent hazard. When evidence of an imminent hazard comes to light, the administrator of the EPA can issue a notice to the manufacturer of the pesticide that use of the pesticide is being suspended. Findings as to the imminent hazard must be included with the notice. The manufacturer then has five days within which to request an expedited hearing before the suspension. If no hearing is requested, the suspension will take place upon termination of the five-day period.

One even stronger action the EPA administrator can take is an *emergency suspension*. If the administrator determines that an emergency exists, he or she may order an immediate suspension of all use, sales, and distribution of the pesticide. The manufacturer, however, is entitled to an expedited hearing to determine whether the suspension was appropriate. As you might guess, emergency suspension has been exercised only a few times.

An interesting issue that arises with respect to cancellation is about what should be done with pesticides that have had their registrations cancelled. The EPA has the authority to allow the sale and use of existing stocks "under such conditions and for such uses as will not unreasonably adversely affect the environment." In many cases, as long as they can use their stock, manufacturers do not protest cancellation. This ability to get an easy cancellation makes it tempting for the EPA to go along with such an arrangement.

Another problem that arises with the cancellation of a registration for a pesticide that has been in use for a long time is that the manufacturer, retailers, and end users may have large supplies of the pesticide on hand. Under the original act, the EPA indemnified or reimbursed the holders (manufacturers and users) of the pesticide for the costs of the cancelled/suspended products, plus disposal of the pesticide if requested, and established standards for its disposal. This provision of the act proved costly. In 1986, for example, the EPA spent $1.5 million on a yet untested chemical method to neutralize the pesticide EDB. Unfortunately, this process released toxic vapors into the air, requiring the EPA to find another way to dispose of it. The 1988 amendments to FIFRA modified this indemnification provision. Consequently, only farmers and other end users are now entitled to indemnification. Under certain extraordinary circumstances, Congress may make a specific line-item appropriation to reimburse a manufacturer or retailer. Otherwise, the retailer or other non–end user may seek reimbursement from the seller/manufacturer. The seller/manufacturer may avoid this liability only by notifying the buyer in writing at the time of the sale that there will be no reimbursement.

Once a pesticide is suspended, the EPA must notify foreign governments through the State Department, providing them with reasons for cancellation and alternatives to the cancelled pesticide. However, the pesticide can still be sold to foreigners, which is one of the criticisms of FIFRA. Even if there were no concern about exposure to others, many foreign growers are using those pesticides on crops that will eventually be exported to the United States. This so-called circle of poison is a major issue in environmental ethics today.

Change of Use Registration. If the EPA decides to change use registration, it must publish its intent to do so forty-five days in advance in the *Federal Register.* The registrant may request a hearing. If a pesticide is classified for restricted use, the registrant may petition the EPA for a change any time. Before any pesticide to be used on a food or feed crop is registered, the EPA must follow one more step. The agency must establish a "tolerance" to pesticide residue. Both locally grown and imported crops are randomly tested to ensure that these tolerances are not exceeded.

Enforcement. The EPA requires manufacturers to keep records showing the quantity sold, date of delivery, and recipient for all pesticides sold. Upon presentation of credentials and a written reason for inspection, the manufacturer or retailer of pesticides must allow an inspection of its facility. Samples

TABLE 7-2 Some Pesticides Taken Off the Market

Pesticides	Use	Concerns
Aldrin	Insecticide	Oncogenicity
Chlordane (agricultural uses; termiticide uses suspended or cancelled)	Insecticide/termites, ants	Oncogenicity; reductions in nontarget and endangered species
Compound 1080 (livestock collar retained; rodenticide use under review)	Coyote control, rodenticide	Reductions in nontarget and endangered species; no known antidote
Dibromochloropropane (DBCP)	Soil fumigant, fruits and vegetables	Oncogenicity; mutagenicity, reproductive effects
DDT and related compounds	Insecticide	Ecological (eggshell thinning); carcinogenicity
Dieldrin	Insecticide	Oncogenicity
Dinoseb (in hearings)	Herbicide/crop dessicant	Fetotoxicity; reproductive effects; acute toxicity
Endrin (avicide use retained)	Insecticide/avicide	Oncogenicity, teratogenicity; reductions in nontarget and endangered species
Ethylene dibromide (EDB) (Very minor uses and use on citrus for export retained)	Insecticide/fumigant	Oncogenicity, mutagenicity, reproductive effects
Heptachlor (agricultural uses; termiticide uses suspended or cancelled)	Insecticide	Oncogenicity, reductions in nontarget and endangered species
Kepone	Insecticide	Oncogenicity
Lindane (indoor smoke bomb cancelled; some uses restricted)	Insecticide/vaporizer	Oncogenicity, teratogenicity, reproductive effects, acute toxicity; other chronic effects
Mercury	Microbial uses	Cumulative toxicant causing brain damage
Mirex	Insecticide/fire ant control	Nontarget species; potential oncogenicity
Silvex	Herbicide/forestry, rights-of-way, weed control	Oncogenicity, teratogenicity; fetotoxicity
Strychnine (rodenticide uses and livestock colar retained)	Mammalian predator control, rodenticide	Reductions in nontarget and endangered species
2,4,5,-T	Herbicide/forestry, rights-of-way, weed control	Oncogenicity; teratogenicity; fetotoxicity
Toxaphene (livestock dip retained)	Insecticide, cotton	Oncogenicity; reductions in nontarget species; acute toxicity to aquatic organisms; chronic effects on wildlife

Oncogenicity, causes tumors; mutagenicity, causes mutation; carcinogenicity, causes cancer; teratogenicity, causes major birth defects; fetotoxicity, causes toxicity to the unborn fetus.

Source: EPA, *Environmental Progress and Challenges: EPA's Update* (1988).

may also be taken following the same procedures. The inspection must be prompt, with a receipt given for samples taken.

If there is a violation of FIFRA, the EPA or state agriculture department must notify the defendant of the civil or criminal proceedings in writing, thereby giving that party an opportunity to be heard orally or in writing before the agency's filing charges.

For minor violations, when it is in the public interest, the EPA may simply give a written warning to the violator. A warning is likely to be used if the violation occurred despite due care and did not cause significant harm to the environment. A stop sale, use, or removal order may also be issued. Or a seizure order may be obtained in federal court. Civil penalties under FIFRA are up to $5,000 per violation by a registrant, wholesaler, distributor, or retailer and up to $1,000 per violation by private user/applicator. Factors the EPA uses to determine the penalty include a comparison of the size of the fine to the size of the business, the effect a fine would have on the violator's ability to stay in business, and the gravity of violation. A private user may use a guarantee from the seller that the pesticide is lawfully registered as a defense.

Criminal penalties may be imposed when there are knowing violations of the act. These fines are up to $25,000 for a firm and $1,000 for a user or applicator. Officials of the firm may also receive up to a one-year jail sentence, and private users may be required to serve up to thirty days in jail.

Federal Food, Drug, and Cosmetics Act

The Federal Food, Drug, and Cosmetics Act aids in the regulation of pesticide use by requiring the administrator of the EPA to establish tolerance levels for concentrations of pesticide residues on commodities consumed in the United States. In establishing these limits, the administrator is to consider "the necessity for the production of an adequate, wholesome, and economic food supply." Theoretically, violations will be caught by the EPA through inspections and by the Food and Drug Administration (FDA) in its routine sampling program. A problem with relying on the FDA, however, is that fewer than 1 percent of fruits and vegetables are inspected. In addition, the FDA does not test for all pesticides. Tests take an average of twenty-eight days; by then, the food is often sold. The shipment from which a sample has been taken is supposed to be held; unfortunately, it rarely is.

Progress under the Acts

The EPA believes that progress has been considerable. Since the enactment of FIFRA, registrations of thirty-four potentially hazardous pesticides have been cancelled, and sixty toxic inert ingredients have been eliminated from use. As figure 7–1 shows, levels of persistent pesticides in humans have significantly declined. A National Pesticide Telecommunications Network has been established. By calling the network's toll-free number (800-858-PEST),

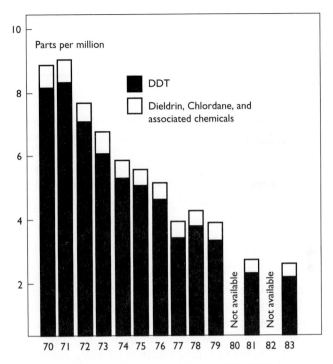

FIGURE 7–1 Levels of Persistent Pesticides in Humans, 1970–1983
Source: EPA, *Meeting the Environmental Challenge* (December 1990), p. 19

one can obtain general information about the use and disposal of pesticides and how to recognize and manage pesticide poisoning.

Not everyone is convinced that pesticide regulation is as effective as it could be, however. Increasingly, FIFRA is coming under fire because under this act, manufacturers do not have to list on their labels the specific inert ingredients, those ingredients that function only to preserve the active, pest-killing ingredients or make them easier to apply. All they have to cite is the broad term "inert ingredients" and the percentage of the total ingredients of all the inert ingredients. This incomplete labeling provides confidentiality for manufacturers to make it more difficult for competitors to discover their formulas.

The problem with this confidentiality is that many of the inert ingredients are among the most toxic substances, including phenol, toluene, and chlorobenzene, and all have been linked to birth defects, liver and kidney damage, or nervous system disorders. Others are suspected carcinogens. The consumer who buys these pesticides for home and garden use has no way to find out what these inert ingredients are because the EPA is required to keep them confidential. This confidentiality requirement is particularly troublesome because in many instances the inert ingredients constitute 80 to 90 percent of the total ingredients.

TOXIC TORTS

Increasingly, common law tort cases are being used to seek compensation for persons injured or killed as a result of exposure to toxic substances. A wide variety of theories are used to seek recovery in such cases. The most common are negligence and strict product liability. Often these cases are referred to as toxic torts, regardless of which theory of liability is being used. In most cases a plaintiff will bring an action attempting to prove both of these theories of liability.

Theories of Recovery

Negligence. To prove a cause of action based on *negligence,* the plaintiff must prove the following: that the defendant owed a duty of care to the plaintiff; that the defendant failed to meet this duty of care; that this failure to meet the duty of care caused the injury to the plaintiff; and that the plaintiff did indeed incur a compensable injury. The duty of care that a manufacturer generally has is a duty not to expose others to an unreasonable risk of harm. This duty may entail such specific actions as properly testing chemical substances for their potentially harmful effects and warning the plaintiff of known or knowable dangers resulting from specific uses of the product.

A typical explanation of what a plaintiff needs to demonstrate in a toxic tort case can be seen in a Maryland judge's statement of what the plaintiffs had to prove in the 1984 case of *Chevron Chemical Company v. Ferebee.*[11] Ferebee had been exposed on numerous occasions over a three-year period to the pesticide Paraquat, manufactured by the Chevron Corporation. Ten months after his last exposure he developed severe lung fibrosis. During the course of the trial, he died, leaving his family to carry on the lawsuit.

In explaining why he found in the plaintiff's favor, the judge said that the plaintiff had the burden of proving, by a preponderance of the evidence, the following elements:

1. That Paraquat proximately caused Ferebee's illness and death;
2. that Paraquat is inherently dangerous;
3. that Chevron knew, or should have known, at the time it sold Paraquat, used by Ferebee, that the chemical was inherently dangerous;
4. that the resulting duty to provide an adequate warning of the danger was not met; and
5. that the inadequacy of the warning proximately caused Ferebee's illness and death.

Strict Product Liability. A special form of liability, *strict product liability,* is most often applicable in cases involving consumers injured by products containing toxic substances. Strict liability, as a general theory of tort liability, requires the plaintiff to demonstrate that the defendant was engaged in an abnormally dangerous activity that caused the plaintiff's harm. The *Restatement (Second) of Torts,* Section 402A, sets out the theory of strict product liability as follows:

1. One who sells any product in a defective condition, unreasonably dangerous, to the user or consumer or to his property, is subject to liability for the physical harm thereby caused to the ultimate user or consumer or to his property, if
   a. the seller is engaged in the business of selling such a product, and
   b. it is expected to reach the consumer without substantial change in the condition in which it is sold.
2. The rule stated in Subsection (1) applies although
   a. the seller has exercised all possible care in the preparation and sale of his product and
   b. the user or consumer has not bought the product from or entered into any contractual relation with the seller.

When looking at the definition of strict product liability, one might naturally ask, When does a defective condition become *unreasonably dangerous*? Because tort law is state law, the precise definition varies from state to state, but most courts rely on one of two tests. The first is the *consumer expectations* test. If a product is more dangerous than the reasonable consumer would expect it to be, then it is unreasonably dangerous. The second test is the *feasible alternative* test. The court asks whether there was some other, less dangerous, reasonably feasible alternative available but the manufacturer chose not to use it. When applying this test, the manufacturer looks at such factors as the utility of the product, the availability of substitutes, the obviousness of the danger, the role a warning label could have played, the avoidability of danger with careful use, and the viability of eliminating the danger without impairing the usefulness of the product.

Problems in Establishing Causation

Regardless of the theory of liability used, the plaintiff must establish that the defendant's conduct caused the plaintiff harm. Proof of causation in toxic tort cases is extremely difficult, for a number of reasons. First, it may be difficult to prove that the chemical in question causes the harm that has resulted, usually cancer, leukemia, or birth defects. Medical science cannot fully explain the causes for many of these diseases. Often there are multiple causative factors.

A few courts have even allowed causation to be proven without statistical evidence. In *Chevron Chemical Co. v. Ferebee,* the appellate judges upheld a jury verdict for which the evidence for causation came solely from the testimony of two expert medical witnesses who based their conclusions about causation on their examination of the victim. The court stated that "as long as the basic methodology employed to reach a conclusion is sound, such as the use of tissue samples, standard tests, and patient examination, product liability law does not preclude recovery until a 'statistically significant' number of people have been injured or until science has had the time and resources to complete sophisticated laboratory studies of the chemical." Not all courts, however, have been equally liberal.

Even if the plaintiff establishes a link between the chemical and the harm, it may still be difficult to demonstrate that the particular exposure to the defendant's chemical caused the plaintiff's specific injury, especially when there are a number of factors that could have caused the plaintiff's harm.

The problems associated with establishing causation in toxic tort cases are discussed in great detail in a district court opinion in the case of *Allen v. U.S.,*[12] a case that arose from the federal government's bomb testing at a Nevada test site between 1951 and 1953. Plaintiffs, all of whom had resided in southern Utah, northern Arizona, and southeast Nevada, claimed to have suffered leukemia or cancer as a result of exposure to radioactive fallout from the bomb tests. Plaintiffs alleged that the government was negligent in conducting the open-air testing, failing to monitor the results, failing to warn people who were in danger of the hazards, and failing to inform such persons of what they could do to minimize their risk from the testing.

In addressing the difficulty of proving that the defendant's action definitely caused the harm, the court stated that if the plaintiff could not establish a cause-in-fact connection, the plaintiff should attempt to establish the most exclusive factual connection between the injury and the defendant. If the defendant's conduct can be found to be a "substantial factor," it may then be judged to be a legal cause. With respect to the particular facts of the case, the judge wrote:

> Where a defendant who negligently creates a radiological hazard which puts an identifiable population group at increased risk, and a member of that group at risk develops a biological condition which is consistent with having been caused by the hazard to which he has been negligently subjected, such consistency having been demonstrated by substantial, appropriate, persuasive, and connecting factors, a fact finder may reasonably conclude that the hazard caused the condition absent persuasive proof to the contrary offered by the defendant.

The judge went on to quote from the *Restatement (Second) of Torts,* §433, as to what factors would be relevant:

> The following considerations are in themselves or in combination with one another important in determining whether the actor's conduct is a substantial factor in bringing about harm to another: a) the number of other factors which contribute in producing the harm and the extent of the effect which they have

in producing it; b) whether the actor's conduct has created a force or series of forces which are in continuous and active operation up to the time of the harm, or has created a situation harmless unless acted upon by other forces for which the actor is not responsible, and c) lapse of time.

The court then went on to discuss the problems related to the use of statistics to demonstrate a causal link, saying that in a case in which a plaintiff tries to establish a factual connection between a particular "cause" and a delayed, nonspecific effect, such as cancer or leukemia, the strongest evidence of the relationship is likely to be statistical in form. "Where the injuries are causally indistinguishable, and where experts cannot determine whether an individual injury results from culpable human cause or nonculpable natural causes, evidence that there is an increased incidence of injury in a population following exposure to a defendant's risk-creating conduct may justify an inference of causal linkage between the defendant's conduct and the plaintiff's injuries . . . whenever there is an increase of observed cases of a particular cancer or leukemia over the number statistically expected to normally appear, the question arises whether it may be rationally inferred that the increase is causally connected to the specific human activity."

The court then went on to describe the scientists' use of the concept of statistical significance, by which they generally mean that the odds of the event occurring as a result of random chance are equal to or less than one in twenty; some researchers use an even more stringent standard of one in one hundred or less. The court was highly critical of the statisticians' requirement of 95 percent probability, and added that the problems of this stringent requirement are exacerbated when the exposed population is fairly small, as is the case with most toxic exposures. The court said that statistical evidence, when combined with other evidence, could "supply a useful link in the process of proof." In discussing the evidence, "the value of the available statistical data concerning radiation and cancer in offsite communities is not confined by arbitrary tests of 'statistical significance.'" The court said that whether causal inferences should be drawn that will carry the case to the additional issues of risk, scope of duty, and culpable breach of duty is a question of judgment resting in part on policy. The court must determine those risks for which the defendant should be held responsible. Thus, the courts are not going to define causation as rigorously as the scientist might, but they cannot clearly articulate the lesser standard of proof they will require.

Enterprise Liability

An additional problem that sometimes arises in toxic tort cases occurs when the exposure was several years before the injury and the toxin was produced by multiple manufacturers. Because of the time lapse, the plaintiff is unable to identify exactly which manufacturer produced the substance to which he or she was exposed. Because of the requirement of establishing the link between the defendant's action and the plaintiff's injury, this lack of knowledge might at first appear to be an insurmountable obstacle. However, some courts felt that to leave a plaintiff in a situation like this would be unfair. So, in the case of *Sindell v. Abbott Laboratories,*[13] the court fashioned the concept of enterprise, or market share, liability, whereby a manufacturer that produced a defective product that was sold interchangeably with other brands of the same product could be held responsible for that percentage of the plaintiff's injuries proportionate to the market share the defendant had at the time of the plaintiff's exposure to the product.

In the *Sindell* case, the plaintiffs' mothers had taken DES during pregnancies that had occurred before the drug was banned. The drug caused cancer and other side effects in the plaintiffs. The eleven defendants had collaborated in testing, promoting, and marketing the drug, and none of the plaintiffs could identify the specific manufacturer of the drugs their mothers had taken, to a large extent because doctors prescribed the drugs generically and pharmacists filled prescriptions with whichever brands they had available.

The court said, in setting out the novel market share theory:

> In our contemporary complex industrialized society, advances in science and technology create fungible goods which may harm consumers and which cannot be traced to any specific producer. The response of the courts can be either to adhere rigidly to prior doctrine, denying recovery to those injured by such products, or to fashion remedies to meet these changing needs.
>
> The most persuasive reason for finding that plaintiff states a cause of action is . . . as between an innocent plaintiff and negligent defendants, the latter should bear the cost of the injury. . . .
>
> From a broader policy standpoint, defendants are better able to bear the cost of injury resulting from the manufacture of a defective product.

Thus the courts removed a potential hurdle that could arise in many toxic tort cases because of the latency of many effects.

Punitive Damages

In most toxic tort cases, regardless of the theory of liability on which the action is based, the primary goal of the plaintiff is to recover compensatory damages, damages designed to place the plaintiff in the position he or she would have been in if the tort never occurred. Such damages include payment for doctor bills, lost wages, property damages, and pain and suffering. In addition, plaintiffs may also seek *punitive damages* when the defendant's conduct may be described as "willful and wanton" or "extremely egregious." Punitive damages are designed, as their name implies, to punish the defendant for his or her wrongful conduct and to provide a strong deterrent to others who might consider engaging in similar activities. In the toxic tort area, punitive damages may also serve to provide an incentive to encourage private citizens to sue to ensure compliance with environmental regulations.

To meet the goals of deterrence and punishment, the amount of punitive damages awarded in tort cases is based primarily on the wrongfulness of the defendant's act and the resources of the defendant. The more egregious the act, the more substantial is the award. The more resources the defendant has, the more substantial the award must be in order for it to have any punitive effect.

In recent toxic tort cases defendants have tried to argue that punitive damages should not be awarded in cases in which a substantial number of potential plaintiffs have been harmed or when the tort occurred in the distant past. Probably the most well publicized of the cases is *Fischer v. Johns-Manville Corporation.*[14] The trial court awarded Fischer punitive damages based on an exposure to asbestos that had occurred forty years before the lawsuit. The defendant, on appeal, raised several arguments as to why punitive damages were inappropriate. First, the defendant argued that the remoteness of the claim made the award unfair because at the time the conduct occurred, different social values might have made the conduct less egregious at that time than the same conduct would appear today. The court dismissed that argument, finding that Johns-Manville's conduct, "knowingly and deliberately" subjecting the plaintiff and other asbestos workers to serious health hazards with utter disregard for their safety and well-being, would have been regarded as equally egregious back then.

The defendant then argued that different officers and managers committed the tort, so punishing the corporation today was unfair. The court likewise did not buy this argument, pointing out that while the officers and managers may have changed, Johns-Manville was the same corporate entity. Officers and managers are merely agents of the corporation. Besides, a goal of punitive damages is general deterrence, which will still be accomplished regardless of who is in command.

The court also did not accept the argument that punitive damages were unfair to innocent shareholders. After all, the shareholders benefited from the misconduct in the past, so it was only fair that they now share in the associated losses. Finally, the argument that mass punitive damages could lead to a corporation's inability to pay later claimants because the firm would have lost all its assets caused slightly more concern on the part of the court. However, the court did not believe this potential problem was insurmountable. First, a defendant could introduce evidence at trial of having paid large punitive damage awards in previous cases so that the jury could take those payments into account when deciding whether to assess punitive damages. Second, if any punitive damage award were so high as to make financial disaster imminent, the defendant could file a motion for *remittitur,* which is a request for damages to be reduced.

It appears that if a plaintiff can overcome the tremendous burden of proving causation, recovery of punitive damages in toxic tort cases is possible. And this threat of potentially unlimited punitive damages awards may provide some incentive for makers of potentially toxic chemicals to test their products more carefully.

CONCLUDING REMARKS

The federal regulatory scheme has been designed both to remove existing toxins from the market and to prevent the introduction of new toxins into commerce. Private law also plays a part in regulating toxins. If one has been harmed by a toxic chemical, he or she can file a toxic tort case, based on either negligence or strict liability. Recovery through such an action will be difficult, although not impossible.

This chapter has focused on toxic chemicals in commerce. We now turn to an examination of toxins in another form—waste—in chapter 8.

QUESTIONS FOR REVIEW AND DISCUSSION

1. Explain the process of risk assessment.
2. Explain the statutory scheme for the regulation of existing toxic chemicals.
3. Evaluate the criticisms that might be made of TOSCA's regulation of new chemicals.
4. List the criteria for registration of a pesticide under FIFRA.
5. Explain why general-use registration is superior to restricted-use registration.
6. Explain how and when a pesticide's registration may be cancelled.
7. Explain two theories of liability on which a plaintiff exposed to a toxic substance might base a lawsuit.
8. What is the rationale for allowing a private party to recover punitive damages in a toxic tort case?

FOR FURTHER READING

ALAN BLOCK & FRANK SCARPITTI, *Poisoning for Profit* (New York: Morrow, 1985).

TROYEN A. BRENNAN, *Causal Chains and Statistical Links: The Role of Scientific Uncertainty in Ultrahazardous Substance Litigation*, 73 CORNELL L. REV. 469 (1988).

PAUL BRODEUR, *Outrageous Misconduct: The Asbestos Industry on Trial* (New York: Pantheon Books, 1985).

MICHAEL BROWN, *The Toxic Cloud.* (New York: Harper & Row, 1987).

DANIEL A. FARBER, *Toxic Causation,* 71 MINN. L. REV. 1219 (1987).

Note, *Toxic Tort Litigation and the Causation Element: Is There Any Hope of Reconciliation?* 40 SW. L. J. 909 (1986).

DAVID ROSENBERG, *The Causal Connection in Mass Exposure Cases: A "Public Law" Vision of the Tort System,* 97 HARV. L. J. 851 (1984).

LAWRENCE TRIBE, *Trial by Mathematics: Precision and Ritual in the Legal Process,* 84 HARV. L. REV. 1329 (1971).

ON THE INTERNET

http://www.seamless.com/talf/txt/penta.html
Information for developing a toxic tort case

http.//www.organic.com/non.profits/F2F/Features/pesticide.report.html
Report on farmers' attitudes toward pesticides

http://www.cais.com/the/neis/lab.html
National Environmental Information Services presents the most requested environmental laboratory documents

http://www.crcpress.com/fcn/ptcnnl/ptcnhome.html
Pesticide and Toxic Chemical News

http://www.atsdrl.atsdr.cdc.gov:8080/HEC/hsphhome.html
Hazardous Substances Public Health Newsletter found at this site

http://www.raleigh.dis.anl.gov:83/
USDA Integrated Pest Management Initiative

NOTES

1. SANDRA POSTEL, *Diffusing the Toxics Threat: Controlling Pesticides and Industrial Waste,* 79 *Worldwatch Paper* 5 (1987).

2. 541 F.2d 1 (D.C. Cir. 1976) (en banc).

3. 647 F.2d 1130 (D.C. Cir. 1980).

4. 824 F.2d 1146 (D.C. Cir. 1987).

5. JOSEPH V. RODRICKS, CALCULATED RISKS: UNDERSTANDING THE TOXICITY AND HUMAN HEALTH RISKS OF CHEMICALS IN OUR ENVIRONMENT (Cambridge: Cambridge University Press, 1992).

6. Postel, p. 7.

7. Ibid.

8. Ibid, p. 8.

9. Ibid.

10. WALTER CORSON, THE GLOBAL ECOLOGY HANDBOOK (Boston: Beacon Press, 1990), p. 80.

11. Toxic Program Commentary: Ohio (1990) (Rockville, Md.: Specialty Technical Publishers, 1990).

12. 736 F.2d 1529 (D.C. Cir. Ct. of Appeals 1984).

13. 588 F. Supp. 247 (D. Ct. Utah 1984).

14. 103 N.J. 643, 518 A.2d 466 (1986).

CHAPTER 8

Waste Management and Hazardous Releases

Chemicals and other agents exhibiting hazardous properties are widely used to meet societal needs and desires. As discussed earlier, regulatory programs are in place governing the introduction of these agents into commerce. However, these regulatory programs are not sufficient to ensure that chemicals are used or disposed of properly. Thus, major regulatory programs have emerged to maximize resource use, manage resulting hazardous and nonhazardous wastes, and provide remedies when hazardous wastes are released into the environment in inappropriate ways. These programs contribute to both prevention and response—encouraging proper management but providing remedies for the inevitable failures of management systems.

In 1976, the U.S. Congress adopted the Resource Conservation and Recovery Act (RCRA). For the first time, the federal government was actively taking responsibility for promoting the proper disposal of hazardous and nonhazardous wastes and the recovery and reuse of wastes as resources. However, as with other environmental management strategies, progress has been slow. Today, we still have unresolved questions of how to implement reasonable waste *management* (not just disposal) strategies that are economically and technologically feasible yet fully protect human health and the environment.

Major federal efforts governing prevention and remediation of hazardous material releases did not start until 1980, with the passage of the Comprehensive Environmental Response, Compensation, and Liability Act (CERCLA). CERCLA provides a complex regulatory system dealing with a continuum of activities ranging from spill prevention through final cleanup of contaminated sites.

This chapter proceeds chronologically, first discussing waste control and RCRA, and then proceeding through CERCLA and hazardous material management. Throughout this chapter, consider that a regulatory distinction often is made between hazardous wastes and hazardous materials. Remember that this distinction is not clear, and that the regulatory structure often overlaps.

WASTE CONTROL TECHNIQUES

When you throw something away, where is "away"? In the United States, *away* usually means putting it in the ground (in a landfill) where it is stored indefinitely. However, using landfills as the primary waste management tool has many disadvantages. Waste entering a landfill may be, or become, hazardous and migrate from the site to the groundwater, surface water, or air. Material placed in landfills as waste probably has lost its potential use as a resource (although there is some interest in mining landfills to recover heavy metals and other resources). Furthermore, people do not want landfills in their neighborhoods. Landfills often decrease property values and are perceived as a threat to health. As the amount of waste increases, and available open space decreases, it becomes increasingly difficult to find acceptable sites for landfill development.

Rather than throwing waste in the ground (which minimizes short-term costs), it is better to prevent it from being generated (which minimizes long-term costs). Reducing waste generation at its source, or source reduction, is the highest priority in EPA's waste management strategy.

Recycling also can be an effective management tool, although less preferable than source reduction. Recycling typically is a reprocessing of a waste product to recover its inherent resource value. For example, recycling of aluminum cans entails recovering the aluminum to manufacture new cans. Not only does this keep aluminum cans out of landfills, but it reduces the need to mine for new aluminum.

Resource recovery also can take the form of incineration, whereby some of the potential energy of a waste can be captured as heat or transformed into electricity. However, this form of resource recovery has less potential to fully maximize the resource value than a reprocessing (recycling) process. Additionally, often the goal of incineration is limited to waste destruction (particularly when destroying hazardous waste), and no attempt is made to harness the waste's potential energy. Substantial concern exists about the by-products of incineration, which may include such toxic chemicals as dioxins in the exhaust gases. Ashes resulting from incineration may also cause disposal problems, particularly if the waste material contains substantial quantities of heavy metals.

A variety of methods are available to change waste into less hazardous forms, reduce it in quantity, or otherwise cause desirable transformations. For example, organic waste may be degraded biologically. This can take the form of composting yard debris, where resulting compost is reapplied to the land. Ideally, both the amount and hazardous characteristics of the waste are reduced.

Chemical and physical treatment methods are important tools for managing hazardous waste. Destroying or reducing hazardous characteristics may make the waste easier to place in a landfill or make it practical to reuse.

However, the majority of municipal waste and significant quantities of hazardous waste are put in landfills.

THE PROBLEM WITH WASTE

Traditionally, waste management has been a local issue. When consumer goods were scarce and people did not live in large communities, the relatively small quantities of waste being produced presented little threat. However, the industrial revolution led to growing urban centers and increased amounts of waste material. Individuals could no longer easily dispose of their waste without threatening the health of the community. Beginning in the late 1800s, cities began to assume some responsibility for waste collection and disposal to counter this threat to public health. By 1880, 43 percent of U.S. cities provided some form of garbage collection.[1]

Both the generation and the recovery of municipal solid waste increased between 1960 and 1988. However, the overall rate of growth was much higher than the increased rate of recovery. Concurrent with this growth in waste was a growing concern that our waste management practices were inadequate. In developing RCRA, the Subcommittee on Transportation and Commerce of the U.S. House of Representatives indicated that forty-eight major cities were projected to have insufficient landfill capacity by the year 1982.[2] A 1986 EPA study indicated that 45 percent of all operating municipal landfills would reach capacity by 1991.[3] Furthermore, the annual municipal waste stream was estimated to grow to 216 million tons by the year 2000.[4] It was becoming increasingly apparent that something needed to be done.

In 1989, the EPA published a national strategy for municipal solid waste management. Three goals were identified: (1) increase source reduction and recycling; (2) increase disposal capacity and improve secondary material markets; and (3) improve the safety of solid waste management facilities. The first two goals deal with issues pertaining to waste quantities: how to reduce generation and how to provide enough capacity to properly manage waste. The third goal recognizes that municipal solid waste properly managed from a regulated perspective still may retain substantial environmental and health risks. The EPA strategy clearly states that the current municipal waste management system is inadequate and that major changes are needed.

Following passage of this strategy, waste generation has continued to increase. EPA reported that almost 207 million tons of municipal solid waste were generated in 1993, an increase of 27.3 million tons from 1988. The rate of recovery has also increased by more than 8 percent, showing the success of recycling programs. Whether this success in increasing recycling occurred at the expense of source reduction programs is one question. It also may be of interest to look at the contents of the current waste stream (table 8–1) and conjecture what strategies might be best in minimizing future municipal solid waste problems.

TABLE 8–1. Generation and recovery of materials in municipal solid waste, 1993

Waste Constituent	Weight Generated (million tons)	Weight Recovered (million tons)	Percent of Generation
Paper and paperboard	77.8	26.5	34.0
Glass	13.7	3.0	22.0
Ferrous metals	12.9	3.4	26.1
Aluminum	3.0	1.1	35.4
Other nonferrous metals	1.2	0.8	62.9
Plastics	19.3	0.7	3.5
Rubber and leather	6.2	0.4	5.9
Textiles	6.1	0.7	11.7
Wood	13.7	1.3	9.6
Other materials	3.3	0.7	22.1
Food wastes	13.8	*	*
Yard trimmings	32.8	6.5	19.8
Misc. inorganic wastes	3.1	*	*
Total Municipal Solid Waste	206.9	45.0	21.7

* Less than 50,000 tons or 0.05 percent

Source: U.S. Environmental Protection Agency, Office of Solid Waste and Emergency Response, Characterization of Municipal Solid Waste in the United States, 1994 Update, Washington, D.C., EPA [1994].)

Providing for the proper management of hazardous waste, a particular kind (or subset) of solid waste, also presents major challenges to the legal and regulatory system. Before 1975, government paid little attention to hazardous waste; only twenty-five states even had hazardous waste programs. There was no consistency among states regarding these limited programs, so companies faced different requirements depending on where they were doing business.

The significance of the problem of hazardous waste production has never been clear. There have been a variety of "official estimates" of the volume of hazardous waste production in the United States, but none are conclusive. More importantly, perhaps, estimates of quantity do little to quantify resultant risk. Recent EPA estimates identify a total of 235,473,584 tons of hazardous waste generated nationally in 1993, from a total of 22,615 generators. Identified in table 8–2 are the ten states with the greatest waste generation.

Quantifying risk from hazardous waste may be unnecessary; however, simply knowing that the risk is substantial was sufficient for Congress to demand (through RCRA and its subsequent amendments) a national hazardous waste management program. Through the 1970s, we began to understand that our industrialized society was producing large amounts of hazardous

TABLE 8–2 Ten States with Greatest Generation of RCRA Hazardous Waste, 1993

State	Thousands of Tons Generated	Percentage of National Total	Number of Generators
Texas	66,747	28.3	1,298
New York	45,471	19.3	2,033
Louisiana	31,683	13.5	347
Michigan	21,014	8.9	778
Illinois	12,494	5.3	1,237
California	7,996	3.4	1,784
Pennsylvania	7,066	3.0	1,139
Washington	6,926	2.9	723
Minnesota	5,993	2.5	300
Kansas	3,145	1.3	297

Source: U.S. Environmental Protection Agency, Solid Waste and Emergency Response [5305], EPA 530-S-95-005.

waste, and much of it was being managed improperly. Locations where improper disposal of hazardous waste had caused, or had the potential to cause, severe health problems became widely known.

REQUIREMENTS FOR MANAGING WASTE

Municipal Solid Waste

RCRA established the framework for a national system of solid waste control. Subtitle D of the act is dedicated to nonhazardous solid waste requirements, while Subtitle C focuses on hazardous solid waste. Remember that solid waste includes solids, liquids, and gases; it is defined in RCRA as:

> any garbage, refuse, sludge from a waste treatment plant, water supply treatment plant, or air pollution control facility and other discarded material, including solid, liquid, semi-solid, or contained gaseous material resulting from industrial, commercial, mining and agricultural operations, and from community activities.

Note that it must be discarded material to be considered waste. Thus, if economics warrant the purification of an industrial by-product for reintroduction into a process, then that material may not be a waste. The same by-product will be a waste if the recycling economics are less favorable. Some material is specifically excluded from being classified as solid waste, including domestic sewage sludge, industrial discharges that are point source discharges regulated under the Clean Water Act, and irrigation return flows.

RCRA directs most of the responsibility for active municipal solid waste management to the states and local governments. The federal role is to set nationwide standards and provide technical and financial assistance. Resource conservation is specified as an important goal of the act, although most attention has focused on waste disposal.

A key condition is that "no reasonable probability of adverse effects on health or the environment" result from solid waste disposal practices. A facility meeting this requirement is called a *sanitary landfill,* while a facility failing to provide this protection is classified as an *open dump.* In 1984, Congress, through RCRA amendments, required the EPA to revise disposal criteria for sanitary landfills. Existing regulations were found to be inadequate, in part because hazardous wastes from small-quantity generators and households can be disposed of (legally) as part of the municipal waste stream. Rather than trying to further limit the types of wastes introduced into sanitary landfills, the EPA elected to require additional landfill controls inhibiting off-site migration of waste.

On October 9, 1991, the EPA promulgated its final rule on municipal solid waste landfills (MSWLFs). These regulations increased requirements on landfill construction, operations, monitoring, and closure. However, these restrictions did not duplicate requirements on hazardous waste landfills (specified in Subtitle C of the act), contrary to the expectations of a number of commentators to the proposed rule. Interest in having MSWLFs meet the same criteria as hazardous waste landfills is based on concern that the two types of disposal facilities share a common potential for damage to human health and the environment.

In establishing the new rules, the EPA required MSWLFs to meet more stringent requirements than previously demanded but less stringent than required for hazardous waste landfills. This distinction was based on the EPA's determination that MSWLFs intrinsically represent a lesser threat than hazardous waste landfills and because the language of the statute and congressional record allowed such a distinction. The EPA argued that the congressional intent of distinguishing between levels of protection at hazardous waste landfills and MSWLFs is evident in RCRA language. For hazardous waste landfills, standards shall be those "necessary for protection of human health and the environment." However, for a facility to be classified as a sanitary landfill, it must only show "no reasonable probability of adverse effects on health or the environment." *Reasonable probability* is interpreted as allowing a less severe standard (that may include economic considerations) than allowed for hazardous waste landfills.

Hazardous and Solid Waste Amendments of 1984

Solid waste management continues to be under state and local control. States are encouraged to seek primacy over their solid waste programs, with the federal role being largely one of guidance, financial assistance, oversight, and enforcement. The EPA maintains an active management role for those states unwilling or unable to assume responsibility for their own program.

Each state (with an approved program) is required to prepare a solid waste management plan. These plans must include methods for encouraging resource conservation or recovery. Each state also must implement a permit program for its solid waste management facilities that receive hazardous waste. Thus, sanitary landfills, which accept such waste as household hazardous waste, must have a permit and meet federal design and operational standards. Substantial flexibility is allowed in the federal standards, however, to allow states to develop specific criteria best suited to the local situation.

The philosophy behind landfill design is that the landfills must prevent movement of any of the waste constituents away from the site. Landfills must be lined with either plastic or clay (usually both) as a barrier to waste migration. Liquids must be minimized, because if liquids build up inside a facility, they result in a force (hydraulic head) that pushes dissolved waste products through the barriers. To keep out water from rain and runoff, closed facilities must have surface liners of the same type as used on the bottom and sides. Leachate collection systems must underlie the landfills to facilitate collection of residual liquids (leachate) that percolated through the waste. In the resulting oxygen-deficient, dry environment, little degradation of waste occurs (although a few facilities put pumped leachate back into the landfill to enhance waste degradation and provide an inexpensive leachate disposal system). Thus, modern landfill design effectively preserves the wastes. Closure plans must ensure that landfills will not fail (allow leakage from the site) for an extended period. While a thirty-year postclosure care period is specified in the federal rule, either a reduction or an extension is allowed depending on local conditions.

Four tools are available to ensure that the state plan complies with federal guidelines. The simplest is the denial of federal funding or technical assistance to noncompliant states. The EPA may seek injunctive relief when solid waste disposal presents an imminent threat to health or the environment, although this authority is somewhat limited because Congress wanted municipal solid waste problems to be solved through local efforts.[5] However, the EPA's power to directly intervene is enhanced by its ability to use hazardous waste enforcement authority in states that do not provide a permit program for MSWLFs receiving household hazardous waste or hazardous waste from small-quantity generators.[6]

The fourth enforcement tool is the citizen suit. Any citizen may bring suit against any government agency or individual alleged to be violating any requirement of the law or the state plan. Suits can be brought against the EPA for failure to perform required duties, as well as for violations of specific facility requirements.[7]

Hazardous Waste

Identification. For material to be regulated as a hazardous waste, first it must be found to be a solid waste, or a combination of solid wastes. RCRA then specifies that solid waste meeting the following criteria will be considered hazardous waste.

1. Waste that causes, or significantly contributes to an increase in mortality or an increase in serious irreversible or incapacitating reversible illness; or
2. poses a substantial present or potential hazard to human health or the environment when improperly treated, stored, transported, disposed of, or otherwise managed.

The definitions of hazardous waste and solid waste clearly reflect the intent of Congress but are too nonspecific to incorporate directly into a regulatory program. Subsequently, the EPA developed language to provide specific direction in determining whether materials need to be regulated as solid and hazardous wastes. The EPA originally defined solid waste in 1980 as "any garbage, refuse, sludge or any other waste material," except for material specifically excluded from consideration. Difficulty with this definition arose because other waste material was interpreted to mean material that sometimes is discarded, by anyone in a similar industry, after serving its original purpose. This interpretation led to confusion regarding the status of intermediate products that were used for later processes and to difficulty in comparing processes to determine when similar materials were sometimes discarded. The EPA expanded and simplified its solid waste definition in 1985 to include any discarded material not exempted from such classification. Discarded material consists of material disposed of in landfills, injection wells, or other facilities where the waste is placed in land or water such that there is potential for migration away from the site. It also includes material that is burned or incinerated and many materials that are recycled.

Hazardous wastes are classified in two ways. Solid waste having characteristics of ignitability, corrosivity, reactivity, or toxicity are considered hazardous waste. (Notice that toxicity is only one of the characteristics for hazardous waste—many people incorrectly use *toxic* waste synonymously with *hazardous* waste.) Alternately, the EPA has listed certain solid wastes as hazardous, so specific characteristics do not have to be measured.

Solid waste must be evaluated for ignitability and corrosivity following specific EPA-designated test procedures. Ignitability is the characteristic of catching fire.[8] Corrosivity is the characteristic of corroding metals and other materials.[9] Reactive wastes are those that are unstable under normal conditions, and can form toxic fumes or explode.[10] It is difficult to describe a specific test procedure that adequately tests reactivity; therefore, the EPA has promulgated a narrative description of reactivity characteristics to assess waste.

Toxicity is the most difficult characteristic to assess. Almost everything is toxic in great enough concentrations, so the regulatory definition cannot include all potentially toxic wastes. Therefore, the EPA had to develop a definition useful as an indicator of potential toxicity, rather than one directly related to all plausible toxic agents.

Waste is evaluated for toxicity by conducting a testing procedure that somewhat simulates conditions found in a landfill.[11] Liquids in a landfill usually are acidic, a condition favorable to the leaching of many heavy metals and other materials from solids. Because liquids are more mobile than solids, the risk of migration of toxics away from landfills is greatly enhanced when the toxics are solubilized. The required test procedure, called the Toxicity Characteristic Leaching Procedure or TCLP, puts the solid waste in a liquid acidic solution under rigidly defined operating conditions. At the end of the test period, the acid is tested for thirty-two organic and eight inorganic chemicals.

The EPA has three lists identifying characteristic hazardous wastes. The source-specific list identifies wastes from specific industrial processes (such as petroleum refining) in which operation is known to produce wastes of known hazards (K-wastes). The non–source-specific list contains hazardous wastes commonly found from a variety of sources, such as degreasing solvents (F-wastes). Discarded commercial chemical products are identified on the final list, which includes off-specification chemicals, containers, and spill residues (P- and U-wastes). Certain solid wastes are not considered hazardous. These exemptions include household waste, agricultural wastes returned to the ground as fertilizer, mining overburden returned to the mine site, and other wastes resulting from the extraction and processing of ores and minerals, utility wastes from coal combustion, oil and natural gas exploration drilling waste, cement kiln dust wastes, and arsenic-treated wood wastes generated by end uses.[12]

Cradle to Grave. Passage of RCRA meant that hazardous waste now needed to be tracked and managed from the point of generation (cradle) to its ultimate fate in the environment (grave). The generator is responsible for identifying whether a material is a waste and whether the waste is hazardous. The generator must ensure that the waste is handled appropriately even after it leaves the generating facility.

Each generator must obtain an identification number from the state agency responsible for maintaining the hazardous waste program (or the EPA if the state does not have primacy for the program). Waste being sent off-site must be listed by the generator on a waste manifest (see appendix B). The waste is characterized following a numerical coding system developed by the EPA. The manifest also contains information on the waste quantity and identifies the generator, transporter, and receiving facility. The generator also must certify that efforts have been taken to minimize the waste quantity and associated hazard. On the manifest, the generator's signature must follow a required statement certifying that efforts have been taken to minimize the waste quantity and associated hazard.

The hazardous waste transporter carries this manifest with the load and gives it to the waste recipient. The recipient checks the manifest to ensure that the waste can be properly handled at that facility and frequently physically checks the waste to make sure it is the same as designated on the manifest. A copy of the manifest is returned to the generator, who is supposed to ensure it has not been altered. Thus, the generator should know that the waste has arrived in an unaltered state at the intended designation, with any problems reported to the appropriate agency in an "exception report." The generator is required to retain a copy of the manifest for at least three years, although most generators will retain them indefinitely.

It is important to remember that while hazardous waste generators have substantial obligations under RCRA, if they do not treat, store, or dispose of waste they do not have to obtain a permit. Because permit requirements can be burdensome (see the following section), many facilities eliminate or avoid practices that would turn them into a Treatment, Storage, or Disposal Facility (TSDF).

Facilities generating less than one hundred kilograms per month are exempt from almost all RCRA requirements. This means that hazardous waste from these sources may legally be deposited in municipal landfills (although municipal landfills are under no obligation to accept such waste). Before 1984, small-quantity generators producing less than one thousand kilograms per month of hazardous waste were also exempt. However, HSWA modified this situation, so that these generators must meet almost all of the same requirements as required for larger facilities.

Permits.   Hazardous waste TSDFs are required to obtain a permit. Congress recognized a problem when implementing a permit requirement: If all TSDFs submitted their applications at the onset of the program, the EPA would not have the resources to provide timely permit review. Therefore, a system was specified to allow TSDFs to operate under an interim permit and a final permit.

All TSDFs in existence on November 19, 1980, that had submitted a Part A application were given an interim permit. The Part A application contains only basic information including the facility location, estimates of waste quantities, and waste management practices. This information has been quite unreliable and of limited value. To obtain a final permit, a Part B permit application needs to be approved by the EPA. Part B permit applications require substantially more operational and organizational detail than Part A permits and may run several volumes in length for major facilities. Initially, Part Bs were submitted only after the EPA requested them for individual facilities. This policy was established to maintain submission of permit applications at a rate coincident with the EPA's ability to provide permit review. However, Congress did not agree with this approach, because few final permits were being issued. After the program's 1980 inception, only twenty-four facilities (out of about eight thousand) had been issued final permits by July 31, 1983.[13] Twenty of these permits had been issued to storage facilities. From the more significant waste management units, only one landfill and three incinerators had been issued permits.

Facility Standards. Treatment, storage, and disposal facilities are all governed by EPA minimum standards, which may be further refined (but not weakened) by individual states. Specific design, construction, and operating standards have been established for hazardous waste facilities with containers, tanks, surface impoundments, waste piles, land treatment units, landfills, incinerators, thermal treatment units, chemical, physical, and biological treatment units, underground injection wells, and miscellaneous units.[14] These standards are technically complex, so their complete discussion is inappropriate in this text on environmental law. It is vital to recognize, however, that if responsible for a TSDF, these standards must be followed precisely.

Before RCRA, the federal system had little impact on disposal practices. Hazardous waste commonly was disposed of in landfills that were not designed for long-term containment of the hazardous constituents. Now, landfills must be highly engineered units providing redundant barriers to waste migration. Furthermore, a comprehensive monitoring program is required to ensure that these barriers are effective.

Landfills do not reduce the intrinsic hazard associated with the hazardous waste. Landfills keep people and wildlife away from the waste and the waste from spreading to uncontrolled parts of the environment. The landfill itself must be designed as a facility that retains its hazardous characteristics in perpetuity.

Because landfills do not destroy waste, they can be viewed as the alternative of choice (along with other land disposal techniques) only after determining that opportunities for reuse, recycling, and treatment are not available or practical. In fact, HSWA banned land disposal of hazardous waste for which alternatives are available. The EPA was directed to determine for all hazardous wastes whether land disposal should be prohibited if pretreatment was not used following best available demonstrated technology.

An elaborate procedure must be followed to close a hazardous waste landfill or a section of a landfill. A written closure plan is part of the facility application, although it may be modified during the active life of the landfill. Technical requirements include capping the top with another liner to ensure that water does not infiltrate the site. Groundwater monitoring must continue, and the site must remain secure from people or animals. However, perhaps the most important part of the entire closure process is that someone must remain identifiable as being responsible for the facility, with financial resources available to remedy any problems.

The owner or operator of the facility must provide an appropriate instrument guaranteeing long-term financial ability to manage the site, even after it has been closed. This instrument may be a trust fund, surety bond, letter of credit, insurance policy, or financial worth test. This financial guarantee became necessary because a past practice of some unethical operators was to charge for waste disposal services but then dump waste illegally and inexpensively. The company would go bankrupt before the practice was discovered, so it could not be forced to pay to clean up the mess. In the mean time, the operators had taken the money for waste disposal and become uninvolved with the company.

Enforcement of RCRA

HSWA greatly expanded the scope of criminal liability for RCRA violations. The key to criminal liability is that the violator must have committed the act "knowingly"; no such requirement is necessary for civil action. Violators may be charged penalties of up to $50,000, receive up to two years imprisonment, or both. Furthermore, anyone who knowingly commits an act that "places another person in imminent danger" may be fined up to $250,000 and receive up to fifteen years imprisonment.

The EPA may take a variety of civil actions to obtain compliance with RCRA. Civil penalties for Subtitle C violations can be up to $25,000 for each day of violation. The EPA also may seek injunctive relief in court or issue compliance orders directly. Failure to comply with administrative orders may result in a company losing its hazardous waste permit.

States (or the EPA in states without primacy over the hazardous waste program) are required to inspect all privately operated TSDFs at least once every two years. This requirement was made part of HSWA because of the lack of an effective existing monitoring program; companies could take the gamble to stay out of compliance because there was a good chance they would not be discovered.

RCRA also established a right for individuals to bring citizens' suits against alleged violators or against the EPA for alleged failure to meet its responsibility. However, citizens' suits are prohibited when dealing with siting and permitting of a TSDF, when the EPA is prosecuting an action, when the EPA or the responsible state is conducting a remedial action, or when the responsible party is conducting the approved remedial action.

Before leaving this section on enforcement, consider why an elaborate program for controlling hazardous waste is needed. Before RCRA, companies frequently disposed of waste using inexpensive techniques. Complying with hazardous waste regulations imposes a substantial financial burden, which may result in a company's product or service becoming economically noncompetitive (or substantially reduce the profit margin). One response to these new burdens is to ignore them. Firms may gamble that illegal practices will not be detected, or, if they are, that the penalties will be less onerous than the compliance costs.

Much of the rationale for imposing criminal sanctions and having a strong enforcement program is to make illegal practices more expensive than compliance. Criminal penalties may be particularly effective, because the expense of a possible jail term—in terms of personal lifestyle costs—would deter most people much more than a personal or company fine. As compliance costs continue to grow, the expense of noncompliance must keep pace to maintain the effectiveness of waste management programs. Ultimately, we will measure success by the magnitude of future problems resulting from today's hazardous waste management practices.

CERCLA: AN OVERVIEW

The key law that brought active federal government involvement to emergency response, site remediation, and spill prevention is the Comprehensive Environmental Response, Compensation, and Liability Act of 1980 (CERCLA or the Superfund Act). Congress intended CERCLA to be comprehensive in its coverage, encompassing both prevention of and response to uncontrolled hazardous substance releases. The act deals with environmental response, providing mechanisms for reacting to emergency situations and to chronic hazardous material releases. In addition to establishing procedures to prevent and remedy problems, it establishes a system for compensating appropriate individuals and assigning appropriate liability. Thus, it is designed to plan for and respond to failures in other regulatory programs and to remedy problems resulting from action taken before we had adequate regulatory protection.

EMERGENCY RESPONSE PLANS AND RIGHT TO KNOW

To begin our discussion of hazardous material releases, we will examine the requirement to plan for emergencies, including consideration of prevention. The federal program requiring comprehensive community planning was established in the Emergency Planning and Community Right-to-Know Act of 1986 (EPCRA), which was passed as part of the Superfund Amendments and Reauthorization Act of 1986 (SARA).

SARA Title III is organized into three subtitles. Subtitle A covers emergency planning, Subtitle B specifies hazardous chemical reporting requirements, and Subtitle C describes how the public will have access to facility information.

State and local governments are required to develop emergency response and preparedness plans. Every state must have an emergency response commission. Each commission must appoint local emergency response planning committees and designate emergency planning districts. Each committee must include, at minimum, representatives from "elected State and local officials; law enforcement, civil defense, firefighting, first aid, health, local environmental, hospital, and transportation personnel; broadcast and print media;

community groups; and owners and operators of facilities subject to the requirements of this subtitle."[15] This requirement makes the local committees fairly large and cumbersome but also ensures that affected parties will have representation.

Each local planning committee was required to have prepared by October 17, 1988, its comprehensive emergency response plan.

At minimum, these plans are designed to determine what extremely hazardous substances are located in or go through a community, who is responsible for them, what resources are available to deal with spills, how spill information will be communicated so that the correct response is taken, and how the entire system has been integrated so that it will work. Ideally, much of this planning will be preventive in nature.

Substantial burden is placed on facilities using extremely hazardous substances. The EPA has published a list of extremely hazardous substances with associated threshold planning quantities. Any facility having any of these substances in more than the designated quantity must notify the state planning commission and the local planning committee that it is subject to provisions of this law. Note that there is a duplicative effort required of the facility, because there is not (by law or regulation) a uniform reporting system to ensure that a single report will be transmitted to all involved agencies.

Facilities also are required to report to the local committee, the state commission, and the local fire department if they have any chemicals regulated under OSHA's hazard communication standard in quantities of ten thousand pounds or greater. For each reportable chemical, the facility must submit either a material safety data sheet (MSDS) or a list of the reportable chemicals providing the following information:[16]

1. the chemical or common name of each chemical;
2. a list of the hazardous chemicals grouped by hazard category; whether the chemical can be considered an "immediate health hazard," chronic health hazard (including carcinogens), fire hazard, hazard from sudden pressure release (such as explosives and compressed gases), or chemical reactives; and
3. identification of "any hazardous component of each" chemical as identified on the material safety data sheet.

Ordinarily, the chemical list and associated information will be more useful than receiving MSDSs for all chemicals. These lists are intended to identify critical information in an organized fashion. MSDSs typically provide such an overwhelming amount of detail as to make them difficult to interpret for pertinent emergency planning and response information.

In addition to this initial reporting requirement, facilities must report annually on the quantities and locations of their hazardous chemicals.[17] To meet "Tier I" requirements this information must include the following:

1. an estimate of the maximum amount of hazardous chemicals in each category at any time during the year (these estimates do not have to be made on a chemical-by-chemical basis, only by category);

2. an estimate of the average daily amount of chemicals in each category present at the facility during the year; and

3. the general location of chemicals in each category.

Local committees, state commissions, or local fire departments can also request Tier II information. Whereas the Tier I data reporting requirements identify categories of chemicals and their general locations, Tier II requirements identify individual chemicals by names and report their specific locations and storage conditions. Companies may elect to protect trade secrets by withholding specific names and locations of chemicals from public reporting. However, community planning agencies must have access to specific names and locations if they request it.

Another list of chemicals is used as the basis for reporting on the presence of toxic materials. Facilities with chemicals greater than threshold quantities on the "Toxic Chemicals Subject to Section 313 of the Emergency Planning and Community Right-To-Know Act of 1986" list must report to the EPA annually. In addition to information identifying the facility, and chemical use at that facility, the report must document the "annual quantity of the toxic chemical entering each environmental medium." The EPA must collect this information and maintain a national toxic chemical inventory available to the public. This information has sparked interest in many communities about the activities of local industry. As these data are released by the EPA and reported by local media, many companies have been faced with a local population outraged by the vast quantities of toxic chemicals being discharged regularly as part of their normal operating practices.

FEDERAL RESPONSE TO CONTAMINATED SITES

Before CERCLA, the federal government had little ability to take an active role in responding to a hazardous material spill or to a site contaminated with hazardous material. CERCLA provided both the necessary authority and a funding mechanism to respond to these types of situations.

Two types of responses are identified in CERCLA, removal actions and remedial actions. Removal actions are intended to stabilize or clean up a hazardous site that poses an immediate threat to human health or the environment. Remedial actions are intended to provide permanent remedies. Removal actions may not eliminate the need for remedial actions, because chronic problems may be ignored while providing immediate protection.

The universe of chemicals regulated by CERCLA is much broader than that regulated under RCRA. CERCLA includes RCRA hazardous wastes and hazardous substances designated under the Clean Air Act, Clean Water Act, and Toxic Substances Control Act. CERCLA also requires the EPA to maintain an additional list of substances not included in these other acts that present a potential threat to human health and the environment.

The Hazardous Substances Response Trust Fund, or Superfund, was established in the 1980 legislation to provide a mechanism for the federal government to finance its emergency response and remedial response activities and recover costs. This was a fund of $1.6 billion, of which 87.5 percent was obtained from the petroleum and chemical industries, with the remaining 12.5 percent coming from general federal revenues. The EPA can use these funds to cover its own costs, or the costs involved with work it orders, in responding to an immediate threat. However, this fund was intended primarily as a rotating fund, with costs incurred in cleanup recovered from the responsible parties.

Congress increased the Superfund to $8.5 billion dollars as part of the Superfund Amendments and Reauthorization Act of 1986 (SARA). While the petroleum and chemical industries continued to finance the bulk of this fund, $2.75 billion and $1.4 billion, respectively, corporate income taxes also provided $2.5 billion. The remainder of the fund came from general federal revenues (1.25 billion), interest (0.3 billion) and recovery of cleanup costs (0.3 billion). If recoveries from PRPs are insufficient, additional funds may be authorized. For example, in 1992 the Superfund received an additional 1.75 billion federal dollars.

Removal Action

If a material is spilled, the EPA can implement a *removal action.* These actions are limited to situations in which there is an immediate threat to human health or the environment. Each action is limited to twelve months and $2 million (before the passage of SARA, these limits were six months and $1 million), although extensions can be granted. An example of a removal action is a collection of leaking drums of explosive material.

Removal actions are not meant necessarily to provide permanent solutions. This means that the EPA may take actions that provide immediate protection and then leave with substantial hazard remaining. Once immediate contact is prevented, the threat becomes chronic rather than acute. Because there are so many sites that present chronic risks, the EPA must follow an elaborate procedure to prioritize them. The EPA reported in 1991 that more than 2,300 cleanups have been started and 1,900 completed since 1980.[18] More than 70 percent of these responses have taken place at sites not currently eligible for remedial actions.

Hazardous substance spills must be reported to the National Response Center, operated by the Coast Guard, if they exceed "reportable quantities." Unlisted hazardous substances generally have reportable quantities of one hundred pounds, although chemicals meeting the EPA criteria for toxicity may have a lower limit.[19] Department of Transportation regulations require reporting spills if the spill results in hospitalization or death, damage exceeds $50,000, pathogens or radioactive materials are involved, the area is evacuated for more than one hour, or the operational flight pattern of an aircraft is altered.[20]

It is important to recognize that the Emergency Planning and Community Right-to-Know Act of 1986 should significantly reduce the need for direct federal involvement in spill cleanup and hazardous substance removals. It is too early to adequately assess the effectiveness of EPCRA and whether it will reduce the need for Superfund removal activities. In evaluating the effectiveness of these programs, you may want to consider the incentives that a spiller might have in *not* reporting an incident.

Remedial Response

Before CERCLA, only common law remedies applied to most sites where hazardous substances had been released and presented a threat to human health and the environment. At many sites, there were a host of uncertainties regarding the nature of the threat and potentially responsible parties. No one seemed to be accountable for determining what kinds of materials were present, how effectively materials were contained, the effects of human exposure to the leaking chemicals, or the long-term effects on the environment.

CERCLA required the EPA to develop criteria for prioritizing among sites needing remediation. The EPA developed (through the Mitre Corporation) a hazard ranking system by which sites were evaluated on the basis of relative risk to human health and the environment (notice that there was no attempt to quantify the actual risk). This is necessarily a complex task because of the many routes by which harm may occur (e.g., surface and groundwater, air, soil, vegetation). Those sites scoring high enough on this ranking system are included on the National Priorities List (NPL). Effective January 17, 1995, there were 1,088 General Superfund sites and 154 sites in the Federal Facilities Section. An additional forty-six sites have been proposed, resulting in a total of 1,288 final and proposed sites. This number could easily rise, because as of 1985, more than thirty thousand potentially contaminated sites had been identified by the EPA, and the states have recognized others that have not been reported to the EPA.[21] Only NPL sites are eligible for the EPA remedial action. However, the EPA is not obligated to pursue sites on the NPL in any particular order. Thus, the EPA site selection can be a very political process, as well as a technically demanding one.

Once a site on the NPL has been selected for remediation, a formal process must be followed to determine and implement appropriate actions. A Remedial Investigation/Feasibility Study (RI/FS) is done first. The conditions at the site must be determined, including the extent of contamination, migration off-site, and potential for human and environmental exposure. A series of specific remediation alternatives must be developed, including specification of costs, technical feasibility, and environmental impacts. This usually is an expensive process, with EPA estimating average costs of approximately $1.35 million for each site.[22] Based on the RI/FS, a Record of Decision (ROD) is written in which the EPA documents and justifies the selection of a particular cleanup option.

The Superfund can be used to finance remedial response (in addition to emergency response, as described earlier). Again, the intended use of the fund is to allow activity to begin before potentially responsible parties (PRPs) are identified. Additionally, if no (financially solvent) PRP can be identified, work may be completely financed from the fund. Ultimately, PRPs should replenish most of the fund, although thus far recoveries from PRPs have been far lower than initially anticipated. Between 1980 and 1989, responsible parties agreed to contribute more than $642 million toward cleanups at 441 sites. The pace of recovery increased in 1990, with the EPA reporting recovery of more than $1 billion from private parties.[23]

PRPs may be legally identified as responsible for waste cleanup even if they had relatively little involvement with the site difficulties. These parties can include present and past owners and operators of the site, transporters of the substances to the site, and generators who produced the substances. Joint and several liability is assigned, meaning that a responsible party may be assigned all, or any part, of the liability. Thus, if a company provided only a tiny fraction of the hazardous substances to an NPL site (but perhaps was the most financially solvent of the potentially responsible parties), the EPA would be acting within its authority to assign the total cleanup costs to that company. Of course, that company could then pursue through the courts cost recovery from the other sources of the hazardous substances. Liability is also retroactive, meaning that companies are responsible for their hazardous substances regardless of the time of disposal (or if they were in compliance with existing laws). Strict liability also applies, meaning that even if a company met all requirements existing at the time of disposal, problems occurring today still put them under the purview of CERCLA.

The definition of *potentially responsible party* has been very broadly interpreted by the courts to expand the net of those who could be held liable. For example, in *United States v. Carolawn Chemical Company,*[24] the district court held that a chemical company that had held title to a hazardous waste disposal site for only *one hour* could be held liable as an owner and operator under the act. The court in that case rejected the chemical company's claim that they had not really been an owner but had merely been a "conduit" in the transfer of title to the site. Other unlikely candidates have also been held responsible as owners under the act. In *United States v. Burns,*[25] a district court in New Hampshire found the trustee of a realty trust liable as an owner. And, in a widely discussed case, *United States v. Fleet Factors Corporation,*[26] the court held that a lender who holds a security interest in a corporation that owns a contaminated site may be liable if that lender is able to "affect hazardous waste disposal decisions" at the site.[27]

Recently, the EPA has provided a mechanism for eliminating liability for owners whose interest in a facility is only financial and does not involve site management.[28] This protection to lending institutions largely applies to "involuntary" acquisitions of property rather than active participation in decisions involving the facility or hazardous material.

The EPA also can limit future liability concerns by granting a "covenant not to sue" or by agreeing to a de minimis settlement. A potentially responsible party that contributed relatively little of the material causing the hazardous condition of a site may enter into an agreement in which it makes a relatively small settlement. As part of this de minimis settlement, the EPA may agree that this party will not be responsible for future liability for activities needed beyond those already specified in the ROD. Because the potentially responsible party will not be responsible for future activities, the EPA will agree not to sue them in the future for cost recovery. These arrangements are intended to allow relatively quick and complete settlement for companies that had little to do with a site and allow concentration of effort to those parties responsible for the majority of the problem.

Another liability issue is whether an officer of a corporation responsible for dumping waste at a site may be held personally liable. In the 1985 case of *United States v. Mottolo*,[29] the court held the president of a chemical company personally liable, stating that those persons who actually arranged for or disposed of a hazardous waste under the act did not need to be owners to be held responsible. Thus, we can see that the court is attempting to extend liability broadly to ensure that the Superfund will be at least partially replenished.

This assignment of liability may seem totally inequitable at first, because companies with very little involvement in a problem may face substantial financial obligations. However, keep in mind that if a responsible party cannot be found, then the burden falls back on the taxpayer. Probably more important is that these liability burdens provide substantial incentive to the generating facilities to ensure that hazardous substances are properly disposed of. Thus, in addition to regulating agencies checking on the performance of treatment, storage, and disposal facilities (TSDFs), companies sending their wastes to these sites have substantial incentive to make sure that they are properly operating. This brings industry expertise to the task of TSDF inspections.

Because of the risk of liability, industry has become somewhat hesitant to move to preexisting industrial sites. This hesitancy often conflicts with local and state land use policies, which promote retention of an active industrial zone to prevent economic stagnation or depression. Furthermore, industry locating in traditionally nonindustrial areas often presents other problems, including the elimination of farmland, destruction of wilderness, or conflict with residential land uses. In response, some states are attempting to entice industrial development by reducing liability associated with site redevelopment. Interestingly, this may be reverting the liability burden back to the taxpayer, in direct opposition to the rationale behind the federal assignment of responsibility.

Furthermore, a recent decision by the Third Circuit Court, *U.S. v. Alcan Aluminum Corp,*[30] may result in an additional mechanism for industry to remove liability from involvement in a hazardous waste site. In this case, the court ruled that Alcan Aluminum must be given an opportunity to demonstrate the portion of harm it was responsible for, rather than having the court indiscriminately impose joint and several liability. If this case serves as a precedent, companies may become less concerned about the status of the disposal sites accepting their wastes, as long as the ultimate fate and impact of their wastes can be clearly identified.

The EPA has encouraged redevelopment of contaminated urban sites and has been promoting its Brownfield Economic Redevelopment Initiative. This initiative attempts to help communities revitalize abandoned contaminated property. Stated objectives of the initiative are "to build the capacity of affected and interested parties to shape how contaminated sites are cleaned up and productively reused; to stimulate a national search for innovative ways to overcome the current obstacles to the reuse of contaminated properties; to coalesce federal, state, and municipal efforts to examine new approaches to achieving cleanup and reuse; and to explore the potential for combining an economic stimulus and a speeded-up environmental cleanup to contribute to achieving environmental justice."[31]

Following passage of CERCLA in 1980, the EPA action affecting remedial cleanup was quite slow. By 1986, only eight sites had been remediated, and the entire Superfund had been spent.[32] This obviously was not the intent of Congress, so it included in SARA a schedule for work to begin at NPL sites.

Congress's demands for increased activity has resulted in a quickened pace for remediation. The EPA has reported that 279 NPL sites have been included on its Construction Completion List through December 1994, signifying completion of remedial activities. To be included on this list, a finding must be made that

1. any necessary physical construction is complete, whether or not final cleanup levels or other requirements have been achieved;
2. EPA has determined that the response action should be limited to measures that do not involve construction (e.g., institutional controls); or
3. the site qualifies for deletion from the NPL.

Additionally (as of November 1994), EPA has conducted 648 removal actions at NPL sites, and 2,331 removal actions at non-NPL sites.

CERCLA provided little guidance on how the EPA should determine the level of removal during a site cleanup. SARA provided the EPA more direction in determining suitable removal levels during a remedial response by providing that cleanups must be protective of human health and the environment, be cost effective, and use permanent solutions, including treatment and resource recovery, as much as practicable. Land disposal is discouraged.

Even within the framework established by SARA, it is difficult to determine appropriate cleanup levels for specific sites. Removal of all of a contaminant is virtually impossible, exceedingly expensive, and involves analytical procedures beyond technical abilities. EPA's regulations promulgated in

1990 provide detailed guidelines to provide more direct guidance, but they may have resulted in a loss of useful site-specific flexibility.

The EPA may use the Superfund to engage in a cleanup while it is negotiating with potentially responsible parties and later recover its costs. Alternately, the EPA may issue an administrative order or go through the courts to force responsible parties to pay directly for site cleanup. Typically, cleanup settlements reflect months or years of negotiations among the EPA and responsible parties to determine appropriate solutions and division of financial responsibility. The EPA encourages parties to decide on their own proper allocation of responsibilities, as long as their settlement covers all costs. Obviously, this is often difficult and the EPA must become involved. One big problem in negotiating is that there is great uncertainty about responsibility (what percentage of the problem is due to each company's waste). Another important complication is that frequently companies that are now insolvent may have contributed significantly. The EPA may use Superfund dollars to cover their portion of the cleanup, although it is not required (or even encouraged) to do so. However, the EPA has shown great reluctance to accept a settlement for less than 100 percent of the total cleanup costs.

Citizen suits permit individuals to sue the government, any company, or individual for alleged violations of SARA.[33] Cases will be heard in the district court in the district where the alleged violation occurred or in the district court for the District of Columbia if the case is against the government. However, to allow time for compliance, no action may begin until at least sixty days after the plaintiff has notified the federal and state governments and the alleged violator of the intent to prosecute. Substantial opportunity and requirement for public involvement is built into this process; the EPA can give grants for up to $50,000 to public groups to hire appropriate people to help them understand the key issues. Obviously, this also makes data available to anyone wishing to pursue litigation. CERCLA does not replace common law liability for personal injury or death under applicable principles of toxic tort laws, as discussed in chapter 7.

UNDERGROUND STORAGE TANK PROGRAM

A program related in nature to emergency planning, although of different regulatory origin, is the underground storage tank (UST) program. The Hazard and Solid Waste Amendments of 1984 (HSWA) provided the framework for a regulatory program designed to help prevent releases from tanks. Most of the underground storage tanks in the United States store gasoline. However, other flammable industrial chemicals (such as degreasing solvents) have traditionally been stored underground to minimize fire hazards. Various estimates put the number of regulated tanks at 1.5 to 2 million, with somewhere between 10 and 30 percent of them leaking. Materials leaking from tanks generally will migrate down to groundwater, and can cause significant contamination. Such leaks are not obvious because the tanks are not visible and because contamination effects may not become apparent for many years.

Underground storage tank leaks can contaminate important groundwater supplies and cost millions of dollars to remediate (even partially). One area that has experienced major problems is the Silicon Valley in Santa Clara County, California, a hub of the semiconductor industry. In the eighteen-month period beginning in April 1980, IBM, Hewlett Packard, Intel, Advanced Micro Devices, and Fairchild all reported tanks leaking organic solvents. These solvents moved to drinking water wells; one well near Fairchild had one organic solvent, 1-1-1-trichloroethane or TCA, at concentrations twenty-nine times the state action level. Cleanup of the groundwater in Silicon Valley will cost millions of dollars and may never be successfully completed. Obviously, the best remedy to this problem would have been prevention.

The federal regulatory program works by establishing tank and leak detection standards. New tanks must have spill and overflow protection devices. The tanks must meet performance standards designed to ensure that the stored material will not corrode the tanks. Because responsibility for these programs is being taken over by the states, actual requirements may be more stringent than these federal minimums. Existing tanks have until December 1998 to meet the new tank standards. This can be accomplished by installing a liner, or cathodic protection, against corrosion. Spill and overflow protection and a leak detection system must be installed. Tanks that store hazardous substances (rather than petroleum products) must have extra protection against hazardous substance release. This may be accomplished through a secondary containment system, a double-walled tank, or an external liner. These devices are intended to keep any release of the inner tank contained, while the leak detection system signals that the inner tank has lost its integrity. The EPA has developed technical guidance documents identifying acceptable methods to meet these requirements.

A significant burden is placed on the owner/operator of a tank to ensure that adequate financial resources are available to respond to a leak. Financial responsibility can be demonstrated through insurance, a letter of credit, a trust fund, a surety bond, or a state-managed financial assurance device where available. Large facilities, handling more than ten thousand gallons of petroleum per month, must have at least $1 million of coverage per occurrence. All other facilities must have $500,000 coverage per occurrence.

The UST program is still in its infancy. Companies are struggling to comply because of the expense and disruption to operations. Tank removal may cost more than $10,000, and complete replacement should cost at least $30,000. Yet, while these costs are high, the costs of remediation following a tank leak may be much higher. Thus, there has been relatively little discussion of the reasonableness of having a UST program, although substantial discussion has focused on specific program provisions and approaches.

CONCLUDING REMARKS

Waste management practices in the United States have changed remarkably over the last two decades. A complex and comprehensive system now governs the fate of waste, with incentives to reduce generation and recycle rather than "dispose" through permanent storage on the land or in the water. Nevertheless, much of our waste stream continues to be put in landfills. Although modern landfills should be effective in containing wastes, even several layers of plastic and clay liners will not last forever. Thus, modern technology may be only deferring liability problems further into the future.

It is clear that progress has been made in providing protection from unintended release of hazardous materials; it is equally obvious that these releases still occur. In addition to the CERCLA and UST provisions, efforts to reduce hazardous waste generation and properly manage waste following RCRA provisions also are important in minimizing risk from hazardous materials. CERCLA followed RCRA because initial concerns focused more on hazardous waste than hazardous materials; much of the public probably still views hazardous waste as presenting the larger threat. The regulatory community recognizes the need to protect the public and the environment from all agents that have a substantial potential to cause harm.

However, the current regulatory framework designed to provide necessary protections are being challenged as overly complex, expensive, and cumbersome. Bills to change our approach to hazardous material management are being actively pursued in Congress, with the Superfund perhaps at greatest risk of large-scale change. Perhaps the only way to stay current on developments is to become involved and influence—rather than just observe—our future directions in managing hazardous materials and wastes.

QUESTIONS FOR REVIEW AND DISCUSSION

1. What is the best solution to the growing problem of waste production?
2. Why should we worry about insufficient landfill capacity? Will market forces drive the completion of new landfills?
3. Why would laws exclude hazardous wastes from households and small-quantity generators from regulation?
4. Should there be a different level of protection at hazardous waste landfills than sanitary landfills? What is the EPA's opinion?
5. Why is CERCLA commonly referred to as *Superfund?* Is this appropriate?
6. What obstacles does the regulated community face in responding to notification requirements of SARA Title III?
7. What groups must be represented in emergency planning? Are there other groups that should be represented?

8. What is the difference between a removal action and a remedial action?

9. How much involvement must you have with a hazardous substance to be considered a CERCLA potentially responsible party?

10. Is the Brownfield Economic Redevelopment Initiative going to help or hinder protection and restoration of environmental quality? What do you suspect are the views of the pertinent interest groups (e.g., industrial organizations, environmental groups, EPA)?

FOR FURTHER READING

J. G. ARBUCKLE, ET AL., ENVIRONMENTAL LAW HANDBOOK (11th ed.)., (Rockville, Md.: Government Institutes, Inc., 1991).

M. A. COHEN, *Criminal Law, Environmental Crime and Punishment: Legal/Economic Theory and Empirical Evidence on Enforcement of Federal Environmental Statutes,* 82 J. CRIM. L. & CRIMINOLOGY 1054–1108 (1992).

R. M. HALL, JR., ET AL., RCRA HAZARDOUS WASTES HANDBOOK (7th ed.). (Rockville, Md.: Government Institutes, Inc., 1991).

L. PECK, *Protection Mechanisms for Lenders against Hazardous Waste Liability,* 18 HOFSTRA L. REV. 89 (1989).

D. L. REBOVICH, DANGEROUS GROUND, THE WORLD OF HAZARDOUS WASTE CRIME (New Brunswick, N.J.: Transaction Publishers, 1992).

W. A. RODGERS, *A Superfund Trivia Test: A Comment on the Complexity of the Environmental Laws,* 22 ENVTL. L.J. 417 (1992).

W. D. ROBINSON, ed. THE SOLID WASTE HANDBOOK, A PRACTICAL GUIDE (New York: Wiley, 1986).

U.S. EPA OSWER. THE SOLID WASTE DILEMMA: AN AGENDA FOR ACTION EPA 530-SW-89-072 (1989).

ON THE INTERNET

http://www.sfref95.org/join.html
Superfund Reform Organization's site

http://www.cais.com/tne/neis/superf.html
The most requested Superfund documents

http://www.house.gov/democrats/ht__environ.html
State-by-state information on Superfund sites

http://www.monitor.net/monitor/free/luftcleanup.html
Information about finding underground storage tank rules

NOTES

1. L. BLUMBERG, and R. GOTTLIEB, WAR ON WASTE: CAN AMERICA WIN ITS BATTLE WITH GARBAGE? (Washington, D.C.: Island Press, 1989).

2. Subcommittee on Transportation and Commerce, Committee on Interstate and Foreign Commerce, U.S. House of Representatives, Resource Conservation and Recovery Act of 1976, 94th Congress, second session; Waste Control Act of 1975; Hearings on H.R. 5487 and H.R. 406 Before Subcommittee on Transportation and Commerce, 94th Congress, first session (1975).

3. U.S. EPA, OSW, SURVEY OF SOLID WASTE (MUNICIPAL) LANDFILL FACILITIES. (August 1986).

4. U.S. EPA, OSWER, REPORT TO CONGRESS, SOLID WASTE DISPOSAL IN THE UNITED STATES, EPA 530-SW-88-011B (1988).

5. 42 U.S.C. § 6073.

6. Pub. L. 898-616, § 302.

7. 42 U.S.C. § 6972.

8. 40 C.F.R. § 261.21.

9. 40 C.F.R. § 261.22.

10. 40 C.F.R. § 261.23.

11. 40 C.F.R. § 261.24.

12. 40 C.F.R. § 261.4(b).

13. Government Accounting Office, INTERIM REPORT ON INSPECTION, ENFORCEMENT, AND PERMITTING ACTIVITIES AT HAZARDOUS WASTE FACILITIES (September 1983).

14. 40 C.F.R. § 264, subparts J–X, § 265, subparts J–R.

15. Emergency Planning and Community Right-to-Know Act § 301 (1986).

16. Emergency Planning and Community Right-to-Know Act § 311 (1986).

17. Emergency Planning and Community Right-to-Know Act § 312 (1986).

18. U.S. EPA, THE SUPERFUND PROGRAM: TEN YEARS OF PROGRESS, EPA 540-8-9-003 (1991).

19. 40 C.F.R. 302.4.

20. 40 C.F.R. 171.5.

21. EPA, ENVIRONMENTAL PROGRESS AND CHALLENGE: EPA UPDATE (1989).

22. EPA, ENVIRONMENTAL STEWARDSHIP: EPA'S FIRST TWO YEARS IN THE BUSH ADMINISTRATION (Washington, D.C.: EPA Office of Communication and Public Affiars, 1991).

23. 21 Env't. Rep. Cases 2124 (D. S.C. 1984).

24. No. C-88-94-L (D.N.H. 1988).

25. 901 F.2a 155 (11th Cir. 1990), *cert. denied,* 111 S.C5.752 (1991).

26. Ibid.,1557.

27. 40 C.F.R. Part 300.

28. 605 F. Supp. 898 (D.N.H. 1985).

29. 964 F.2d 252.

30. SIDNEY M. WOLF, POLLUTION LAW HANDBOOK—A GUIDE TO FEDERAL ENVIRONMENTAL LAWS (New York: Quorum Books, 1988).

31. SARA, Sec. 310.

32. 106 NJ 557, 525 A.2d 287 (1987).

33. J. M. LOGSDON, *Collaboration to Regulate L.U.S.T.: Leaking Underground Storage Tanks in Silicon Valley,* 23 J. BUS. RES. 99–111 (1991).

CHAPTER 9

Energy and Natural Resources

No nation seems more endowed with natural resources than the United States—abundant water, fertile soil, a benign climate, an incredible variety of plant and animal species, and stores of energy resources, including natural gas, coal, oil, and uranium. Yet these resources are not unlimited. Without careful management, many will become depleted or destroyed. This chapter focuses on how we protect these important natural resources, with special emphasis on energy.

We begin by examining energy law and policy, the area of law attempting to manage energy needs. This area is very complex because we must consider not only issues of resource depletion, but also the effects of alternate forms of energy on the environment. Next we examine U.S. policies with respect to preservation of land, protection of coastal areas and wetlands, and the protection of plant and animal species.

ENERGY POLICY: A HISTORICAL OVERVIEW

The U.S. energy policy has been anything but consistent. We seem to bounce back and forth between complacency and crisis, at least with respect to aspects of energy policy designed to ensure that the nation's demand for energy can be met. Many fear that this cycle may be continuing and we are heading for the next energy crisis.

As you examine energy policy, you should be aware of the major conflict in philosophies that underlies our shifting policies. On the one hand, the belief in unlimited resources or unlimited technological developments tends to encourage the full development of energy resources. On the other hand, the view that energy is a limited resource favors policies that encourage conservation and demand reduction.

Before the 1970s, energy policy received little consideration. Although the possibilities of nuclear energy had begun to be explored, we were still complacently relying on what seemed to be an unlimited access to worldwide stores of fossil fuels: coal, petroleum, and natural gas.

218

The Crisis Begins

Not until 1973 did the phrase *energy crisis* enter the American vocabulary. The "crisis," which would last until 1978, began in October 1973, when the United States was importing 38.8 percent of its daily petroleum consumption. The Organization of Petroleum Exporting Countries (OPEC) voted to cut its oil production by 5 percent monthly until Israel made fundamental changes in its Arab policies. The day after that vote, Saudi Arabia, OPEC's major producer, cut its oil exports by 10 percent and ended all petroleum shipments to the United States until the Nixon administration altered its pro-Israel policies. The loss of 2 million barrels of oil a day shocked Americans into suddenly recognizing how dependent they had become on foreign oil and also what political, economic, and military risks this dependence entailed. From an environmental standpoint, the situation was a crisis because if the oil shortage continued for long, the United States might be compelled to increase greatly its mining of coal, with potentially disastrous ecological consequences.[1]

In response to the OPEC oil embargo, Nixon took the first steps in U.S. history toward comprehensive national energy planning. He established the Federal Energy Office (FEO) within the White House staff in late 1973. The next year he established the Federal Energy Administration, which was given authority to initiate federal policy and take whatever steps the White House deemed necessary for national energy needs. Congress, likewise, contributed to a developing national energy policy by creating the Energy Research and Development Administration (ERDA) to consolidate all federal energy research in a single agency.

Until his forced resignation in 1974, Nixon continued to urge legislation designed to increase the federal role in energy management. He proposed laws restricting public and private energy consumption, providing unemployment insurance for those who lost jobs because of the energy crisis, temporarily relaxing air pollution standards for automobile emissions and power plants, and imposing a windfall profits tax to keep companies from making excess profits by rapidly increasing energy prices. He used powers granted to him by Congress to impose mandatory allocations of selected fossil fuels, as well as to set up an allocation program and price guidelines for crude oil and petroleum.

By the end of Nixon's term, he and Congress had also required national daylight savings time and the fifty-five-mile-per-hour speed limit as conservation efforts. They had funded new federal programs for research into solar energy and had encouraged private development of nuclear energy. Nixon had also invented Project Independence, a hastily crafted program designed to ensure that by the end of the decade the United States would be able to meet all of its own energy needs. Many of the proposals were technologically infeasible, and some were contradictory.

The energy crisis continued through the Ford administration, with Ford submitting a package of measures in his 1975 Energy Policy and Conservation Act focusing on programs designed to give flexibility to the administration in handling energy problems. Carter came into office making energy policy his number one priority. A month after taking office, he set forth his National Energy Plan (NEP), organized around four broad objectives:

1. to centralize federal energy planning through institutional reform;
2. to achieve greater energy efficiency through selective use of market forces and a major expansion of federal regulatory policy;
3. to increase rapidly federal spending on research and development of new technology for energy conservation and productivity; and
4. to ensure that environmental protection and social equity would be important in these new programs.[2]

More than two hundred separate proposals were considered by Congress in relation to NEP. Many were defeated, and the program was perceived by many as hastily constructed and too complex. But by the end of his term, Carter had made some significant changes in federal energy policy: The Department of Energy (DOE) had been created; domestic gas and petroleum prices had been decontrolled; increased government funding had been provided for federal research and development for new energy technologies; and more environmental safeguards on energy use had been established.

A Return to Complacency

Reagan's victory signaled the end of the energy crisis, at least as perceived by the executive and the general public. In his first National Energy Plan, Reagan informed the public that the forecast for energy supplies was not as bad as some had thought; there were going to be no more "wars on energy." And Reagan's program of regulatory relief was going to be applied to energy policies and other regulatory actions. Within a few years, energy policy had been dramatically altered. There was a return to the preembargo days of abundant energy. This new philosophy continued through the Bush administration.

Reagan tried to abolish the DOE, but Congress would not go along and he had to be content with reducing the agency's authority. He slashed the budget of the Office of Strip Mining, weakening its ability to enforce regulations. His secretary of state attempted to lease more public land on the outer continental shelf and in federal wildlands for energy exploration than had been leased in the entire period before Nixon's election. Funding for energy conservation programs and research for renewable sources of energy such as solar and wind power was slashed.

By mid-1985, energy no longer appeared in public opinion polls as a major concern. By 1990, Americans were no longer interested in energy-efficient houses; many developers had quit building them because of lack of demand. In 1986, residential energy demand had exceeded industrial demand for the first time ever. By the end of Reagan's term, funding for research and development of renewable energy sources had fallen to 18 percent of 1980 levels, and federal tax credits for the use of these alternate energy sources had expired.

What Now?

Today, the energy situation in the United States is similar in many ways to what it was at the time of the 1973 embargo. The United States is importing 46 percent of its daily petroleum consumption, an increase over the 38.8 percent that was imported in 1973. Domestic oil production is decreasing; in 1989, U.S. production was at its lowest level since 1963 and was not expected to increase significantly, if at all. Only about 1 percent of U.S. electrical power comes from renewable sources. Many states have increased the fifty-five-mile-per-hour speed limit, and our per capita energy consumption continues to increase.

There were some indications that the 1990s might see a renewed interest in a national energy policy. The 1990 invasion of Kuwait, which made Americans again aware of the danger of dependence on foreign oil, may have served as a partial stimulus. Nonetheless, in February 1991 Bush introduced his National Energy Strategy (NES), an attempt to achieve roughly equal measures of new energy production and conservation. Summaries of the various initiatives under the NES are given in table 9–1.

In April 1991, Bush issued an Executive Order on Federal Energy Management.[3] If fully implemented, the order is projected to save taxpayers up to $8 million in annual energy costs and cut federal energy consumption by the equivalent of up to 100,000 barrels of oil per day.[4] The three primary elements of the order are the following:

1. Energy use in federal building must be reduced to 25 percent below 1985 levels by 1995;
2. gasoline and diesel use in government fleets of 300 or more must be reduced to 10 percent below 1991 levels by 1995; and
3. all federal agencies must secure the largest practicable number of alternative-fuel vehicles by the end of 1995.[5]

With a new administration in 1993 and a growing awareness of some of the problems associated with fossil fuels, it is possible that the United States may attempt to develop a comprehensive energy plan that incorporates the often conflicting objectives of providing sufficient inexpensive energy to satisfy demands, lessening energy dependency on foreign nations, and not causing further environmental degradation.

In the next sections, we look at where this energy goes. Then we examine the types of energy we have to choose from, along with the problems of each and the temporary solutions at which we arrive. Though it may seem strange to examine each type of energy independently when we need a strategy combining all of them, you will see that as a nation we have indeed

TABLE 9–1 National Energy Strategy

In February 1991, President George Bush issued a National Energy Strategy (NES) to lay the foundation for a more efficient, less vulnerable, and environmentally sustainable energy future. In barrel-of-oil equivalents, NES initiatives will provide roughly equal measures of new energy supplies and increased conservation. With maximum reliance on markets as a keystone of the strategy, NES initiatives address five interlocking areas:

- *Energy security.* When fully implemented, NES will make the nation less prone to economic damage from sharp fluctuations in either the supply or the price of petroleum.
- *Energy and economic efficiency.* NES initiatives aim to lower energy costs to consumers, reduce energy-related emissions, maintain or enhance standards of living, and promote a strong economy.
- *Energy supplies.* To secure future energy supplies, NES will develop and use renewable energy sources; increase reliance on low-emission energy sources such as natural gas; develop a new generation of safer nuclear technology; and continue development of domestic coal and oil supplies in an environmentally responsible manner.
- *Environmental quality.* Initiatives will increase the efficiency of energy-producing and consuming technologies, reduce solid and hazardous wastes, and improve energy-related practices.
- *Technology and competitiveness.* NES initiatives fortify the nation's foundations in science and engineering research, technology development, and education; establish federal research and development priorities; strengthen research in universities, industries, and international collaboratives; accelerate technology transfer from federal laboratories to private industry; and enhance U.S. mathematics, science technology, and engineering education.

The strategy complements such developments as the 1990 Clean Air Act amendments, natural gas price decontrol in 1989, incentives provided to domestic energy producers in the fiscal 1991 budget agreement, international cooperation forged during the recent Persian Gulf crisis, and the secretary of energy's science and mathematics education initiatives.

Source: Council on Environmental Quality, *Twenty-Second Annual Report* (1992), p. 75.

chosen to treat each independently—and perhaps that is part of our inability to establish a coherent energy policy.

ENERGY CONSUMPTION

One of the reasons that lack of a coherent, long-term energy policy is problematic is that as a nation, we have extremely high energy demands, consuming about one-fourth of the world's energy production. Consumption of energy is consistent with our high standard of living, large land mass, low population density, and historically abundant, relatively low-cost energy resources. The great demand for energy can be understood a little better if we examine the four economic activities that place the greatest demands on our energy resources: residential, commercial, industrial, and transportation.

Because of the large number of single-family dwellings, the relative spaciousness of these dwellings, relatively small average family size, a desire for heating and cooling systems to maintain uniform indoor temperatures year-round, and a wide range of labor-saving devices, U.S. energy use per dwelling is among the highest in the world. More than half of that use is for heat and hot water; approximately 20 percent is used to run major appliances.

Commercial energy use is primarily for heating and cooling commercial buildings. More than one-third of the nation's energy demands comes from industry. Seventy percent of that demand can be traced to the nine most energy-intensive industries, including steel, paper, and chemicals. Finally, transportation of goods and people accounts for more than one-fourth of energy consumption. Most of this energy comes from the petroleum used to power automobiles, planes, trains, ships, and trucks.

COAL: THE OLDEST ENERGY SOURCE

Coal is this nation's most plentiful fossil fuel, constituting approximately 90 percent of U.S. hydrocarbon reserves. At one time providing more than 80 percent of our energy needs, today coal supplies about 25 percent. At present rates of consumption, we have sufficient reserves to last approximately 250 years. Coal is extremely important because it is used to generate more than half the nation's electrical power, and the percentage of electricity generated by coal seems to be increasing. Most of the coal reserves are located in three regions of the country: the seven-state Appalachian region, the midwestern plains, and the western plains and grasslands. Roughly half the coal reserves are in the west, and approximately 60 percent of those are on public lands. Most of the coal on these western reserves is low in sulfur content; most of the coal in the eastern reserves is privately owned and has a high sulfur content.

Because coal is so plentiful and its use would therefore reduce U.S. dependence on foreign oil, and because an increase in coal production could increase employment, every president since Nixon has, in some way, sought to increase our reliance on coal. Congress has also jumped on the bandwagon for greater use of coal.

Under the 1978 National Energy Act, five statutes were passed by Congress that were designed to increase dependence on coal. The most significant of these was the Powerplant and Industrial Fuel Use Act (PIFUA).[6] This act required certain electrical power generating plants and major fuel-burning installations to switch from oil or gas to coal. The DOE was authorized to require facilities, both individually and by category, to convert to coal or other alternate fuels when two conditions were met: (1) the conversion was financially feasible and (2) the facilities had the technical capability to be converted without substantial physical modifications or reductions in capacity. Individual plants in categories subject to conversion were to be granted permanent exemptions if the plant would have difficulty, because of its location, in getting access to alternate fuels. Also, conversion would not be required if it would cause a violation of any state or federal environmental regulations. The EPA was charged with making sure that no proposed conversions would result in NAAQS violations.

Problems with Coal

Given the plentiful nature of coal and its positive impact on employment, one may wonder why the United States does not more wholeheartedly endorse a policy that emphasizes the use of coal. The reason is that a number of environmental problems are associated with the use of coal, especially the high-sulfur coal of the eastern reserves. Recall the discussion of acid rain in chapter 6, and that one of the major factors in acid rain is sulfur dioxide emissions. Increased use of coal, especially high-sulfur coal, may increase acid deposition.

One of the biggest problems associated with the use of coal is that coal mining can have disastrous environmental effects, especially strip or surface mining. There are three basic types of surface mining: contour mining, area mining, and open pit mining.

Contour mining is the main type of mining used in Appalachia. The miner excavates a portion of the hillside where the coal seam intersects the surface. Then the soil that covers the seam is stripped off, following the seam along the contour as far into the mountain as possible. The excess dirt unearthed to reveal the coal is thrown downhill from where the coal is removed. In flat or rolling terrain, area mining is used. The earth is stripped off the coal and piled up to one side in a ridge along the area from which the coal has been removed. Open pit mining is similar to area mining except that the area from which the coal has been stripped is much deeper than the thickness of the land that was stripped off, so the stripped-off land, called the overburden, is not thick enough to replace the coal that was removed; consequently, a deep depression is left.

If unregulated, the results of strip mining are acres of barren, sterile land. Unregulated strip mining may cause soil erosion, pollution of streams from mining runoff, destruction of the land for agricultural purposes, destruction of ecosystems, and loss of habitat for numerous species. By some estimates, more than 1.5 million acres in more than thirty states have been disturbed by strip mining, and more than a million of these acres remain abandoned wasteland, no longer claimed by those who took the coal and no longer productive.[7] More than one thousand more acres are being ravaged each week by further mining.

Given these disastrous environmental consequences, why has strip mining remained such a viable activity? The answer lies to a large extent in the fact that surface mining is much cheaper, less labor intensive, more efficient, more profitable, and safer than underground mining.

Regulation of the Mining Industry

In an attempt to contain some of the disastrous consequences of strip mining, Congress passed the Surface Mining Control and Reclamation Act of 1977 (SMCRA). Vetoed twice by President Ford and strongly opposed by the mining industry, the act was finally signed into law by President Carter. The primary objective of the act, as indicated by its name, was to force the mining industry to return the land from which it stripped the coal to a level of productivity equal or superior to its condition before mining.

The act contains strong provisions that were pleasing to environmentalists; but the implementation of the act, from an environmentalist perspective, has been a disaster. Under the act, a number of environmental protection performance standards were established, regulating a broad range of activities including the removal, storage, and redistribution of topsoil; siting and erosion control; and drainage and protection of water. These standards were to be implemented in two stages: an interim and a permanent phase.

A new executive agency, the Office of Surface Mining Reclamation and Enforcement (OSM), was created within the Department of the Interior to enforce the act. To ensure that this agency was not captured by the mining industry, the OSM could, by statute, employ only individuals from other agencies who had no association with any authority, program, or function intended to promote the use or development of coal. The primary means of enforcing the SMCRA is through a permit system that can be administered by the states if they adopt programs for enforcing the act that are at least as stringent as the federal program.

Despite the fact that the SMCRA reads like a strong piece of environmental regulation, its effectiveness is highly questionable. The act has been fraught with problems from the beginning. Under the Carter administration, many strong regulations were drafted, a number of which were strongly opposed by the mining industry. One of the industry's most common arguments was that the OSM exceeded its authority to establish performance standards for mine sites when it set standards for both the types of controls to be used and the standard of performance to be met. It also argued that standards were too rigid and did not allow for enough local flexibility.

Industry's complaints were heeded shortly after the Reagan administration came to power. Under the auspices of Interior Department Secretary James Watt, approximately 90 percent of the regulations promulgated under the Carter administration were rewritten. The OSM also underwent massive downsizing, making serious enforcement of the law almost impossible. The OSM also suffered from instability at the top; in its first eight years it had six acting directors.

The OSM's record of enforcement, especially under the Reagan administration, has been abysmal and has subjected the agency to congressional investigations and litigation by environmental groups. In 1983 and 1984, congressional hearings revealed that state enforcement was inadequate in several states in light of evidence that mining activities were causing severe environmental deterioration. There was, obviously, a strong incentive for states not to strictly enforce the regulations. Compliance was costly, so mining companies in those states with loose enforcement would be at a competitive advantage.

In 1984, in response to a lawsuit brought by a number of environmental groups, the Department of the Interior agreed to establish a computerized system to monitor mine operators that violated the act and prevent them from obtaining permits in the future. The settlement also allowed plaintiffs to monitor the Interior Department's enforcement actions. This settlement took place at a time when there were about 1,700 cease and desist orders against violators that had never been enforced.[8] In 1985, a House Government Operations subcommittee cited the OSM for failing to collect more than $150 million in fines for violation of the SMCRA.[9] What is incredible about the OSM's inaction is that approximately $72 million of the fines were fully processed, undisputed, and unappealable.[10]

Clearly, the SMCRA is not the success for which its advocates had hoped. There is some evidence that the act has helped maintain environmentally safe conditions in some states, including Montana, Pennsylvania, and Wyoming,[11] but in states such as West Virginia and Kentucky minimal enforcement means minimal impact.[12] Some people, however, question whether the act's overall objective can actually be accomplished, even with the most vigorous enforcement program. Some scientists believe that the disruption of subsurface hydrology and the drainage of acids and salts that occurs during mining may cause irreparable damages.[13]

In light of all the controversy over the potential environmental destruction resulting from strip mining, it is no wonder that another problem with the use of coal is over the extent to which the federal government should lease exploration and mining rights to coal companies. Remember that more than half the coal reserves in the western states are on public lands.

Under the Mineral Leasing Act of 1920, the secretary of the interior may lease federal lands to private companies for oil, gas, and mineral exploration and production. Until the 1960s, very few leases were sought for energy production. There was a slight increase in interest in leases for coal production during the 1970s. During the Reagan administration's tenure, however, Secretary of the Interior James Watt announced his intention to increase lease sales from the Carter administration's 771 million tons of new coal to 2.2 billion tons. In 1982, Interior received almost $55 million in bids on almost 1.6 million acres of reserves, the largest coal lease sale in U.S. history. Congressional Democrats fiercely opposed the leases, as did the governors of many western coal states. Some congressional staff reports alleged that the leases were being offered for far less than fair market value.

Because of the controversy, Watt appointed a special panel to study federal coal leasing policies. The panel, called the Linowes Commission, after its chairman, concluded that the government had offered too many leases, many at less than fair market value. The commission recommended that Interior revise its schedule of leases to respond better to changes in the coal market. Shortly before the commission issued its report, Watt resigned. Since his resignation, other Interior secretaries have been less eager to lease federal coal reserves. Thus, for now, at least, leasing federal lands is not a major concern. An increase in demand for coal, however, could reignite the controversy.

PETROLEUM AND NATURAL GAS

Since 1955, petroleum and natural gas have been the primary sources of energy for the United States, supplying more than two-thirds of our energy needs. Petroleum has been a chief energy source primarily because of its low cost. Natural gas is a fossil fuel that, like petroleum, burns cleanly and efficiently, producing few pollutants. It constitutes about 30 percent of domestic energy production. Approximately one-fourth of this domestic production satisfies about 40 percent of residential energy needs. Reserves of natural gas in the United States, however, are not extensive. In the mid-1980s, known reserves of natural gas were sufficient to last for twenty to forty years at then-current rates of consumption. Petroleum and natural gas share common problems, primarily related to production and transportation.

Onshore Development Problems

Production and transportation of petroleum and natural gas necessitate large refineries and terminals, as well as miles of pipelines. Construction of these facilities often causes conflicts over land use. Many times the terminals and refineries are near coastal areas, which many people believe should be preserved as natural areas or used only for recreation. The environmental balance in these areas is delicate, and many fear disruption of this balance from the construction. There are those who are fearful of spills at these facilities. Even though such spills are not common, their environmental consequences can be devastating.

Offshore Development Problems

Even more controversies have been generated over offshore development, primarily in conjunction with the federal leasing of land in the outer continental shelf (OCS) for energy exploration. The federal government, primarily through the Department of the Interior, exercises authority over the approximately 1.1 billion acres of the continental shelf beginning three miles from the coastline and extending ten to twelve miles farther offshore. As custodian of this public land, the government leases some of it to private firms for exploration and production of oil. To ensure that states have some say in the development of submerged land off their shores, and to help ensure that multiple interests are taken into account when leasing decisions are made, Congress passed the Outer Continental Shelf Leasing Act (OCSLA).

As amended in 1978, OCSLA requires the secretary of the Interior to establish a five-year leasing program that includes as many details as possible about plans for leases during that period. Details include the time, location, and sizes of leases that the secretary believes are necessary to meet the nation's energy needs. In developing the leasing plan, the secretary is to take into account four basic principles. First, the OCS must be managed in a manner that reflects a balancing of economic, social, and environmental values. The impact of exploration on the marine, coastal, and human environment must be taken into account. Second, choice of locations for development must be based on an equitable sharing of developmental benefits and environmental risks among the various regions, with special attention given to the laws, goals, and policies of the affected states as communicated by their governors to the secretary. In selecting timing and location of leases, the secretary must balance the potential for environmental damage, the potential for the discovery of oil and gas, and the potential for adverse impact on the coastal zone. Finally, the federal government must receive fair market value for the land.

The steps for developing the leasing program are laid out by the act. When initially drafting the program, the secretary of the interior must "invite and consider suggestions" from governors of any states that might be affected by the leasing program. The proposed program finally drafted must then be submitted to the governors of the affected states for their comments. If any governor makes any suggestions that the secretary denies, the reasons for the denial must be provided, in writing, to the governor.

The next step is publication of the proposed program in the *Federal Register.* Any interested parties, including representatives of the affected states, have ninety days to submit written comments to the secretary. The secretary will then forward the proposed program, along with the comments, to Congress and the president. If any suggestions from a state were not incorporated, the secretary must include an explanation for rejecting the state's advice.

Sixty days after submitting the proposed program to the president and Congress, the secretary may finally approve the program. Anyone who participated in the administrative process that led to the adoption of the leasing program and who will be adversely affected by it then has sixty days to challenge the program in the Circuit Court of Appeals for the District of Columbia. When reviewing the actions of the secretary, the court must take the secretary's findings as conclusive if supported by substantial evidence on the record. After the process of judicial review has been completed, the secretary of the interior will then propose and conduct competitive bidding lease sales. Once land has been leased, leasees submit to the secretary their exploration plans, followed by development and production plans. Throughout these stages, the secretary must still operate in accordance with the four principles described previously.

OCSLA is not the only law designed to ensure a balanced development of coastal and subcoastal lands. The Coastal Zone Management Act (CZMA) aids in this process by providing financial assistance for states that develop and administer management programs that achieve a balance between energy development and environmental and coastal zone factors. NEPA also comes into play, because leasing is a major federal activity. Therefore, the secretary of the interior generally will have to prepare an EIS when proposing a lease sale. Many times, in fact, environmental groups will challenge an EIS as a way to at least delay proposed leases.

Oil Spills

One of the worst problems associated with oil and petroleum, or at least one that captures the public's attention, is oil spills. To try to reduce the harm from oil spills when tankers run aground, break up in heavy weather, or collide with other vessels, President Carter issued an executive order in 1976 requiring all tankers more than twenty thousand tons that sailed in American waters to be fitted with double hulls and bottoms by 1982. As of 1992, the order has not been fully implemented. Congress has been considering legislation to effectuate the same goal by 2005. Shipowners argue that the expense is too great considering the low likelihood of a wreck; and these costs, they add, would have to be passed on to the consumers.

Oil spills in conjunction with production of oil on the OCS are also a concern. The 1978 amendments to OCSLA impose strict liability for cleanup costs and damages resulting from OCS activities on owners and operators of offshore facilities and vessels carrying oil from such facilities. Liability is limited to $250,000 for a vessel and $35 million plus government removal costs for a facility. The act also created the Offshore Oil Spill Pollution Protection Fund, which pays for all losses that cannot be covered by the responsible parties. The fund receives its income from per barrel tax imposed on purchasers of OCS oil.

Additional liability was also imposed by the Clean Water Act. Section 311 held vessel operators strictly liable for cleanup costs incurred by the government unless the operator can prove that the cause of the spill was an act of God, act of war, act or omission of a third party, or negligence of the federal government. Government removal costs under this act include restoration or replacement of natural resources damaged or destroyed by the spill. Damages were limited, however, to $125,000 for inland barges, $250,000 for other vessels, and $50 million for onshore and offshore facilities. The limits would not apply if the accident were caused by "willful negligence or willful misconduct within the privity and knowledge of the owner."

Liability of responsible parties was broadened by the Oil Pollution Control Act of 1990. Under this law, each responsible party, defined as owners and operators of vessels, onshore facilities, or pipelines, is liable for removal costs, damage to natural resources, damages for injury to or economic losses from destruction of real or personal property, and lost profits caused by the injury or destruction of any real property, personal property, or natural resources. The measure of damages to natural resources was clearly spelled out under the act. It includes the cost of restoring, rehabilitating, rejecting, or acquiring the equivalent of the damaged resources; the diminution of value of those resources pending restoration; and the reasonable cost of assessing those damages.

Liability limits under the Oil Pollution Control Act were increased to $10 millon for ships weighing more than three thousand gross tons and $75 million for owners of offshore facilities. Limits are inapplicable if the spill is caused by gross negligence, willful misconduct, or a safety violation. A $1 billion oil spill trust fund is also established under the act.

NUCLEAR ENERGY

Nuclear energy once offered a dream of cheap, unlimited electrical power. In many people's opinion that dream has now been dimmed because numerous problems have developed during the almost forty years of attempts to harness nuclear power to satisfy energy needs. As originally conceived, uranium ore would be mined, processed, used in nuclear reactors, reprocessed, and used again in nuclear reactors—all in a continuous, closed cycle. The cycle did not work that way, however, leading to perhaps the most serious problem of nuclear energy: nuclear waste.

History of Nuclear Energy Development

Development of nuclear energy as a fuel really began in the mid-1950s. The federal government invested a great deal of money to subsidize early research and development. To encourage industry further in developing nuclear power, Congress even passed the Price-Anderson Act in 1957 to limit liability for any nuclear reactor accident. By 1975, the high point of nuclear energy, fifty-six commercial reactors had been built, sixty-nine were under construction, and there were plans for 111 more. By 1986, ninety-five nuclear reactors were licensed and operating. Then came the near-catastrophe of Three Mile Island, which alerted the public to the potential risks of nuclear accidents and also called attention to a lot of other problems in the nuclear industry.

By 1990, 112 commercial reactors were generating electricity in the United States, providing about 20 percent of the energy for peak summer consumption. Half these generators are scheduled to be closed down between 2005 and 2015; the remainder will be shut down by 2075. No new reactors have been ordered since 1979, so it is conceivable that nuclear energy will be only a memory by the year 2075. Still, another oil crisis might spur the redevelopment of this industry.

Problems with Nuclear Energy

A major problem with the nuclear industry is safety. Many of the materials and designs currently in use in reactors have failed safety tests; and many reactor parts have aged faster than projected. A 1988 survey by the GAO revealed that one-third of the plants it inspected had prematurely deteriorating pipes; the GAO consequently recommended inspection of pipes at all facilities. Horror stories about mismanagement and incompetence of managers and technicians in the industry abound. Those within the industry, however, point out that, in terms of accidents, the nuclear industry has a good safety record.

The nuclear industry has also been beset with economic problems. Costs were underestimated, and many of the facilities completed during the 1980s and early 1990s were 500 to 1,000 percent over budget. The licensing procedures caused costly delays in start-ups, with many plants taking four to eight years to obtain all the necessary permits.

The most troublesome problem with nuclear energy, perhaps, is nuclear waste. Four types of wastes are created, all of which present problems. First are the high-level radioactive liquids created during the reprocessing of reactor fuels. Stored along with the high-level wastes are transuranic wastes. These are by-products of reactor fuel and military waste processing. Some have a half-life of more than two hundred thousand years. A third category is spent nuclear fuel, which is currently being stored in cooling ponds at reactor sites. Many of these ponds are nearly full. This category of waste was never expected to be so large, because this spent fuel was supposed to have been recyclable. Unfortunately, the necessary technology for recycling did not develop. Finally, there are low-level radioactive wastes. This category includes such items as clothing, tools, and equipment that have become radioactive through exposure at reactors.

As the nuclear industry was developing, those in the industry assumed they would discover the technology to reprocess and then safely contain the waste. When the technology did not develop, the industry was, and still is, unprepared to handle all the hazardous wastes. A major problem is finding permanent sites to dispose of the waste.

Not only is waste disposal a problem, but the cost of decommissioning these plants now appears to be much higher than anticipated. The first nuclear plant to be taken apart began being decommissioned in 1993. That relatively small plant, located at Fort St. Vrain, in Colorado, cost $224 million to build in the 1970s; it is now being taken apart at a cost of $333 million. To make matters still worse, many plants are wearing out far earlier than their projected forty-year life span, after having never consistently produced the low-cost energy they were designed to produce. Closed plants now operate an average of 12.7 years.

Currently, at least fourteen nuclear plants have closed and are being mothballed until a lower cost method of dismantling them can be developed. The NRC will allow plants to sit idle for up to sixty years before the owners must dismantle them. However, maintaining, inspecting, and securing a closed nuclear facility can cost up to $15 million a year.

Regulation of the Nuclear Industry

The Atomic Energy Act of 1954 is the primary legislation that gives the federal government the authority to protect human health and the environment from excessive exposure to radiation. The agency responsible for regulating the nuclear industry is the Nuclear Regulatory Commission. Created in 1978 to replace the old Atomic Energy Commission, the NRC issues licenses for the construction and operation of nuclear facilities, as well as for the possession, use, handling, and disposal of nuclear wastes. The NRC has generally been staffed by people who believe in nuclear energy and is cited by some as an example of a captured agency.

In 1980, Congress passed Public Law 96–295. The law provided funding to train additional federal inspectors who would be stationed at nuclear power plants. The law also required the agency to draw up a plan for agency responses to nuclear accidents, as well as to issue new regulations to improve safety at reactors.

The Nuclear Waste Policy Act of 1982 was passed to resolve the problem of siting and developing permanent repositories for high-level nuclear waste. By 1985, the DOE was to nominate five sites. After extensive public hearings, the president was to make a recommendation to Congress. If the site were approved by the selected state or Congress, the DOE was to apply to the NRC for a repository license. Until the permanent facility was established, an interim storage program was to be maintained.

After spending two years and $500 million on preliminary work, the DOE announced that it was abandoning its initial repository plan. The DOE projected it would be at least the year 2010 before it would have a repository ready to accept high-level waste.

RENEWABLE FUELS

Because the so-called traditional fuels present a number of environmental problems—and they are bound to be depleted someday—many argue that the government needs to encourage more research into renewable fuels, sources of energy that are continuously renewed. Those renewables most heavily used today include hydropower, solar power, wind, and the burning of waste for steam. Briefly, these sources offer the benefits of generally being less polluting and being available domestically, so they reduce dependence on foreign oil.

Hydropower

The most popular renewable fuel is hydropower, that is, the power to generate electricity from running water. In 1990, hydropower from dams generated about 10 percent of the electricity used in the United States. Increasingly, however, environmental groups have been raising concerns about the environmental effects of dams.

Dams are licensed by the Federal Energy Regulatory Commission (FERC). The 1986 Electric Consumers Act requires the FERC to give environmental and recreational factors equal weight with power generation when granting and reviewing licenses.

Solar Energy

The sun can provide energy in different ways. Solar energy can be used at one centralized location to create electricity, or it can be used in individual residences or commercial buildings to directly satisfy energy needs. Because solar energy requires sunshine, it is obviously not a source that could satisfy anyone's energy needs completely. And places where there is sufficient sunlight year-round to justify construction of a solar energy plant are extremely limited.

Solar energy systems used at individual sites are generally referred to as passive or active. Passive solar energy is really a matter of designing a structure so that it will become a solar collector. For example, you would have big south-facing energy-efficient windows that would capture the heat of the sunlight. Active systems are ones that use moving parts to generate energy for heating, producing hot water, and sometimes even powering air-conditioning. Active systems generally use some sort of collector to absorb the sunlight and transfer its heat to some other medium for distribution or storage.

The legal system can encourage or discourage the use of solar energy, primarily through the funding of research into solar energy and through the tax system—directly by providing tax breaks for installing solar technologies or indirectly by increasing taxes on the use of fossil fuels.

Wind Energy

Another form of renewable energy, which, again, can be used in only appropriate climates, is energy from the wind. Again, because federal support for this nontraditional technology is not strong, its development is unlikely.

Biomass Energy

Biomass conversion simply means burning organic matter such as agricultural waste, municipal garbage, grains, animal manure, and wood to generate energy. Burning of wood creates pollution problems, but other biofuels are much cleaner than fossil fuels. As air pollution standards become more stringent, use of these alternate fuels becomes more desirable.

Geothermal Energy

Geothermal energy refers to the use of heat that is trapped within the Earth. Technically, it is not a renewable fuel but is often thought of as one because it is such a vast source. The most common form of geothermal energy is hydrothermal energy. Naturally occurring hot water reservoirs are tapped for their energy.

PROTECTING PUBLIC LANDS

As the preceding sections have revealed, use of one of our major energy resources—fossil fuels—often comes into conflict with alternate uses of one of our most important natural resources, the land. This section focuses on a particular segment of land resources—public lands. When examining the laws developed to regulate our public lands, it is important to remember that, historically, the purpose of these laws was to preserve the land for sustained exploitation.

More than a half billion acres of public lands are managed by federal agencies. Many conflicts arise over the appropriate use of these lands. Some argue that we should take a purely economic view of the use of public lands. If the Sierra Club is willing to pay more for Yellowstone National Park, then it should have it to preserve for nature lovers' enjoyment. But if the strip mining companies will pay more, then perhaps the best disposition of the land is to sell it to the strip mining companies.

Of course, many people will say that we cannot take a purely economic viewpoint with respect to use of public lands. Those who advocate consideration of other values tend to fall into two categories: conservationists and preservationists. Conservationists tend to focus on conserving resources, using them in a sustainable way, so that they will be available for future generations. Plant and animal species should not be reduced to the extent that they can no longer serve human needs. Conservationists have an instrumental view of nature; its purpose is to serve humans. Preservationists, on the other hand, want to preserve wilderness areas just as they are for their inherent value. They see nature as having value beyond its usefulness to humans. Both preservationists and conservationists tend to be especially concerned about protecting certain types of land, namely, forests and wilderness.

Forests

Forests are complex ecosystems, made up of interdependent communities of plants, animals, and microbes. They are vital because they provide recreational opportunities, watersheds, wildlife habitats, wilderness, timber, and minerals. Forests also provide food and raw materials for pharmaceuticals.

There are numerous types of forest, from the scrub forests of the arid interior West to the lush forests on the coasts. A major concern today is the declining amount of forests in the United States. Obviously, when the nation was young, forests were cleared with abandon. But even during the 1970s and 1980s many acres of forestland were lost. Many were cleared for agricultural use as a result of a rapid growth of agricultural exports during that period. Despite consequent recognition of the need to protect these areas, their acreage loss has been slowed, but not halted. The EPA in 1990 estimated a further decline of 4 percent by 2040. This figure represents an annual decline of half a million acres per year, an improvement over the decline of 1.5 million acres per year from 1970 through 1987.

Of particular concern is the loss of a special type of forest, old-growth forests. Old-growth forests contain trees that are hundreds, and even thousands, of years old. Some of the fir trees are up to 300 feet tall. These old-growth forests are considered valuable by conservationists because they contain a much greater diversity of plant and animal species than do younger, so-called secondary forests. In 1990, only about 15 percent of the old-growth forests that once covered the United States remained, and some conservation groups fear that at current rates of cutting, most of the old-growth forests of the United States will be gone within fifteen to twenty years.

One of the causes of the rapid depletion of forestland is a process known as *clear-cutting*. Clear-cutting occurs when a logging firm moves into a twenty-five- to fifty-acre area and cuts down every tree in that area. Clear-cutting is favored by the timber industry over the alternative, selective cutting of individual trees in a forest, for several reasons. With selective cutting, the company must search through the forest to identify small groups of single intermediate or mature trees to be cut. This method, which preserves a "whole" forest with multiple-aged trees, is extremely expensive and time-consuming. Clear-cutting is cheaper and requires less skill. Fewer roads must be built into the area, and replanting is relatively easy. Also, the company knows that in a given number of years it can come back and reharvest a huge acreage of relatively similar size trees. Clear-cutting does not require a great amount of planning.

When clear-cutting was initially proposed, some thought that it would be ecologically superior. After all, it left some areas of forest completely undisturbed. Soon, however, problems began to materialize. First, removal of big swatches of trees affects the ecological balance in the adjacent areas. If the clearing is done on sloped land, there can be extreme erosion problems: flooding from melting snow and heavy rains, and landslides. Today, an estimated two-thirds of the annual timber harvest is done by clear-cutting. At present, there are no viable measures available to limit this ecologically devastating process.

Rangelands

Much of public land is rangeland. The Bureau of Land Management oversees more than 170 million acres of range. The Forest Service also manages 104 million acres, about half of which is timbered. The primary issue with respect to rangeland is the extent to which such land should be leased to farmers for grazing. While the government takes in a substantial amount of revenue from grazing fees, more than $18 million in 1991, there is a question about the extent to which grazing should be viewed as the dominant use of these lands, especially when the land is to be managed under a multiple-use concept (described in the next section).

Regulation of Public Lands

No comprehensive statutory scheme for regulation of public lands exists, and management of these lands is fragmented among a number of agencies housed under different departments. The primary agencies responsible for land management are the Bureau of Land Management, Forest Service, Fish and Wildlife Service, and National Park Services. Also, the Department of Defense is responsible for managing 6 million acres of forestland.

The management activities of these agencies are directed by diverse statutes. To discuss all of them would take an entire book, so our discussion will be limited to the most influential laws affecting the management of public lands, starting with the earliest laws, so that you can follow the historical development of public lands policies.

Initially, the attitude of the federal government toward public lands was "sell and develop." Early homestead acts conveyed large tracts of public lands to farmers and ranchers who were willing to develop those lands. The Mining Law of 1872 provided that anyone who discovered a valuable mineral deposit (excluding oil, gas, coal, and oil shale) on public land could obtain a mining claim on that land; further provisions of the act allowed the miner also to obtain title to the land on which the claim was located, hence encouraging mining of formerly public lands.

In 1891, the president was first authorized to set aside land for national forests.[14] An 1897 statute declared the purposes for establishing such forests were to be water control and "a continuous supply of timber."[15] In 1920, the exploitation of land for the extraction of oil and gas was encouraged by the Mineral Leasing Act of 1920, described earlier in this chapter.

In more recent years, land use regulation took on a less singularly developmental tone. In 1960, Congress passed the Multiple-Use Sustained Yield Act. This act provides that national forests should be managed to fulfill a multiplicity of purposes: outdoor recreation, timber, and provision of wildlife habitats. No particular weight is given to any of these uses by the act.

In 1964, Congress passed what many preservationists consider one of the most significant pieces of legislation for the protection of land—the Wilderness Act, the law that created the National Wilderness Preservation System. The act defines a wilderness as having four characteristics. First, there has been no noticeable human impact on the land. Second, the area offers opportunities for solitude or primitive recreation. Third, the area consists of at least five thousand acres or a sufficient size to make preservation possible. Finally, although this characteristic is not mandatory, the area has ecological, geological, or other value. The act itself specifies certain areas to be designated wilderness and other forests to be reviewed for consideration as wilderness in the future. Under this law, once land is designated wilderness, its use is sharply restricted. The agency administering the land must preserve the "wilderness character" of the area and make sure that the area is devoted to "the public purposes of recreational, scenic, scientific, education, conservation, and historical use." Unless specifically provided for by statute, no commercial enterprises or permanent roads may be constructed in any wilderness area. An exception in the act, however, provided for the continuation of mining in wilderness areas until 1983. By 1990, 94 million acres had been designated wilderness under the National Wilderness Preservation System.

In 1976, greater protection for public lands was encouraged by the Federal Land Policy and Management Act. This act requires the secretary of the interior, when managing the public lands, to take any action necessary to "prevent unnecessary or undue degradation of the lands."[16] This act also requires the Bureau of Land Management to prepare land management plans for the 450 million acres of land it administers.[17] Similar management plans for national forests were required of the secretary of agriculture in legislation passed by Congress in 1974 and 1978.[18]

WETLANDS, ESTUARIES, AND COASTAL AREAS

Although the need to regulate public lands has been recognized, to some extent, since the late 1800s, preservation of wetlands, estuaries, and coastal areas is of more recent vintage. A wetlands is an area of land covered with water all or part of the year. When covered with saltwater, these areas are known as coastal wetlands; when covered with fresh water, they are inland wetlands. The wet tundra that covers 58 percent of Alaska is also a wetlands. Figure 9–1 depicts the typical features of a wetlands.

An estuary is a coastal area where the fresh water of rivers and streams mixes with seawater.

Coastal wetland make up about 30 percent of the wetlands and 16 percent of the coastline. Figure 9–2 shows the types of coastal wetlands, the regions where they are located, and the states with the greatest coastal wetlands acreage. Despite the fact that they are viewed by many as useless

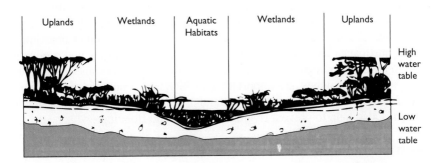

FIGURE 9–1 Identifying Features of Wetlands

Source: Council on Environmental Quality, *Environmental Trends* (Washington, D.C., 1989), p. 97.

Habitat

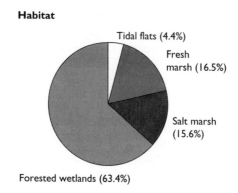

Tidal flats (4.4%)

Fresh marsh (16.5%)

Salt marsh (15.6%)

Forested wetlands (63.4%)

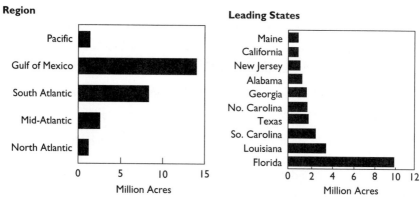

Region

Pacific
Gulf of Mexico
South Atlantic
Mid-Atlantic
North Atlantic

0   5   10   15
Million Acres

Leading States

Maine
California
New Jersey
Alabama
Georgia
No. Carolina
Texas
So. Carolina
Louisiana
Florida

0   2   4   6   8   10   12
Million Acres

FIGURE 9–2   Coastal Wetlands by Habitat, Region, and Leading States

Source: Council on Environmental Quality, *Twenty-Second Annual Report* (1992), p. 36.

homes for mosquitoes, coastal wetlands are highly productive ecosystems. They provide a habitat for numerous plant and animal species, including a number of endangered species. Roughly 70 percent of the nation's commercial seafood is spawned in coastal wetlands. Coastal wetlands also dilute water pollutants, thereby helping to improve the quality of the adjacent water.

Both coastal wetlands and estuaries help prevent erosion of coastlines. When hurricanes and tropical storms hit coastlines, estuaries and wetlands help to absorb the impact of the waves. Inland wetlands, commonly referred to as bogs and marshes, are important as habitats for a number of fish (most inland sport fish spawn in inland wetlands), waterfowl, and wildlife. Inland wetlands also help to prevent riverbank erosion and flooding.

Destruction of Wetlands

Wetlands were once plentiful in the United States, but since the eighteenth century, more than half of them have been lost, with some states losing up to 80 percent of their wetlands. From the mid-1950s to the mid-1970s, wetlands in the lower forty-eight states were lost at a rate of approximately 458,000 acres per year. During the next decade, this loss fell to approximately 290,000 acres per year.[19] Alaska's wetlands losses have not been as severe, with only about 1 percent being lost. However, in coastal areas around major cities, losses have been about 50 percent.[20]

Coastal wetlands and estuaries are being lost in part because of development exacerbated by increasing coastal populations. Almost half the country's population in 1990 lived in coastal counties, which make up only 11 percent of the nation's total land. By the year 2010, this coastal population of 110 million is projected to grow to 127 million. Not only are wetlands being filled for development, but runoff, including sewer overflows, are polluting these fragile areas. The heavier the population, the more severe the pollution problem becomes.

Loss of inland wetlands can be primarily attributable to filling in the wetlands for agricultural use. Additional losses are due to a desire to develop wetlands for industrial or residential use.

Regulations to Preserve Coastal Areas and Wetlands

A number of regulations and federal programs have been implemented to preserve wetlands and coastal areas. Preservation of wetlands is in some ways more difficult than protecting wilderness and forest areas because many of the wetlands are on private property. The main regulatory tool for preserving wetlands is Section 404 of the Clean Water Act. This provision requires that any landowner seeking to add dredged or filled material to a wetland receive a permit from the Army Corps of Engineers or risk being subject to both civil and criminal penalties. To obtain such a permit, the landowner must demonstrate that the activity satisfies the environmental criteria established by the EPA and that the activity is in the public interest. In many states the landowner must also comply with state regulations governing wetlands.

Marine Protection, Research, and Sanctuaries Act. The 1972 Marine Protection, Research, and Sanctuaries Act allows the National Oceanic and Atmospheric Administration to designate specific areas as marine sanctuaries. Such sanctuaries are the marine equivalent to national parks, and they are to have protective management of their recreational, ecological, historical, educational, and aesthetic values. Figure 9–3 shows where existing and proposed marine sanctuaries were located as of 1991 and provides a description of some of them.

Coastal Zone Management Act (CZMA). In 1972, to encourage the prudent management and conservation of the coastal zone, defined as state land near the shorelines of the coastal states and the coastal waters, extending to the outer limits of the U.S. territorial sea, Congress passed the Coastal Zone Management Act. The act, like NEPA, is a planning statute. Under CZMA,

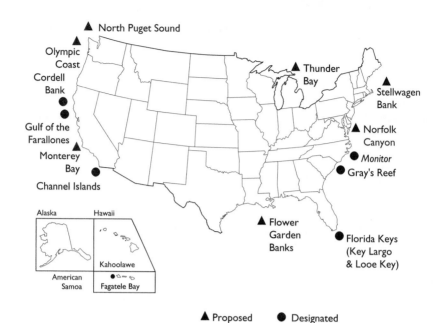

North Puget Sound ▲

Olympic Coast ▲

Cordell Bank ●

Gulf of the Farallones ●

Monterey Bay ▲

Channel Islands ●

Thunder Bay ▲

Stellwagen Bank ▲

Norfolk Canyon ▲

Monitor ●

Gray's Reef ●

Flower Garden Banks ▲

Florida Keys (Key Largo & Looe Key) ●

Alaska

Hawaii

Kahoolawe

American Samoa

Fagatele Bay

▲ Proposed   ● Designated

Marine Sanctuary	Location	Description
1. Channel Islands	Santa Barbara, CA	1,253 square nautical miles of offshore, nearshore, and internal habitats.
2. Cordell Bank	San Francisco, CA	397 square miles of ocean waters surrounding a submerged mountaintop.
3. Fagatele Bay	Tutuila Island, American Samoa	25 square miles of terraced coral reef ecosystem typical of Pacific islands.
4. Gray's Reef	Sapelo Island, GA	17 square miles of submerged live-bottom coral reef.
5. Gulf of the Farallones	Along the northwest California coast	948 square nautical miles of diverse habitat for marine mammals and seabirds.
6. Key Largo	Upper Florida Keys	100 square miles of coral reef.
7. Looe Key	Lower Florida Keys	5.32 square miles of the Florida reef tract.
8. *Monitor*	Cape Hatteras, NC	A circular area, 1 nautical mile in diameter, over the wreck of the *U.S.S. Monitor.*
9. Florida Keys	Upon final designation, it will incorporate Key Largo, Looe Key, and other coral reef areas off Florida.	2,600 square nautical miles designated by Congress and the president in 1990; an environmental impact statement is being prepared.

FIGURE 9–3 National Marine Sanctuaries System

Source: Adapted from Council on Environmental Quality, *Twenty-Second Annual Report* (1992), pp. 39, 40.

the federal government will provide matching funds to a coastal state, including Great Lakes states, to assist the state in developing a management plan for its coastal lands and waters. CZMA specifies nine elements that must be included in the plan. Some of the more substantive elements include

- A definition of what will constitute permissible land uses within the coastal zone that will have direct and significant impact on coastal waters
- Broad guidelines on the priorities of uses in particular areas
- A description of the organizational structure to implement the proposed management plan
- A definition of *beach* and a planning process for protection of and access to public beaches and other public coastal areas of environmental, recreational, historical, aesthetic, ecological, or cultural value
- A planning process for studying and controlling erosion

The plan must give full consideration to ecological, cultural, historical, and aesthetic values, as well as to needs for economic development. The National Oceanographic and Atmospheric Administration reviews the plans submitted by the states. If the plan is approved, the state will receive additional funds to administer the plan. Approval of a state plan also means that any federal activity within the state's coastal zone must be consistent with that state's management plan, "to the maximum extent possible." As an incentive to the state to adhere to its plan, funding can be withdrawn if the state fails to do so.

In 1990, CZMA was amended to require each state to develop a nonpoint source pollution-control program. Recall that one of the major problems along the coasts is nonpoint source pollution.

Swampbuster Provisions of the 1985 Food Security Act. Many people argue that one of the most effective measures for protecting wetlands, particularly inland wetlands, has been what is commonly referred to as the *Swampbuster bill.* This provision was an attempt by Congress to slow the conversion of wetlands to agricultural land. It provides that any persons who produce crops on wetlands that were converted after December 23, 1985, will be ineligible for most federal farm benefits.

"No-Net-Loss" Policy. In August 1989, President Bush announced a no-net-loss of wetlands policy. Much of the policy involved improving funding with respect to existing nonregulatory wetlands programs, such as the North American Waterfowl Management Plan, which was designed to help restore declining waterfowl population by the acquisition and restoration of wetlands that provided breeding grounds and resting areas for these waterfowl.

Bush's policy of no-net-loss of wetlands was mitigated by the fact that no-net-loss really meant except when the loss was "unavoidable." If the loss were unavoidable, the developer had the option of creating roughly the same amount of wetlands elsewhere. This option completely overlooks the significance of a loss in a particular area. Also, if the loss were "insignificant," a clearly vague term, then no replacement was necessary. Finally, in a move many believed was clearly directed toward Alaska, replacement was unnecessary if it would be impracticable to create more.

ENDANGERED SPECIES

In 1973, Congress recognized that the wide variety of plants and animals constitute an important natural resource, and they passed what has since become one of the most controversial, and some say most effective, pieces of environmental legislation ever enacted: the Endangered Species Act (ESA). In setting forth its findings to justify the ESA, Congress declared that

1. various species of fish, wildlife, and plants in the United States have been rendered extinct as a consequence of economic growth and development untempered by adequate concern and conservation;

2. other species of fish, wildlife, and plants have become so depleted in numbers that they are in danger of or threatened with extinction;

3. these species of fish, wildlife, and plants are of aesthetic, ecological, educational, historical, recreational, and scientific value to the Nation and its people.[21]

Congress went on to state that the purpose of the ESA was to provide a means to preserve the ecosystems in which endangered species survive, to provide a program to conserve such species, and to enter into appropriate treaties for species protection on an international level. Thus, the ESA has both a national and an international focus. This chapter discusses the national aspect; chapter 10 addresses the international aspect.

Under the ESA, the secretary of the interior is required to list species of animals and plants that are both threatened and endangered, a task that he has delegated to the Fish and Wildlife Service (FWS) and the National Marine Fisheries Service (NMFS). A species can become threatened or endangered because of a number of factors: "present or threatened destruction, modification or curtailment of its habitat or range; overutilization for commercial recreation, scientific, or educational purposes; disease or predation; the inadequacy of existing statutory mechanisms; or other natural or manmade factors affecting its continued existence."[22] As of January 1996, 956 species of plants and animals in the United States were listed as threatened or endangered. Once a species is listed as endangered, it cannot be "taken"; that is, it cannot be harassed, harmed, pursued, hunted, shot, wounded, killed, trapped, captured, or collected. Violation of the prohibition against taking can result in criminal sanctions.

A major issue under the ESA until the summer of 1995 was the definition of harm. The secretary of the interior interpreted harm in the definition of a taking under the act to mean "an act which actually kills or injures wildlife. Such act may include significant habitat modification or degradation where it actually kills or injures wildlife by significantly impairing essential behavior patterns, including breeding, feeding or sheltering."[23] This broad interpretation of harm was challenged by a plaintiff that included citizens' groups, lumber companies, and lumber trade associations. The plaintiff argued that the secretary had exceeded his authority by issuing that definition of harm because the ESA had excluded habitat modification from the specific list of prohibited actions that constituted takings of species.[24] In July of 1993, environmentalists received a temporary victory when the Court of Appeals upheld the secretary's broad interpretation. However, in an unusual move, the Circuit Court subsequently agreed to rehear the appeal, and this time ruled that the secretary's interpretation was in fact not a reasonable interpretation of the statute.[25]

In the summer of 1995, however, the U.S. Supreme Court, in a six to three decision, overturned the Court of Appeals decision and ruled that the secretary's interpretation was in fact reasonable. Thus the broad interpretation of harm stands, and a private property owner may not develop or use his or her land in a way that modifies the habitat of an endangered or threatened species to such an extent that species may die because the habitat modification or degredation will impair essential behavior patterns.

While this Supreme Court decision was a significant victory for environmentalists, it was considered a major setback by property rights advocates. Some believe the decision may have helped motivate more property rights advocates to put pressure on Congress to pass legislation to reduce the power of the ESA.

The ESA was supposed to have been reauthorized in 1993, but a lack of consensus as to whether it needed to be strengthened, weakened, or significantly modified led Congress to simply fund the act for another year with the hope of making necessary modifications in the act in 1994. That year saw much debate over a broad range of bills, yet ended once again in simply refunding the act for another year. A third year of unresolved debate over the future of the ESA occurred in 1995. While there seemed to be growing support for reauthorization bills that reduced the protections provided by the ESA, especially after the Republicans became the majority party in Congress in 1994, by the start of 1996 no bill had yet been able to garner sufficient support for passage.

While much of the focus of the debate over the ESA reauthorization is on the impact of the act on private property owners who might own land on which an endangered species resides, perhaps an equally important aspect of the ESA is Section 7, which requires all federal agencies to take actions necessary to ensure that activities authorized, funded, or carried out by them do not jeopardize the continued existence of endangered or threatened species. This section of the act has become a powerful tool to protect the habitat of endangered species, which many environmentalists believe is the key to protecting the species. So powerful is this section that many accuse environmentalists of using, or abusing, it to prohibit developments they primarily oppose for other environmental reasons.

Because many habitats are on public lands, this law also helps regulate the use of public lands and protect old-growth forests and wilderness areas. Most Americans probably became aware of the controversy over protection of old-growth forests as well as endangered species as a result of the application of the ESA in a highly publicized case involving the northern spotted owl.

The controversy began during the late 1980s, when the Forest Service, charged with perpetuating vertebrae species native to the national forests, discovered through its research that the population of the northern spotted owl was shrinking because of the destruction of its forest habitat by logging. The Forest Service recognized that if the spotted owl were placed on the endangered species list, a virtual cessation of logging in the Northwest could be mandated. So the agency proposed setting aside 550 spotted owl habitats in Oregon and Washington, along with two hundred areas in northwestern California. Each habitat area consisted of approximately 2,200 acres of old-growth forest. The plan was criticized immediately by environmentalists, who claimed that this was insufficient habitat area.

After discussing in its findings of fact the importance of logging and the record of violations by the Fish and Wildlife Service, the court acknowledged the likelihood of irreparable harm from continued logging: the extinction of a species. The court then discussed the balancing of equities necessary in an environmental case and issued an injunction ordering the Forest Service to come up with a plan to preserve the species by March 5, 1992, and to prohibit the selling of further logging rights in spotted owl habitats until they were in compliance with the law.

That same year, the issue became more than "owls v. jobs." Environmental groups sought to have the Pacific Yew, the bark of which provides an extract that can be used in a potent drug to fight cancer, listed as an endangered species. The tree, one of the slowest-growing species in the world, is found exclusively in old-growth forests. In June 1990, after considerable controversy, and under court order, the Fish and Wildlife Service listed the northern spotted owl as a threatened species under the Endangered Species Act. This precipitated a massive publicity campaign by the timber industry, forecasting the loss of thousands of jobs.

On February 26, 1991, the federal district court once again ruled that the FWS had violated the law. This time, it had violated the ESA by failing to designate critical habitat with the listing of the spotted owl, and it had failed to comply with the deadline of September 30, 1990, for adopting a plan for ensuring the owl's survival. The Audobon Society then filed an action seeking a permanent injunction against any further sales of logging rights in northern spotted owl habitat until the Forest Service adopted guidelines and regulations to ensure that a viable population of the species is maintained in the forest.

Subsequently, an interagency team of federal, state, and university representatives met to develop a plan for the recovery of the species. In January 1992, the Fish and Wildlife Service adopted regulations designating 6.9 million acres in Oregon, Washington, and California critical habitat for the owls. Thus, a tentative resolution was reached. Loggers were allowed to exercise the logging rights they had previously obtained, but future logging right sales, at least in a limited area, were temporarily halted.

The controversy continued into 1993, when President Clinton called a special summit for affected interests to try to discuss the ongoing controversy. Whether any real changes will result from this attempt to get the parties talking to one another remains to be seen.

The controversy will never really end, however, because the timber industry may always return to argue that logging in this or that area will not adversely affect the owl's habitat.

Perhaps a compromise reauthorization bill will be reached at some point. In May 1995, the National Research Council of the National Academy of Sciences released a report on the ESA that had been requested by members of both congressional parties four years previously. The report concluded that the ESA is "critically important" and "based on sound scientific principles," but changes are needed in the way biological populations and habitats are designated. The most dramatic change recommended in the report is to permit federal officials to designate a "survival habitat" for species immediately upon their designation as threatened or endangered. This designation would prevent further losses. The report also stated that "habitat protection is essential not only to protect those relatively few species whose endangerment is established, it is also in essence a preemptive approach to species conservation that also in essence can help to avoid triggering the provisions of the ESA." The report also encouraged the protection of distinct populations.

Another document that may have an impact on Congress as they deliberate in 1996 over the proposals for reauthorization is the House Republican Policy Committee's principles for reauthorization, which they adopted in August 1995. These principles include:

- using accurate, "non-politicized" science in the listing process and implementation process;
- including social and economic considerations in the conservation plan process;
- using incentives to encourage private property owners to enhance habitat and protect species;
- compensating property owners "when practical use of their land has been taken from them"; and
- enhancing the state and local role in endangered species protection.

Of course, these principles are by no means shared by all members of the House of Representatives, but the setting forth of these principles may provide a focus for debate over the reauthorization of this controversial piece of legislation.

CONCLUDING REMARKS

Energy policy and resource protection, while not often thought of as part of traditional environmental law, are important to environmental conditions. We need energy, and though some say that the United States uses more than its share, our consumptive behaviors are not likely to change soon. Therefore, the best the law can do is to try to regulate use of energy in ways that allow us to extend the life of current resources and not create environmental damage through the extraction and use of those resources.

Other natural resources besides energy also need protection. Therefore, legislation attempts to protect the forests, ranges, wetlands, and estuaries. We have even come to recognize species of plants and animals as natural resources and are according them protection under the Endangered Species Act. When we think about issues of resource protection, however, it really makes no sense to think in terms of national resources alone. Resource protection is really a global issue, as you will realize when reading chapter 10.

QUESTIONS FOR REVIEW AND DISCUSSION

1. Explain why we have come to rely heavily on coal as an energy source at so many times in our history.
2. Explain the main problems associated with coal as a fuel and how we try to solve those problems.
3. Explain the primary problems associated with petroleum as a fuel and how we try to solve those problems.
4. Explain the primary problems associated with nuclear energy as a fuel and how we try to solve those problems.
5. What is an old-growth forest, and why are such forests important?
6. What are wetlands, and why are they important?
7. Explain the purpose of the Coastal Zone Management Act.
8. Explain the similarities and differences between Section 7 of the ESA and the EIS requirement of NEPA.

FOR FURTHER READING

ROBERT BURCHELL, & DAVID LISTOKIN, ENERGY AND LAND USE (New York: Transaction Publishers, 1981).

JOHN BYRNE, & DANIEL RICH, eds. ENERGY AND GLOBAL ENVIRONMENTAL CHANGE (New York: Transaction Publishers, 1992).

CHARLES HALL, ET AL., ENERGY AND RESOURCE QUALITY: THE ECOLOGY OF THE ECONOMIC PROCESS (Boulder: University of Colorado Press, 1992).

BARBARA KEELER, ENERGY ALTERNATIVES (San Diego: Lucent Books, 1990).

CHRISTOPHER MANE, GREEN RAGE (Boston: Little, Brown & Co., 1991).

MOHAN MUNASINGNE, ENERGY ANALYSIS AND POLICY (Stoneham, Mass.: Butterworth-Heinemann, 1990).

GARY MEYERS, *Of Woodchips, Wildlife, and Wetlands: A New Ecological Ethic for a Planet in Crisis,* 12 ENVTL. PLANNING L.J. 211 (1995).

RODERICK NASH, WILDERNESS AND THE AMERICAN MIND (New Haven: Yale University Press, 1967).

WILLIAM J. SUTHERLAND, & DAVID A. HILL, MANAGING HABITATS FOR CONSERVATION (New York: Cambridge University Press, 1996).

RAY VAUGHN, *State of Extinction: The Case of the Alabama Sturgeon and Ways Opponents of the Endangered Species Act Thwart Protection for Rare Species,* 46 ALA. L. REV. 569 (1995).

ON THE INTERNET

http://www.mit.edu/afs/athena.mit.edu/c/ceepr/www/ceepr.htm
Home page of the Center for Energy and Environmental Policy Research at MIT

http://www.emanifesto.org/
Tools for Resource Policy in the Public Interest page

http://www.newsdata.com/
Indexes information on electrical and natural gas energy production

http://www.sierraclub.org/policy/
Sierra Club conservation policies

http://www.econet.apc.org/endangered
Information about legislation and other actions on behalf of endangered species

http:/www.tribnet.com/environ/env_biod.htm
Contains a current list of endangered species and information about biodiversity

http://hisurf.com/~/lena/Research.html
Information about endangered species in Hawaii

http://econet.apc.org/endangered/kempworth.html
Analysis of Kempworth Endangered Species Conservation Act of 1995

http://www.sdsc.edu/1/SDSC/Research/Comp_Bio/ESA/ESA.html
The home page of the ESA, from which you can read the ESA Newsletter and weekly environmental policy updates

NOTES

1. U.S. Department of Commerce, Bureau of the Census, Statistical Abstract of the United States (1989), p. 563.
2. WALTER A. ROSENBAUM, ENERGY, POLITICS, AND PUBLIC POLICY (Washington, D.C.: Congressional Quarterly Press, 1987), p. 6.
3. Council on Environmental Quality, Environmental Quality: The Twenty-Second Annual Report (1991), p. 80.
4. Ibid.
5. Ibid.
6. 42 USCA §§ 8301–8433 (1978).
7. WALTER A. ROSENBAUM, ENVIRONMENTAL POLITICS AND POLICY (2d ed.). (Washington, D.C.: Congressional Quarterly Press, 1991).
8. ROSENBAUM, ENERGY, POLITICS, AND POLICY.
9. Ibid.
10. Ibid.
11. ROSENBAUM, ENVIRONMENTAL POLITICS AND POLICY, p. 264.
12. Ibid.
13. Ibid., p. 265.
14. 16 USCA §471.
15. 16 USCA §475.
16. 43 USCA §1732(b).
17. 43 USCA §1701–1784.
18. 16 USCA §1601 et seq.
19. Council on Environmental Quality, pp. 193–94.
20. Ibid., p. 194.
21. 16 USCA §1531.
22. 16 USCA §1533.
23. 50 C.F.R. Sec. 17.3 (1994).
24. Sweet Home Chapter of Communities for a Great Oregon v. Babbitt, 1 F.3d 1 (D.C. Cir. 1993).
25. 17 F.3d 1463, 1464 (1994).

CHAPTER 10

International Environmental Law

Thus far, we have been examining the environmental law of the United States. Environmental protection, however, if it is to be truly effective, must have an international dimension.

THE NEED FOR INTERNATIONAL ENVIRONMENTAL LAW

Over the past two decades there has been growing recognition of the need for international environmental law, primarily because of an increasing awareness of the severity of certain worldwide environmental problems. These problems are discussed first. The next section explains the unique nature of international law, followed by descriptions of the sources of environmental law and the primary institutions that carry out those laws. The final sections address how international environmental law is attempting to remedy some specific environmental problems and speculate about the future of international environmental law.

Overpopulation

One of the most severe problems in the world today is overpopulation. This problem necessitates an international solution because without a worldwide solution, extremely adverse consequences will result. The threat of overpopulation was set forth originally in the now famous book of Thomas Robert Malthus, *On the Principle of Population.* Published in 1798, Malthus's work argued that population, which grows geometrically, will eventually outstrip food production, which grows arithmetically, resulting in mass starvation. Though Malthus's timetable for disaster may have been disrupted by unanticipated agricultural developments, many believe that the ultimate impact of those developments is simply to delay the point at which our inability to provide sufficient foodstuffs will occur.

Added to this original concern, and more important to stimulating the development of international environmental law, is the effect that a larger population has on the overall ability of the planet to sustain life: More people use more energy, more land, and more water. This greater use of resources may lead to their depletion. A huge influx in population also creates more pollution. Burning wood and low-sulfur coal contributes to the buildup of carbon monoxide. Rapid urbanization, occurring in most Third World nations today, leads to massive traffic jams, overcrowded slums, and clogged waste disposal systems, all of which degrade the environment.

Some social scientists, most notably Julian Simon, believe that population growth is good for humanity, primarily because human intellect is our most valuable resource: The more people, the greater the intellect pool from which society can draw. Those who do not believe there is a population problem point out that whenever apparently fixed resources become scarce, we seem to figure out a way to replace them. It could be argued from history that every apparent shortage is just a stimulus for the development of new resources, new resources that in the long run may be cheaper than the old ones.[1]

Whether we agree with those who see increased population as a blessing or a curse, we can all agree that the population of the planet is increasing at an unprecedented pace. Perhaps as a society we have always been able to handle increases in population and increasing demands on resources, but it is only logical that at some level a breaking point must be reached. For years the air managed to cleanse itself, but then its self-cleansing properties were overcome by excess pollutants. The same phenomenon occurs with bodies of water. And many fear that despite our successes in the past, we are nearing the carrying capacity for Earth.

Regardless of whether we perceive population increases as nearing crisis levels, certainly the fact that an increasing number of people are using common resources means that we are more likely to interfere with one another's use of these resources. Hence there is a need for an international body of law to respond to questions regarding use and abuse of the global environment.

Loss of Biological Diversity

Whereas some see overpopulation as the preeminent global problem today, others consider loss of biological diversity an even greater problem. Scientists have classified approximately 1.4 million living species, of which roughly 750,000 are insects, 41,000 are vertebrates, 265,000 are plants, and the rest are invertebrates.[2] No one knows how many millions more exist that have not been classified. The more we learn about these diverse species, the more we discover ways that they can improve and maintain our lives. Some plants and animals provide food, medicine, and industrial raw materials. For example, more than 40 percent of prescription drugs contain chemicals originally derived from wild species. Other species provide flood control, pest control, and natural recycling of waste. Ninety percent of agricultural crops are pollinated exclusively by insects.

Yet, just as we are starting to learn about many of these species and how they can benefit the planet, we are destroying them. At least two-thirds of all land-dwelling species inhabit the tropical rain forests that are being rapidly destroyed. As the rain forests are being destroyed, so are the species that inhabit these areas. Some researchers project that by the year 2000, we may lose more than 1 million species.[3] In Germany, the Netherlands, Denmark, and Spain, more than 20 percent of the bird species[4] and 40 percent of the mammalian species are classified as threatened.[5]

As noted, however, the greatest losses are occurring in tropical forests, where most of the various species reside. These losses are occurring because increases in population, endemic poverty, the need for fuel wood, and the failure to use sustainable agriculture methods have led to massive clearing of these forests. Essentially, it is human activity that destroys habitats and leads to the loss of species.

The Global Commons

The term biosphere refers to the thin shell where the atmosphere, hydrosphere, and lithosphere connect; in this context life and its products exist. The biosphere constitutes a symbol of the unity and interrelationships of living things and their physical setting. The biosphere calls to mind a complementary relationship between humans and the physical environment. That environment is not viewed primarily as a set of independent, strictly bounded territories but, rather, as one related unit, divided if at all, into natural components—air, water, and land—each having interactive relationships with one another and with humans. Space travel permitted the first real view of Earth as a biosphere. From outer space we could see Earth as a single, unitary whole, set against the blackness of the universe. When we view Earth as a biosphere, we can see that the land, air, and water are interconnected and, in fact, represent a sort of global commons.

Obviously, the oceans and seas constitute a major part of the global commons. Problems associated with the destruction of these shared resources are potentially numerous: Human health may be placed directly at risk by contamination of seafood; reproductive cycles of species of animal life may be disrupted; human health may also be adversely affected as a result of direct contact with polluted water; aesthetic qualities of coastal environments may be destroyed.

Potential destruction of the ocean environment comes primarily from three sources: ocean shipping, land-based pollution, and the dumping of wastes in the oceans. The primary problem caused by marine shipping is pollution created by marine oil. Ninety percent of this oil is from standard ship operations, deballasting, and tank washing. Only about 10 percent results from tanker accidents, although it is these accidents that tend to generate the greatest publicity. Recall from chapter 6 that water pollution from land-based activities can be point or nonpoint source. The same two categories apply to pollution of oceans. Point source discharges occur when manufacturers along a coast discharge insufficiently treated or untreated water directly into the ocean. Nonpoint source pollution comes primarily from runoff from cropland, urban areas, and construction and mining sites. Wastes being dumped at sea include sewage sludge, industrial waste, and dredge spoils. These wastes may contain a plethora of heavy metals, synthetic chemicals, and other toxic materials.

Air is another important part of the global commons. Because of air currents, substances one country emits into the atmosphere are likely to travel to other countries. The three primarily global problems associated with air (described in chapter 5) are acid deposition, depletion of the ozone layer, and the greenhouse effect.

Environmental Disasters and Transboundary Pollution

During the past twenty years, a number of dramatic environmental disasters have made people recognize the potential that our advanced levels of technology have for allowing one nation to wreak havoc on the environment worldwide. These catastrophes make it very clear that no nation, regardless of the precautions it takes, can protect its environment by itself. Thus, people question whether there should be some international agreement on how to respond to such disasters when they arise and, even more importantly, how to prevent their occurrence.

Transboundary pollution, on the other hand, has been around for years. Transboundary pollution generally arises in two ways. First, pollution is generated in one area and transported a great distance before falling to earth in another nation. A typical example would be where a U.S. firm uses tall stacks to disperse air pollutants, which causes the air pollutants to settle in Canada. The second type of transboundary pollution occurs when two or more nations border on a common resource and one nation pollutes the common resource to the detriment of the other. An example would be Mexico's dumping sewage into the Tijuana River, resulting in damage to wells and crops in California.

Solutions to these wide-ranging problems are being sought through international environmental law. Before we examine international environmental law, per se, however, we need to understand how international law in general compares to domestic law.

THE NATURE OF INTERNATIONAL LAW

International law is unlike any other area of law in that there is disagreement over whether there can even be a body of law known as international law, and if there is, what that can contain. There is no international superlegislature to establish these laws and no effective international mechanism with enforcement authority.

International law is generally viewed as being derived from two sources: treaties and other agreements freely entered into by nation-states and principles derived from long-standing practices. Laws from treaties are referred to as *conventional laws;* those from long-standing practice are called *customary laws.* The primary actors in the international law system are the nation-states, as represented by their governments. Intergovernmental agencies also play an important role in the international law system, as do nongovernmental organizations (NGOs). Also, individuals and corporations are sometimes participants.

Enforcement is where international law presents the greatest difficulty. The Security Council of the United Nations is most often viewed as the primary source of enforcement of international law. The council has limited executive authority to enforce the provisions of its charter and to maintain peace and security. However, it does not have any enforcement authority over international law in general. It is also limited because it requires unanimity of all of its members before acting.

The United Nations has established an International Court of Justice. However, the impact of this court has been limited by the fact that it decides only cases submitted by parties who agree to be there. The parties between whom there is the greatest disagreement are therefore unlikely to be before the court because they will not agree to submit their dispute. Thus the parties who need the court the most arguably will be the least likely to use it. In some cases the court has the authority to issue advisory opinions only, which may be, and frequently are, freely ignored.

Given the ineffectiveness of these sources of enforcement, parties have sometimes turned to the courts of the nation-states to seek enforcement of international law. As long as the court will assume jurisdiction, this approach may be the most effective.

SOURCES OF INTERNATIONAL ENVIRONMENTAL LAW

As noted in the preceding section, international law comes from both treaties and practices. International environmental law likewise draws from these two sources. Its conventional law comprises some twenty multilateral treaties governing environmental issues and more than 275 bilateral agreements that contain references to environmental issues.

Conventional Law

Conventional international environmental law can trace its roots back to the UN Conference on the Human Environment in Stockholm in 1972. This two-week meeting produced the Stockholm Declaration of the conference, which was subsequently adopted by the twenty-seventh session of the UN General Assembly by a vote of 114 to 0, with 10 abstentions. This document contained twenty-six principles, an action plan consisting of 109 recommendations, and a resolution on institutional and financial arrangements. The topics covered by the principles included fundamental human rights (Principle 1), management of human resources (Principles 2–7), the relationship between development and the environment (Principles 8–12), planning and demographic policy (Principles 13–17), science and technology (Principles 18–20), state responsibility (Principles 21–22), respect for national environmental standards along with the need for state cooperation (Principles 23–25), and the threat of nuclear weapons to the environment.[6]

The principles are important because they consolidated the existing rules of international environmental law while also providing guidance for the future of this body of law. Principle 21 is a good example of the tone of these principles and also reflects a recognition by the drafters of the existence of a body of international environmental law. Principle 21 reads as follows:

> States shall cooperate to develop further the international law regarding liability and compensation for the victims of pollution and other environmental damage caused by activities within the jurisdiction or control of such states to areas beyond their jurisdiction.

A second important agreement, the World Charter for Nature,[7] was adopted by the UN General Assembly in 1982, by a vote of 111 to 1, with the United States casting the only dissenting vote. The charter contains a preamble and twenty-five principles. The first five are general principles. Principles 6 through 13 provide detailed rules for planning and management of the natural environment. Finally, Principles 14 through 24 contain implementation rules that specify obligations for members of the international community.

Customary Law

Customary law is defined by the statute of the International Court of Justice, Article 38,[8] as having its source in state practice, in the "general principles of law that are recognized by civilized nations, and in the judicial decisions and teachings of respected jurists." Think of customary law as analogous to common law in the U.S. legal system.

Four basic principles seem to have evolved as customary international environmental laws. These customary laws are reinforced by treaty provisions. Attempts to codify these customary rules have been undertaken by two private organizations: the International Law Association and the International Law Commission.

A first principle is that of good neighborliness—the rule that no state is entitled to use its land in a way that would infringe on the rights of others. This principle, often cited in its Latin form, *sic uter tuo alienum non laedas,* can be viewed as an international application of the U.S. common law of nuisance, discussed in chapter 4. The doctrine of good neighborliness seems to have been initially granted its status as a customary law in the Trail Smelter arbitration.[9] Trail Smelter arose from a situation in which sulfur dioxide fumes from a smelter in Trail, British Columbia, were damaging farmland and crops in the state of Washington. The United States complained to Canada in 1927. After years of negotiations, Canada accepted liability and agreed to arbitrate the issue of damages. In 1941, the decision was handed down that contains the often quoted principle of good neighborliness as applied to transboundary pollution: "Under principles of international law, as well as the law of the United States, no state has the right to permit the use of its territory in such a manner as to cause injury by fumes to another country or to the properties or persons therein where the case is of serious consequence and the injury is established by clear and convincing evidence." This decision is sometimes criticized because of two requirements that limit the rule's application: the description of the consequences as serious and the standard of clear and convincing evidence.

Further support for this customary law can be found in several treaties that incorporate the principle of good neighborliness. For example, the preamble to the Charter of the United Nations states the desire of member states to "live together in peace with one another as good neighbors." Article 74 of the same document encourages member states to conduct their social, economic, and commercial policies in accordance with "general principles of good neighborliness."

A second principle is the duty of due diligence—the obligation to protect the rights of other states. In the environmental area, this duty has been extended to mean a duty to use due diligence to prevent and abate pollution. This principle has not been interpreted as an absolute prohibition on pollution but, rather, a mandate that the state take the measures expected under "good government" to prevent pollution.

Another important principle is that of the equitable utilization of shared resources—the requirement of the reasonable use of shared resources. The obvious question that arises with respect to this principle is how one decides whether a use is reasonable. In fact, if one decides that reasonableness may be derived from past practice, one may in fact be sanctioning the very activities that gave rise to the environmental problems in the first place.

This customary law of equitable utilization was first set out in the River Oder case.[10] In that case the Permanent Court of International Justice laid down the rule by stating that "this community of interest (of riparian states) in a navigable river becomes the basis of a common legal right, the essential features of which are the perfect equality of all riparian states in the use of the whole course of the river."

This principle was reinforced by its inclusion in the Helsinki Rules.[11] Article IV states: "Each basin state is entitled, within its territory, to a reasonable and equitable share in the beneficial uses of the waters of an international drainage basin." The Helsinki Rules attempt to provide some guidance as to what is considered reasonable use by listing some factors that should be taken into account—for instance, geographic and climatic conditions, social and economic needs of the neighboring states, comparative costs of alternate ways to satisfy those needs, availability of the technological means to reduce the impact on the environment, and the practicality of compensation as a means of adjusting the burden. The rules do not suggest any order of importance for these factors, indicating that their relevance depends on the individual circumstances of each case.[12]

A final principle is the duty to inform and cooperate. The duty to give prior notice is recognized in such often cited cases as the Corfu Channel case.[13] This case arose when two British warships traveling through the Corfu Channel, part of Albania's water, were damaged by mines that had been placed there by the Germans. Albania was believed to have, at minimum, knowledge of the mining. The International Court of Justice, in ruling that Albania had to compensate the British for the damage to property and life, stated that "the obligations incumbent upon the Albanian authorities consisted in notifying . . . the existence of a minefield in Albanian territorial waters and in warning the approaching British warships of the immediate danger to which the minefield exposed them."

Adoption of the duty to inform is evidenced by this principle's inclusion in many treaties. For example, Article XXX of the Helsinki Rules recommends that states "furnish any other basin state the interests of which may be substantially affected, notice of a proposed construction or installation which would alter the regime of the basin."[14]

INSTITUTIONS THAT EFFECTUATE AND INFLUENCE INTERNATIONAL ENVIRONMENTAL LAW

United Nations

The most influential intergovernmental organization in the development of international environmental law is the United Nations, an organization established in 1945. Its primary bodies include the General Assembly, the Security Council, and the Economic and Social Council. Technically, all the United Nations can do is make recommendations; the individual members must adopt their own policies. However, the articulation of treaties and policies by the United Nations is a powerful first step toward the worldwide adoption of environmental policies. The United Nations also sponsors several programs that have a significant impact on international environmental law.

United Nations Environmental Program. The United Nations Environmental Program (UNEP) is a special body created by the UN General Assembly that has done much to effectuate worldwide environmental policies.

Created at the same time was the Environmental Fund. Both UNEP and the Environmental Fund were mandated by Resolution 2997 (XXVII) in 1972 to put into effect the action plan set forth in the Stockholm Declaration.

UNEP's structure has three distinct entities: the Governing Council, the Environment Secretariat, and the Environment Fund. The Governing Council comprises delegates from the fifty-eight member states that are elected on a rotating basis by the General Assembly. The main responsibilities of the Governing Council are to promote international cooperation in environmental matters and provide general policy guidance for the direction and coordination of environmental programs within the UN system. The council also annually reviews and approves the allocation of money from the Environment Fund. Every year the council receives from the executive director, the state of the environment report, which it uses to identify environmental issues and to decide on future initiatives. The Governing Council reviews the impact of environmental policies on developing countries and promotes contributions from the scientific and other communities to program formulation and development. The council reports UNEP's activities to the General Assembly through the Economic and Social Council, with special attention paid to questions of coordination and to the relationship of environmental policies and programs within the UN system to overall economic and social policies and priorities.

The Environment Secretariat is composed of approximately two hundred people and is headed by UNEP's executive director, who is elected by the General Assembly. The tasks of the secretariat include coordinating environment programs in the UN system and reviewing and evaluating their effectiveness, providing advisory services for promotion of international cooperation, advising intergovernmental bodies of the UN system on environmental programs, and administering the Environment Fund.

The Environment Fund receives about $5 million in funds annually from the United Nations to cover operating expenses, but relies on voluntary contributions from governments to build up funds to be used for financing initiatives taken within the United Nations.

UNEP's mandate is to assess, monitor, and protect the human environment by seeking solutions to pollution and human-made contamination and promoting environmentally sound economic and social developments in urban and rural areas. UNEP is primarily a catalyst and coordinating agency. As such, it collaborates with other environmental agencies, as well as running some of its own programs.

The Global Environmental Monitoring System (GEMS) is one of the most important UNEP programs. GEMS is responsible for the collection, storage, retrieval, analysis, and dissemination of environmental data related to a wide range of potential pollutants. It functions through a network of national monitoring stations, each of which is coordinated by an appropriate UN specialized agency.

The Regional Seas and Oceans Program (renamed Oceans and Coastal Areas Program) is one of UNEP's most successful endeavors. This program involves more than 120 countries through eleven regional sea treaty agreements. The objectives of the program are to foster communications among nations sharing coastal and marine problems, to provide training in oil spill management and emergency response, and to develop marine science centers. The program is also attempting to create common calibrations for monitoring coastal water pollution.

UNEP also engages in a wide range of cooperative ventures with other organizations such as the International Council of Scientific Unions. For example, UNEP publishes the *International Register of Potentially Toxic Chemicals,* which provides detailed information and policy proposals for more than eighty thousand chemicals.

World Commission on Economic Development.   The World Commission on Economic Development (WCED, sometimes referred to as the Brundtland Commission) was created by the General Assembly of the United Nations in fall 1983 to formulate long-term strategies to attain sustainable development by the year 2000 and beyond. The prime minister of Norway was named chair; the prime minister of the Sudan was named vice chair. These two appointed the remaining twenty-one members, with more than half from developing nations.

On October 13, 1984, the newly organized WCED met and adopted a mandate to "re-examine critical issues of environment and development and formulate innovative, concrete, and realistic action proposals to address them, strengthen international cooperation on environment and development and assess and propose new forms of cooperation that can reshape existing economic patterns and influence policies and events in the direction of needed change; and raise the level of understanding and commitment to action on the part of individuals, voluntary associations, businesses, institutions, and governments."[15]

The major accomplishment of WCED, thus far, has been the publication of *Our Common Future.* The report was based on data gathered from public hearings in a dozen cities around the world and information from several advisory panels. The report concluded that "humanity has the ability to make development sustainable—to ensure that it meets the needs of the present without compromising the ability of future generations to meet their own needs."

World Bank

The World Bank is one of the primary sources of funding for projects in developing countries. As such, it has the potential to play an extremely influential role in environmental policies worldwide.

Before the mid-1980s, environmental factors were not a consideration in the World Bank's lending decisions. And, in fact, many have criticized the bank for lending money without considering the social impacts of the projects, for example, lending money for projects that led to deforestation and to governments that do not care about indigenous tribal minorities. In 1987, however, the bank was reorganized and an environmental department was established. As a result, potential borrowers were asked to prepare an environmental issues paper for each loan they wished to obtain. The contents of these papers were to be considered when loans were being made.

In 1979, the impact of potential environmental effects was given even more prominence by an operational directive on environmental assessments of proposed projects. Now, when a project is being considered, a preliminary screening is done by the environmental department of the World Bank. The project is rated according to its potential impact on the environment. Not only are these assessments taken into account when the bank is considering action on loan requests, but a summary of the project's environmental impact is included in a supplement to the bank's monthly operational summary, the main document the bank uses to convey its future plans to interested parties.

In 1991, the World Bank's commitment to environmentally sound lending practices was strengthened by its adoption of a new policy on tropical rain forests. No further bank funding is to be made available for commercial logging in the remaining tropical forests. In 1995, the bank established new environmental guidelines that place stricter controls on air, waste water, and solid waste pollution, shifting the bank's focus from pollution control to prevention. These new guidelines will be phased in "progressively." The World Bank, while not a party to making law, still has a tremendous influence on international environmental policy. A law prohibiting logging in tropical rain forests may be evaded, but if the funding for such projects is not readily available, evasion will be much more difficult.

European Community

The European Union (EU) is a union of fifteen European nations. Their overall objective is to do away with internal tariffs among member states and create uniform external tariffs to be applied to nonmember states. The EU wants to "level the economic playing field" among member states and achieve the free movement of goods, capital, and people across member states' borders. See table 10–1 for a list of the member states of the European Union.

The EU has been given the authority, by its member states, to negotiate treaties that directly bind the members without further ratification by members' separate legislatures. The EU consists of a council, whose members are ministers from the member nations, a commission, and a parliament, which is made up of representatives directly elected by member states. The commission proposes legislation, and the council adopts it after receiving input from the parliament. The legislation passed by the EU is in two forms—regulations and directives. Regulations have the force of a national law and are directly enforceable in each nation's court. Directives are broader and bind nations to ends that are to be achieved.

TABLE 10–1 Nation-States of the European Community

Belgium (1958)	Finland (1994)
France (1958)	Sweden (1994)
Germany (1958)	
Italy (1958)	
Luxembourg (1958)	
Netherlands (1958)	
Denmark (1973)	
Ireland (1973)	
United Kingdom (1973)	
Greece (1981)	
Portugal (1986)	
Spain (1986)	
Austria (1994)	

The EU first began to address environmental policy explicitly in 1972, influenced to a great extent by the Stockholm Conference. Legislation is adopted in accordance with the EU's environmental action program. The program, which has been redefined four times since its inception, establishes principles in accordance with which environmental legislation is to be adopted. Eleven principles have been established; the following are typical examples of those principles: Activities in one nation should not cause deterioration of the environment of another, and the effects of environmental policies in member states should take into account the interests of developing nations. By 1992, the EC had adopted more than 280 pieces of environmental legislation. These regulations cover a broad range of environmental issues, from drinking water standards to limits on sulfur dioxide emissions for controlling acid rain.

From the perspective of those concerned about environmental issues, one of the biggest concerns about the expansion of the European Community into the European Union and its continued growth is the impact that joining the EU has on environmental regulation of member states. Remember that the objective of the European Union is to remove trade barriers among member states. What this means in terms of environmental protection is that no state can set up environmental standards that would keep another member state from competing in its markets or keep its firms from competing in other states' markets. The problem from environmentalists' perspective is that the northern European community states have traditionally had much more stringent environmental regulations than do the southern European states. Many fear that as the states unify their laws the southern European states will block the northern European states from imposing their more stringent requirements on the entire community and may have to reduce some of their standards.

The EU also acts as negotiator for its member states in negotiations for treaties (often referred to as conventions) with nonmember nations. As a representative of many nations, the EU has greater clout than any single nation would have. Although the EU is an active and influential participant in these treaty negotiations, the EU does not actually bind member states to most conventions; member states independently determine whether they will become signatories to such agreements. In some cases, however, member states give the EU the authority to bind them to a proposed treaty. When given such authority, the EU has even greater power at the negotiating table.

ADDRESSING SPECIFIC INTERNATIONAL ENVIRONMENTAL PROBLEMS

In this section we examine how international environmental law attempts to solve some specific problems. Treatment of these problem areas relies on both customary and conventional law, neither of which is very satisfactory. The customary law is plagued by the uncertainty of its principles. Treaties, because they require agreement of parties with conflicting interests, are often very weak, imposing few absolute rights or obligations. Both types of law are victims of the overall problem of weak enforceability.

Transboundary Pollution

Transboundary pollution occurs when pollution generated in one nation is transported to another nation, or when two countries share a common resource and one contaminates that resource to the detriment of the other. Establishing an international law for transboundary pollution is difficult because of two conflicting perspectives on state sovereignty. One is a concept of absolute sovereignty, under which a nation is free to do whatever it wishes with resources within its boundaries. Most nations denounce this absolutist position, but, still, in practice, it describes many nations' behavior. The opposing view is that of absolute territorial integrity. This view holds that no state may engage in activities that would in any way damage the territory of another nation.

The development of international environmental law regarding transboundary pollution can be seen as an attempt to find a way to recognize these two competing notions of territoriality. The current tentative resolution of this conflict seems to be that the rights emanating from territorial sovereignty imply a reciprocal duty to take into account the impact of one nation's behavior on other nations. Recognition of the need to incorporate both concepts of territoriality is perhaps best exemplified by Principle 21 of the Stockholm Declaration. The principle reads as follows: "States have, in accordance with the Charter of the United Nations and the principles of international law, the sovereign right to exploit their own resources pursuant to their environmental principles, and the responsibility to ensure that activities within their jurisdiction or control do not cause damage to the environment of other states or areas beyond the limits of national jurisdiction."

Finding a definitive statement of the law of transboundary pollution is not easy. In *Restatement (Third) of the Foreign Relations of the United States,* we find the following statement of liability for transboundary pollution:

§902 Interstate Claims and Remedies

(1) A state may bring a claim against another state for violation of an international obligation owed to the claimant state or to states generally, either through diplomatic channels, or through any procedure to which the two states have agreed.

(2) Under Subsection (1), a state may bring claims, inter alia for violations of international obligations resulting in injury to its nationals or to other persons on whose behalf it is entitled to make a claim under international law.

Because of the confusion surrounding the issue of liability of nations for transboundary pollution, the UN General Assembly requested that the International Law Commission (ILC) report on liability for transboundary pollution when the acts giving rise to the injury were not illegal, per se. (The ILC is a body of the United Nations composed of thirty-five representatives who are elected by the General Assembly by geographic location.) The conclusions reached by the ILC seem to be reflective of what we have seen as the principles of customary international environmental law.

Four duties appear to be imposed on nations: to prevent transboundary harm, to inform other nations of accidents that might cause transboundary harm, to enter into negotiations to attempt to develop a convention to determine how the situation should be handled, and, if no convention can be adopted, to negotiate in good faith with respect to the rights and obligations of the parties. When harm has resulted, liability should be determined by considering a number of factors, including the amount of damage, the degree of control exercised by the responsible state, the reasonableness of the parties' conduct, and the relative costs of preventing the injury.

Choice of Forums

A question may arise when one reads that statement of law in the preceding paragraph: Where should such a case be brought? Earlier we made reference to the fact that one of the problems of international law is its lack of an effective forum for both dispute resolution and the subsequent enforcement of any judgment that may be obtained. That problem is reaffirmed in our examination of the alternate forums in which transboundary pollution disputes may be brought.

Whenever one thinks of resolving a transboundary pollution dispute, the first forum that comes to mind is the International Court of Justice, which has the jurisdiction to decide cases that are submitted to it. Also, the court may render advisory opinions at the request of the General Assembly or any other competent body of the United Nations. One major problem is that when one party is the transgressor, that partly is obviously going to be reluctant to submit the dispute to the court. And if the court is asked to render a nonbinding advisory opinion, the effect of that advice is likely to be nil, especially if the opinion suggests the payment of reparations. The rarity of disputes coming before this forum is reflected by the low number of opinions rendered by this court. From 1945 to 1986, only seventy-two cases were submitted, with forty-five judgments and seventeen advisory opinions issued.[16]

Even if a judgment is rendered, enforcement is difficult. The UN Security Council can, "if it deems necessary, make recommendations or decide upon measures to be taken to give effect to the judgment."[17] However, because of the uncertainty of this clause, the Security Council has been reluctant to take action under it. Therefore, states have felt fairly free simply to ignore the judgments of the International Court of Justice.

Perhaps the most effective forum for resolution of these disputes is the court of the nation in which the harmful conduct took place. The major problem solved by this approach is that there exists an effective means of enforcement; the power of the state lies behind the judgment. This approach, however, is most likely to be effective when the plaintiff state is suing a private party residing in the state where the offense occurred rather than actually suing the state itself, because a state court is more likely to rule against one of its residents than to rule against the state government.

The UNEP Draft Principles of Conduct express a preference for the use of national courts for the resolution of transboundary pollution problems. Principle 14 provides as follows:

> States should endeavor, in accordance with their legal systems and where appropriate, on a basis agreed by them, to provide persons in other states who have been or may be adversely affected by environmental damage resulting from the utilizations of shared resources with equivalent access and treatment in the same judicial and administrative proceedings and make available to them the same remedies as are available to persons within their own jurisdiction who may have been or may be similarly situated.

The UN Organization for Economic Cooperation and Development (OECD), in its 1977 Recommendation for Implementation of a Regime of Equal Right of Access and Non-Discrimination in Relation to Transfrontier Pollution, reflects a similar view. The OECD recommends that equal access to information be given to foreign nations, as well as equal access to all public authorities, courts, and administrative agencies. In private treaties, some nations are adopting this equal access approach with respect to transboundary pollution. One example of such a treaty is the Convention on Protection of the Environment, the so-called Nordic Convention, entered into by Sweden, Denmark, Finland, and Norway. Article 3 of the convention provides that any person who is affected or may be affected by a nuisance caused by environmentally harmful activities in another contracting state shall have the right to bring before the appropriate court or administrative authority of that state the question of the permissibility of measures to prevent damage, and to appeal against the decision of the court or administrative agency to the same extent and on the same terms as a legal entity of the state in which the activities are being carried out.

An alternate forum to the courts themselves is the use of international arbitration. To make the decision binding, disputants enter into a compromise or agreement that sets forth the subject matter of the dispute, the method for selecting the arbitration panel, and the procedures to be followed during the arbitration. Again, however, because of the need for an agreement to arbitrate, the most hotly contested cases may not come before the arbitrator. Also, once the award is made, if one of the parties disagrees with the award and refuses to comply, there is no available mechanism for enforcement.

A final and perhaps most common way of resolving conflicts arising out of transboundary pollution is diplomacy. Diplomatic solutions are generally compromises brought about through negotiations between the countries in conflict. Frequently they are aided by representatives from an international or regional organization, so that the procedure for resolution in fact becomes a form of mediation.

Problems of the Global Commons

Recall that the global commons refers to those areas of Earth that cannot easily be partitioned, those resources that belong to no one but preserve and maintain the lives of all. If we all simply use the commons without taking care to preserve it, the global commons will be destroyed. The primary problems associated with the global commons have been discussed earlier in this chapter. Here we will consider attempts to solve some of these problems. As you will see, the primary approach has been through multilateral treaties.

Destruction of the Ozone Layer.   Although this problem has been considered a national problem, it is, in fact, global in nature. The United States could totally ban the use of ozone-destroying CFCs, but if other nations did not follow suit, the ozone layer would still be destroyed. We cannot separate "our" portion of the ozone layer.

The worldwide response to ozone depletion has been remarkably swift. On September 16, 1987, twenty-four nations and the EC signed the Montreal Protocol on Substances That Deplete the Ozone Layer. The primary objectives of the treaty were as follows:

1. In 1987, to hold increases of ozone-depleting chlorofluorocarbons and halons to 10 percent of 1986 levels.

2. Within four more years, to reduce the production of CFCs and halons to 80 percent of 1986 levels.
3. By July 1, 1999, to reduce CFC and halon production to 50 percent of 1986 levels.

The protocol provided an exception for developing countries. The treaty also provided that there would be no trade in controlled substances with any nation not a party to the treaty. A Montreal Protocol Multilateral Fund was also set up in conjunction with the treaty. This fund provides aid to assist developing nations in the transition from ozone-depleting chemicals. At a June 1990 meeting in London, the parties to the protocol agreed to phase out CFCs, carbon tetrachloride, and nonessential uses of halons by the year 2000 and the use of methyl chloroform by 2005.

Between November 23 and 25, 1992, representatives from the more than one hundred signatories to the Montreal Protocol held the Fourth Meeting of the Parties to the Montreal Protocol on Substances That Deplete the Ozone Layer. Ultimately, the parties agreed to speed up the dates for reduction of CFCs. They agreed that by 1994, there would be reduction of CFC production by 75 percent of 1986 levels, and a complete elimination of CFC production by January 1, 1996.

At that meeting, representatives agreed that there was a need to look closely at the substances being used as substitutes for CFCs. Most frequently used are HCFCs, which are not as harmful to the ozone layer as CFCs; however, they contain some chlorine and destroy some of the stratospheric ozone. They are, therefore, not a permanent solution to the CFC problem. Some parties argued that the main goal is to eliminate the use of CFCs as quickly as possible, and therefore HCFCs need to be available as a "lesser-of-two-evils" alternative until a better substitute can be developed.

Others argued that there already were better alternatives available, but as long as HCFCs could be used, there would not be the motivation to invest in technologies to use the alternate substances. In the end, the parties agreed to

1. cap the use of HCFCs in January 1996 at a level equal to the sum of their use in 1989; and
2. subsequently reduce their use of HCFCs by 35 percent by 2004, by 65 percent by 2010, by 90 percent by 2015, by 99.5 percent by 2020, and by 100 percent by 2030.

The late date of the final phase out can be seen as evidence of the power of those who want to continue using the HCFCs as long as possible. The United States was particularly concerned about being able to continue to uses HCFCs because they play an important role in air-conditioning of big buildings.

After that meeting, there was pressure to add methyl bromide as a controlled, ozone-depleting substance. Methyl bromide is an insecticide that is primarily used to fumigate stored produce and grain, soil, and structures. Many believe that the scientific evidence of methyl bromide's ozone-depleting effects is undeniable. By far, the greatest production of that chemical is in North America, where approximately 42 percent is produced. Europe produces roughly 29 percent, and Asia 22 percent.

At the 1995 meeting on the Protocol, representatives agreed to phase out the use of methyl bromide in industrialized nations entirely by 2012, and to gradually phase out its use during the fifteen years before that deadline. Use in developing nations is to be frozen in the year 2002 at annual levels equivalent to the average of the annual volume of domestic use from 1995 through 1998. Representatives also agreed to look at this issue again at the 1997 meeting. Many environmental organizations were upset by the failure of the 149 parties to the protocol to take more urgent action when, according to a UN report, the quickest and most efficient way to reduce future ozone loss would be to ban the use of this pesticide. Some scientists estimate that the chemical is fifty times more destructive to the ozone layer per atom than CFCs.

Under the Clean Air Act, the United States was already required to phase out the domestic use and production of methyl bromide by the year 2001. However, at the time this book went to press, Clinton was asking Congress to amend the Clean Air Act in such a way as to not require the complete phase out of the insecticide until the date mandated under the Montreal Protocol. The argument of Clinton and the EPA (and, many would argue, the agribusiness interests) was that there is no guarantee that an adequate substitute for all of the chemical's uses will be found by the year 2002, and if the United States is required to cease use of this chemical before other nations are, it will put the United States at a competitive disadvantage against other nations. Other nations, however, including the Netherlands, Austria, Indonesia, and Italy, have either eliminated their major use of methyl bromide or are planning to do so by the year 2000.

Opponents of extending the deadline argue that the effects on the ozone layer clearly justify the early deadline, and that the best way to ensure that substitute products are found is by having firm, early deadlines and creating a definite market for the substitutes. Some argued that if industry had spent as much time and money on research as they did on lobbying to change the law, substitute products would have already been found by now. They also pointed out that farmers throughout the world are already using innovative alternatives to methyl bromide.

Global Warming. Figure 10–1 depicts the global warming or greenhouse effect. As you can see from the figure, carbon dioxide is the primary contributor to global warming, and the United States is a primary source. In May 1992, the problem of greenhouse gas emissions was temporarily resolved by the signing of a treaty by representatives of 142 nations to attempt to reduce the level of emissions of greenhouse gases (carbon dioxide, methane, nitrous oxide) by developed nations back to 1990 levels by the year 2000. The treaty

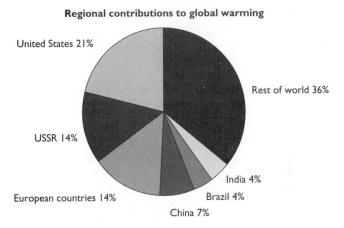

FIGURE 10–1 Global Warming, 1980s

Source: EPA, *Meeting the Environmental Challenge* (1990), p. 12.

will set up a procedure for monitoring scientific advances so that modifications can be undertaken if necessary. Developing nations will adopt policies that will limit the increase in their emissions, although these emissions will still increase substantially, and developed nations will provide financial and technical aid to developing countries.

This treaty was actually much less stringent than originally proposed; many environmentalists argued that the treaty had been gutted by the United States. President Bush had used this treaty for leverage to bargain with other nations at the Earth Summit. Bush agreed to attend this major international conference on the environment only if stipulations in the original treaty that absolute curbs on carbon dioxide levels would be enforced were removed.

Marine Pollution. As with most global commons problems, the primary approach to protecting the oceans and seas has been through the use of treaties, with one of the more important treaties being the 1982 Convention on the Law of the Sea. Restatement (Third) of Foreign Relations Law of the United States, Part VI, the Law of the Environment (1988), reiterates some of the important aspects of this convention.

Section 603, State Responsibility for Marine Pollution, obligates a state to "adopt laws and regulations to prevent, reduce and control any significant pollution of the marine environment that are no less effective than generally accepted international rules and standards" and to "ensure compliance with the foregoing by ships flying its flag, imposing adequate penalties on the captain or owner of the ship that violates such rules." Part (2) of Section 603 provides that "a state is obligated to take, individually and jointly with other states, such measures as may be necessary, to the extent practicable under the circumstances, to prevent, reduce, and control pollution causing or threatening to cause significant injury to the marine environment."

Remedies for marine pollution caused by violating Section 603 are given in Section 604, which provides that any state responsible to another state for violating Section 603 is subject to general interstate remedies "to prevent, reduce, or terminate the activity threatening or causing pollution and to pay reparation for the injury caused." The state must ensure that a remedy is available through its legal system "to provide prompt and adequate compensation or other relief for an injury to private interests caused by pollution of the marine environment."

This section gives coastal states the additional authority to detain and institute proceedings against foreign states navigating its territorial seas and violating one of the state's antipollution laws or violating international antipollution laws that resulted in a discharge that caused or threatened a major injury to the state. A port state may institute proceedings against a foreign ship that voluntarily entered its port for "a violation of that states anti-pollution laws . . . if the violation occurred in the port state's territorial sea or exclusive economic zone"; or for "a discharge in violation of applicable international anti-pollution rules and standards that occurred beyond the limits of national jurisdiction of any state." A port state also has the obligation, as far as practicable, under Section 604(c), to investigate whether a ship that voluntarily entered into its port was responsible for a discharge in violation of applicable antipollution rules and standards, when asked to do so by either the states in whose waters the discharge allegedly occurred or by the flag state.

Another important international treaty dealing with marine pollution is the International Convention for the Prevention of Pollution from Ships of 1973, as modified by its protocol of 1978, and generally referred to as the MARPOL Convention. The MARPOL convention has been ratified by more than forty countries and thereby regulates more than 80 percent of the world's merchant fleet. The convention is divided into five sections, called *annexes,* with each attempting to regulate a different potential problem: pollution by oil; noxious liquid substances carried in bulk; harmful substances carried in packages; ship sewage; and ship garbage. Many of the treaty's directives involve standards for design and equipment. For example, Annex I requires ballast tanks of all oil-carrying vessels to be strategically located around the outer periphery of the hull of the vessel. Discharges are also regulated under the MARPOL Convention. For example, oil tankers may discharge no more than sixty liters of oil per mile, and discharges must take place at least fifty miles from land. Under the convention the disposal of plastics at sea is completely prohibited. The disposal of other types of garbage is restricted to certain distances from land. Domestic garbage cannot be dumped within three miles of land, and if it is to be dumped within twelve miles, it must first be sent through a grinder.

Ocean dumping is regulated by the London Convention on the Prevention of Marine Pollution by Dumping of Wastes and Other Matter, effective since December 29, 1972. This treaty prohibits the deliberate dumping of high-level radioactive waste at sea. Other compounds that parties may wish to dump are divided into annexes and regulated accordingly: Matter from Annex I cannot be dumped. Matter listed in Annex II can be dumped only with a "special permit," the criteria for which are specified in Annex III. All matter not mentioned in Annex I or II may be dumped with a prior general permit.

Land-based pollution, in general, is simply regulated by the state of origin. Article 207 of the UN Law of the Sea Convention, however, obliges parties to adopt necessary laws to prevent and control land-based sources of marine pollution.

By 1991, the United States had ratified three additional treaties that are important for protecting the marine environment. The first was the International Convention on Oil Pollution Preparedness, Response, and Cooperation; this treaty establishes a worldwide network of expertise and resources to prevent and respond to oil spills. The second treaty, the 1989 Salvage Convention, provides compensation for persons who take steps to preserve the environment while salvaging a ship or cargo at sea. The third treaty was the International Convention on Standards of Training, Certification, and Watch Keeping for Seafarers, which sets standards for ship officers and crew so that accidents will be less likely to occur.

Preservation of Biological Diversity

The primary way that we are attempting to preserve biological diversity is through treaties. See table 10–2 for a listing of some of these treaties.

Convention on International Trade in Endangered Fauna and Flora (CITES). The Convention on International Trade in Endangered Species of Wild Fauna and Flora has been characterized by some as "perhaps the most successful of all international treaties concerned with the conservation of wildlife."[18] Ratified by ninety-six nations as of 1987, the treaty is de-

TABLE 10–2 Treaties That Help Preserve the Global Commons and Biological Diversity

Treaty	Purpose
Convention on Regulation of Antarctic Mineral Resource Activity	Regulate exploitation of mineral resources in Antarctica
Declaration on Arctic Environmental Protection	Encourage cooperation in areas of pollution, marine environmental protection, emergency response, conservation of flora and fauna, and research and monitoring in the Arctic
Convention for the Protection of the Environment in the South Pacific	Encourage cooperation in addressing water treatment programs, management of coastal zones and wastes, lagoon and coral reef restoration, and climate change issue
International Whaling Convention	Phase out commercial whaling by 1986, except when meat and products are used for local consumption by aborigines
Treaty for Amazonian Cooperation	Obtain agreement among eight countries with territories in Amazon to balance economic growth and environment protection
Convention in International Trade in Endangered Species	Prohibits international trade of endangered plants and animals
United Nations Convention on Biodiversity	Stimulates the transfer of technology and sharing of benefits of technology to preserve biodiversity

signed to prohibit the international trafficking in wildlife species and products that are endangered. Under the CITES, species are listed under Appendixes I, II, and III. Appendix I species are endangered, and trade in these species will be authorized under only the most extraordinary circumstances. Appendix II contains those species that are not now threatened with extinction but may become so if traded. Appendix III consists of species that a nation protects within its jurisdiction and is seeking the cooperation of other nations to protect that species from exploitation. Only under extremely strict conditions specified in CITES can a listed species be traded. Enforcement is left to the signatory parties.

Although the CITES looks good, the problem with it lies in its enforcement, which is almost nil. Studies of enforcement of the treaty have found that most inspectors in signatory nations are not trained well enough to be able to enforce the treaty.

In the United States, CITES is implemented through the Endangered Species Act, which many call the most stringent environmental statute in the world. As explained in chapter 9, it prohibits the import, export, sale, or shipment of any endangered or threatened species in the course of a commercial activity, as well as the possession of any species taken in violation of the act.

Only with a special permit can one cause any harm to an endangered species or its habitat. The act is enforced by the U.S. Fish and Wildlife Service with respect to animals and by the Animal and Plant Health Inspection Service with respect to plants.

Today, 956 domestic species are listed in the act as threatened or endangered. Another 3,700 are candidates for listing, but the Fish and Wildlife Service has not yet had time to study them or add them to the list. Additionally, during 1995, Congress placed a moratorium on the listing of new species, as mentioned previously. Since the law's passage, only one species—the American alligator—has recovered as a result of being protected. Seven listed species have become extinct, 10 percent are recovering, and 37 percent are declining.

The act is up for reauthorization and is generating considerable debate. Some argue that there is not enough money to save all species, as the act tries to do, and that under the new law certain species should be targeted so that the money can be used more efficiently to save the targeted species. Many argue that the way the decision as to what biological species or subspecies are to be preserved must be revised. Currently subspecies and even distinct populations of subspecies may be listed. This issue was raised when the preservation of one of twenty-five subspecies of the red squirrel halted the construction of an observatory. Some people are even arguing that the species-by-species approach is wrong; instead, focus should be on creating and preserving habitats. Given all these conflicting views, it should be an interesting reauthorization process.

Man and the Biosphere Program.   The United Nations Educational, Scientific, and Cultural Organization (UNESCO) has tried another approach to preserving our biological diversity. In 1976, UNESCO's Man and the Biosphere (MAB) program became operational. Participating countries create and protect biosphere reserves—protected areas designed to combine conservation and sustainable use. In the center of a reserve is a core area where there is minimal disturbance of an ecosystem characteristic of a major type of natural environment. This core is surrounded by a buffer zone wherein activities are managed in ways that will help protect the core. Outside the buffer zone is the transition area, which combines conservation and sustainable activities such as forestry and recreation. As of early 1987, more than 110 countries were participating in the MAB program, and 260 biospheres reserves had been created. The United States established its first reserve in 1974 and now has forty-four.

Debt for Nature Swaps.   One new way to try to protect diversity is an innovative contractual arrangement called *debt for nature swaps.* In simplest terms, a debt for nature swap occurs when conservation parks or sustainable use areas are set aside and legally protected by a foreign government in exchange for which a portion of that country's foreign debt is canceled. An intermediary group, generally a conservation organization, facilitates the swap by paying off the debt at a deeply discounted rate.

By November 1991, twenty-two debt for nature swaps had been completed in eleven countries, and several other swaps were being negotiated. The three conservation organizations most frequently involved in swaps, Conservation International, the Nature Conservatory, and the World Wildlife Foundation, were responsible for nineteen of the twenty-two swaps. With $17 million of privately raised funds, they retired $99 million worth of debt through these swaps.

The typical debt for nature contract attempts to achieve its environmental goals by specifying the environmental activities that are to be undertaken by the host government. Many include provisions allowing the conservation organization to undertake specific activities on the newly protected area. The debtor nation is usually required to set aside a specific fund of money to be used in managing the protected area.

These projects seem to have potential, but, again, the major problem is their enforceability. The developing country may mismanage the funds set aside for protecting the area; the host country may simply be incompetent and not manage the area appropriately. Or, in some less stable nations, the government that agreed to the swap may be overthrown and the new government unwilling to carry out the contract.

If the host country breaches the agreement, the organization that retired the debt may always sue for breach of contract in the host country. That country's willingness to rule against its own government is somewhat unlikely, however. Alternately, the conservation group may hold out the threat of refusing to carry out any further swaps with the nation in question if compliance is not attained. Another possibility is to include in the contract a provision that if compliance by the host country is lacking, that country becomes liable to the conservation organization for the amount of debt retired by the organization.

Another problem with the debt for nature swaps is that their use on a large scale may be impossible. Part of the reason why these swaps can be done is the willingness of banks to discount debt. Banks may do so when they feel they will never get full payment anyway. But their willingness to discount loans is not unlimited.

In spite of these potential problems, many believe debt for nature swaps are an important tool for retaining biodiversity. First, when successful, land is set aside that otherwise might have been developed. Second, deforestation in areas other than the swapped region may be prevented because one of the reasons for deforestation is that developing countries are often forced to exploit their natural resources to service their debt. Without the massive debt, much exploitation may be unnecessary. Because swaps are new, it is too early to speculate as to their effectiveness. For now, we can only wait and see.

THE FUTURE OF INTERNATIONAL ENVIRONMENTAL LAW

The Rio Summit

From June 1 through June 12, 1992, delegates from more than 120 nations met in Rio de Janeiro for the United Nations Conference on Environment and Development (UNCED), commonly referred to as the Rio Summit. With two years of negotiations leading up to the summit, the participants in the meeting had established a lofty goal for themselves: to agree on a set of principles and conventions to set the world on a new environmental course and perhaps some day eradicate the pollution that is threatening our planet.

It is too early to know what real impact, if any, the summit will have on worldwide environmental policies. Some participants are claiming that it has already been a success because, if nothing else, the two years of preparation brought the idea of sustainable development—progress without destruction of the environment—before hundreds of officials from developing nations. Others applauded the creation of a UN Sustainable Development Commission, modeled on the Human Rights Commission, that will use public criticism and pressure to hold governments accountable for achieving the goals laid out at the summit.

Five documents came out of the summit. Whether the agreements will have any impact on international environmental law depends on the agreements' ratification and enforcement.

Agenda 21. Agenda 21, an eight-hundred-page blueprint for environment-friendly development, covers a diverse range of issues, including hazardous waste, human health, ocean pollution, and advancement for women. The heart of this document is a program of aid to Third World nations to help them clean up their pollution and replant their forests, at an estimated cost of $125 billion per year.

Rio Declaration. The Rio Declaration is a six-page statement containing twenty-seven principles that calls for a link between environmental protection and development, spelling out the "rights" of poor nations to develop in responsible ways. This document was designed to encourage new levels of cooperation among states.

Biodiversity. The agreement that aroused the most debate in the United States was the biodiversity agreement, the United Nations Convention on Biological Diversity. This treaty requires signatory nations to establish policies to slow the loss of plant and animal species. Developed nations with technology will cooperate with nondeveloped nations that have the diverse species of rain forest flora and fauna to develop new pharmaceuticals. President

Bush created an uproar among environmentalists by opposing the treaty on the grounds that it would not adequately protect biotechnology and other patents and would excessively regulate the biotechnology industry. He also argued that the treaty was unnecessary because the U.S. Endangered Species Act was already providing much greater protection than would be provided under this treaty. When President Clinton took office, he said that he would sign the biodiversity treaty, and on June 30, 1993, he did so, after having drawn up interpretive language that he claimed would protect U.S. patents.

The battle for ratification of the treaty in the House and Senate, however, has been a long one. As of mid-1996, the treaty still had not been ratified. Its primary opponents initially came from organizations of cattlemen and ranchers, who feared that signing the treaty would make it more difficult for Congress to weaken the Endangered Species Act. Additional opposition came from firms in the biotechnology industry who feared loss of some of their patent rights, although they have since changed their position and now support ratification of the treaty.

While the treaty still awaits ratification in the United States, it went into effect for signatory nations on December 29, 1993.

Climate Change.   The industrialized nations, including the United States, agreed to reduce emissions of greenhouse gases to 1990 levels by the year 2000. Developing nations are to develop policies to control their emissions. When fifty nations sign, this treaty becomes effective.

Forest Protection.   A statement of principles called for sustainable forest management and asked nations to avoid excessive cutting of trees.

It was clear from the meeting that some changes from all nations are going to be needed if Rio's agreements are to be successfully ratified and implemented. Poor nations tended to place all blame for the world's woes on developed nations and asserted that the polluters should pay developing countries to protect their ecosystems. Clearly, the World Bank, the primary distributor of money to developing nations, will have to do a better job of integrating environment and development in its investments. Only time will tell, however, whether the world will be able to live up to the goals set forth at the Rio Summit.

Environmentalism and Trade

Traditionally, the only treaties environmentalists really worried about were those designed to address specific environmental problems, such as the treaties we have examined in this chapter. Increasingly, however, some environmental groups are beginning to see the value of having input into international trade agreements, although not surprisingly, not all environmental organizations agree about how environmental interests can best be protected through these treaties.

The negotiations of two treaties designed to make trade freer, the 103-nation General Agreement on Tariffs and Trade (GATT) (initially negotiated almost fifty years ago and strengthened by several renegotiations, culminating in the formation of the World Trade Organization) and the North American Free Trade Agreement (NAFTA), have caught the interest of environmentalists. One issue that negotiators must resolve is the potential conflict that arises when a nation's "green" laws have an adverse effect on commerce. For example, Germany passed a law requiring that all packaging be recyclable. Because other nations do not require recyclable (and, thus, more expensive) packaging, an extra burden is placed on foreign competitors that do not do a significant amount of business in Germany yet would probably, for efficiency, have to change the packaging of their products or leave the market.

The key provision of GATT related to this issue is the statement that nations have the right to enact any environmental, health, and safety laws they choose, as long as the laws are "necessary" and are the "least trade restrictive" way of resolving the problem. NAFTA additionally requires that the laws be based on "scientific principles" and "risk assessment." Because U.S. laws are often based on political compromise as well as science, one can see how some of this nation's laws might not meet these standards.

In fact, the United States has already lost two environmental law battles under GATT. GATT disputes are resolved by a GATT panel of trade judges. In 1991, such a panel ruled that the United States violated GATT by banning the import of tuna caught in the type of net that kills dolphins, a ban required by the Marine Mammal Protection Act. Fortunately, the United States and Mexico, the nation challenging the ban, reached a settlement satisfactory to both. But this adverse ruling was sufficient to alarm many environmentalists, as was the similar ruling in 1993 against a U.S. boycott of tuna caught by fishing methods that killed dolphins.

A subsequent ruling in a 1994 case, however, is cited by some as evidence that environmentalists need not fear the strengthening of GATT under the recently negotiated World Trade Organization. In 1993, the European Union challenged the 1975 corporate average fuel economy standards (CAFE standards) established under the Clean Air Act, as well as a 1978 "gas guzzler" tax on automobiles that taxed those vehicles that had a fuel efficiency of less than 22.5 miles per gallon. These laws hit the German Mercedes Benz corporation particularly hard. The laws were held to not violate the GATT.

U.S. Trade Representative at the time, Mickey Kantor, saw the decision as evidence that the GATT's trade rules can be compatible with environmental protection.[19] Likewise, the Director of the Yale Center for Environmental Law and Policy said that the decision "shows GATT is learning to accommodate ecological concerns."[20] However, the director of the Natural Resources Defense Council was not convinced by that decision that the agreement would not ultimately be used to bar enforcement of more stringent environmental laws.

As noted previously, the GATT has undergone a number of revisions. The most significant round of negotiations, known as the Uruguay Round, was completed in 1993. This round of negotiations established the World Trade Organization, which became operational on January 1, 1995. Additional negotiations in 1994 led to the formation of the Committee on Trade and the Environment, which will operate under the auspices of the WTO. Many environmentalists saw the creation of this committee as a significant improvement in the treatment of environmental analysis under the GATT/WTO. However, there is still a great deal of concern about the wisdom of entering into this agreement.

Ralph Nader questioned the wisdom of entering into an agreement that gives substantial legislative, executive, and judicial authority, including the authority to impose sanctions, to an international body in which the United States would have equal voting power with every other member and no veto power. Never before had the United States entered a comparable international organization without having either veto power or weighted voting.[21]

Another concern raised by Nader and many others was the wisdom of entering into an agreement with a mandate based on the supremacy of trade matters over consumer, worker, and environmental safeguards, an arrangement under which countries could not be in violation by treating the environment too harshly, but they could be subject to trade sanctions for being too protective of the environment.[22]

Some people, including Max Baucus, the head of the U.S. Senate's trade subcommittee, argue that for purposes of trade, lax environmental regulation should be seen as a governmental subsidy because it will be cheaper to produce when a firm does not have to meet stringent environmental standards. Therefore, many argue, nations with strict environmental standards should be able to place a duty on those goods made under relaxed regulations to increase their price to what it would have been without the subsidy. His position, however, is a minority position among those who negotiated the WTO.

A key issue during the Uruguay Round was that of dispute resolution. The final mechanism for dispute resolution under the agreement is viewed by many environmentalists as being inferior to the method for resolving environment/trade conflicts under NAFTA. Under the Dispute Settlement Understanding, a three-person arbitration panel hears the claim and issues a report that contains its decision. If both parties accept this report, it becomes the final decision. The parties, however, have the option of appealing the decision to the Settlement Body. A final appeal may be made to the Appellate body (the "Supreme Court" of the WTO), and if they still uphold the decision, the party must comply with the ruling or face trade sanctions, which have not as of yet been determined.

In terms of the procedures, there are a few aspects of the process that are not seen as favorable by many environmentalists. For example, while the arbitration panel *may* request information and technical advice from any source they deem appropriate, disputing parties cannot unilaterally call on experts to present information to the panels. An even greater concern is that the burden of proof in challenges that an environmental regulation adversely affects trade lies with the party seeking to defend the regulation.

The opportunity to examine how these processes work came up sooner than many had anticipated. On January 17, 1996, in the first complaint brought before the body since it came into existence on January 1, 1995, a WTO panel ruled against the United States in a challenge brought against the U.S. EPA's rules for implementing the Reformulated Gasoline Program. The regulations at issue required foreign refiners to use EPA baseline data for calculating necessary reductions in certain fuel components, whereas U.S. refiners could opt to use their own data rather than the more stringent EPA data. The EPA had said that they needed to require the foreign firms to use EPA data because those firms did not keep sufficient records to allow them to use their own data. Not requiring them to use EPA data could lead to the import of a reformulated gasoline that is less clean than that expected from U.S. refiners.

Mickey Kantor, U.S. Trade Representative, was not happy with the ruling and promptly declared that a WTO ruling has no force under U.S. law, although he did indicate an intent to appeal. Regardless of the outcome of the appeal, this first ruling does not bode well for those concerned about protecting the environment. Trade officials were more concerned about Kantor's reaction, saying that a rejection of a ruling of the WTO by Washington would send a negative signal regarding U.S. intentions regarding the WTO.

Regardless of the outcome of this debate, certainly environmental groups are beginning to recognize the need to try to influence the negotiation of trade agreements.

CONCLUDING REMARKS

This chapter clearly demonstrates that many of our major environmental concerns—acid rain, the greenhouse effect, transboundary pollution, and the loss of biodiversity—are really global problems. World population is growing at an unprecedented rate, and this increase in population only exacerbates these problems. International environmental agreements appear to be the best approach to solving these problems. As we see how these treaties work, we may begin to understand the extent to which we may be able, through international cooperation, to solve the most pressing environmental problems. We can also continue to try innovative ideas such as the debt for nature swaps. The United States is a small part of a complex biosphere; thus, we must remember that we cannot solve our environmental problems in isolation.

QUESTIONS FOR REVIEW AND DISCUSSION

1. Identify four major problems that international environmental law needs to address.
2. Discuss the two primary sources of international law.
3. Why does international law tend to be ineffective?
4. Explain the four primary principles of customary international environmental law.
5. How does UNEP function?
6. Explain why it has been difficult to establish a satisfactory way to handle transboundary pollution problems.
7. What are the purpose and provisions of the Montreal Protocol?
8. Explain how international law is addressing the problem of pollution of the oceans and seas.

FOR FURTHER READING

JOHN ANSBRO, *The EC Regulation on Waste Shipment: In Conflict with the Free Market and Contrary to Environmental Comparative Advantage,* 3 CARDOZO J. INT'L. & COMP. L. 405 (1995).

JOHN F. BEGGS, *Combating Biospheric Degradation: International Environmental Impact Assessment and the Transboundary Pollution Dilemma,* 6 FORDHAM ENVTL. L.J. 379 (1995).

JOHN BERMINGHAM, *Recent Books about World Population Growth,* 6 COLO. J. INT'L. ENVTL. L. & POL'Y. 395 (1995).

ROBERT CONSTANZA, ET AL., *Sustainable Trade: A New Paradigm for World Welfare,* ENVT. (June 1995), at 16.

DAVID FAVRE, *Tension Points within the Language of the CITES Treaty,* 5 B.U. INT'L. L.J. 247 (1987).

TAUNYA L. MCLARTY, *The Applicability of NEPA to NAFTA: Law, Politics, or Economics?* 19 MD. J. INT'L. L. & TRADE 121 (1995).

B. JOHN OVINK, *Transboundary Shipments of Toxic Waste: The Basel and Bamako Conventions: Do Third World Countries Have a Choice?* 13 DICK. ENVTL. L.J. 281 (1995).

DONALD REBOVICH, DANGEROUS GROUND: THE WORLD OF HAZARDOUS WASTE CRIME (New Brunswick, N.J.: Transaction Publishing, 1992).

WILIAM K. REILLY, *Debt-for-Nature Swaps: The Time Has Come,* 2 ENVTL. AFF. 134 (1990).

ALLEN SPRINGER, THE INTERNATIONAL LAW OF POLLUTION (Westport, Conn.: Quorum Books, 1983).

RODNEY WAGNER, *Doing More with Debt for Nature Swaps,* 2 INT'L. ENVTL. AFF. 160 (1990).

BROCK WILLIAMS, *Trade and the Environment,* 62 FOREIGN AFF. 1037 (1988).

World Commission on Environment and Development, OUR COMMON FUTURE (New York: Oxford University Press, 1987).

DAVID A. WIRTH, *The Rio Declaration on Environment and Development: Two Steps Forward and One Back, or Vice Versa?* 29 GA. L. REV. 599 (1995).

DONALD ZANG, *Frozen in Time: The Antarctic Mineral Resource Convention,* 76 CORNELL L. REV. 722 (1991).

ON THE INTERNET

http://iisd1.iids.ca/didgest
Summaries of articles shaping the international development dialogue

http://www.indiana.edu/envdec/envirolaw.html
A source for international trade policies and treaties

http://www.planeta.com/
Information about ecological threats in Latin America

http://www.bio.bris.ac.uk/research/bats/croc_cat.htm
Information about CITES

NOTES

1. JULIAN SIMON, *Population Growth Is Not Bad for Humanity,* PHI KAPPA PHI J. 12 (Winter 1990).
2. EDWARD WILSON, *The Current State of Biological Diversity* in BIODIVERSITY, (Edward O. Wilson, ed., Washington, D.C.: National Academy Press, 1988).
3. Ibid., p. 13.
4. United Nations, Organization for Economic Cooperation and Development, The State of the Environment (1985).
5. Ibid.
6. LOUIS SOHN, *The Stockholm Declaration on the Human Environment,* 14 HARV. J. ENVTL. L. 423 (1973).
7. GA Res. 37/7, 37 UN GAOR Supp. (No. 51) at 7, U.N. DOC. A/37/51 (1982).
8. I.J. Acts and Documents 77 (1978).
9. *Trail Smelter Arbitration,* ENCYCLOPEDIA OF PUBLIC INTERNATIONAL LAW INSTALLMENT 2 (1983), pp. 267–80.
10. P.I.C.J. Ser. A. No. 23 at 27 (1929).

11. Comment to Article IV, Helsinki Rules on the Uses of Waters of International Rivers, ILA, Report of the Fifty-Second Conference (Helsinki, 1966), p. 487.

12. Ibid., comment to Article X, p. 497.

13. I.C.J. Reports (1949), 4.

14. International Law Association, *Legal Aspects of the Conservation of the Environment.*

15. Council on Environmental Quality, Environmental Quality: Twentieth Annual Report (1990).

16. RICHARD LEVY, *International Law and the Chernobyl Accident, Reflections on an Important but Imperfect System,* 36 KAN. L. REV. 81 (1987).

17. Ibid.

18. JOHN HEPPES & ERIC McFADDEN, *The Convention on International Trade in Endangered Species of Wild Fauna and Flora: Improving the Prospects for Preserving Our Biological Heritage,* 5 B.U. INT'L. L. J. 22 (1987).

19. TIMOTHY NOAH, *GATT Backs Fuel Efficiency Rule, Recognizing U.S. Environmental Laws,* WALL. ST. J. (October 3, 1994).

20. Ibid.

21. RALPH NADER, *WTO Means Rule by Unaccountable Tribunals,* WALL ST. J. (August 17, 1994).

22. Ibid.

APPENDIX A Sample Page of Drinking Water Standards and Health Advisories

Chemicals	Standards Status Reg.	MCLG (mg/l)	MCL (mg/l)	Status HA	10-kg Child One-day (mg/l)	Ten-day (mg/l)	Longer-term (mg/l)	70-kg Adult Longer-term (mg/l)	RfD (mg/kg/day)	DWEL (mg/l)	Lifetime (mg/l)	mg/l at 10^{-1} Cancer Risk	Cancer Group
ORGANICS													
Acenaphthene	—	—	—	—	—	—	—	—	0.06	—	—	—	—
Acifluorfen	T	zero	—	F	2	2	0.1	0.4	0.013	0.4	—	0.1	B2
Acrylamide	F	zero	TT	F	1.5	0.3	0.02	0.07	0.002	0.007	—	0.001	B2
Acrylonitrile	T	zero	—	D	—	—	—	—	—	—	—	0.006	B1*
Adipate (diethylhexyl)	F	0.4	0.4	D	20	20	20	60	0.6	20	0.4	3	C
Alachlor	F	zero	0.002	F	0.1	0.1	—	—	0.01	0.4	—	0.04	B2
Aldicarb**	D	0.007	0.007	D	—	—	—	—	0.001	0.035	0.007	—	D
Aldicarb sulfone**	D	0.007	0.007	D	—	—	—	—	0.001	0.035	0.007	—	D
Aldicarb sulfoxide**	D	0.007	0.007	D	—	—	—	—	0.001	0.035	0.007	—	D
Aldrin	—	—	—	D	0.0003	0.0003	0.0003	0.0003	0.00003	0.001	—	0.0002	B2
Ametryn	—	—	—	F	9	9	0.9	3	0.009	0.3	0.06	—	D
Ammonium sulfamate	—	—	—	F	20	20	20	80	0.28	8	2	—	D
Anthracene (PAH)***	—	—	—	—	—	—	—	—	0.3	—	—	—	D
Atrazine	F	0.003	0.003	F	0.1	0.1	0.05	0.2	0.035	0.2*	0.003*	—	C
Baygon	F	—	—	F	0.04	0.04	0.04	0.1	0.004	0.1	0.003	—	C
Bentazon	T	0.02	—	F	0.3	0.3	0.3	0.9	0.0025	0.09	0.02	—	D
Benz(a)anthracene (PAH)	—	—	—	—	—	—	—	—	—	—	—	—	B2
Benzene	F	zero	0.005	F	0.2	0.2	—	—	—	—	—	0.1	A
Benzo(a)pyrene	F	zero	0.002	—	—	—	—	—	—	—	—	*0.0002*	B2*
Benzo(b)fluoranthene (PAH)	—	—	—	—	—	—	—	—	—	—	—	*0.0002*	B2
Benzo(g,h,i)perylene (PAH)	—	—	—	—	—	—	—	—	—	—	—	—	D
Benzo(k)fluoranthene (PAH)	—	—	—	—	—	—	—	—	—	—	—	*0.0002*	B2
bis-2-Chloroisopropyl ether	—	—	—	F	4	4	4	13	0.04	1	0.3	—	D
Bromacil	L	—	—	F	5	5	3	9	0.13	5	0.09	—	C
Bromobenzene	L	—	—	D	—	—	—	—	—	—	—	—	—

* Under review.

** NOTE: The HA value or the MCLG/MCL value for any two or more of these three chemicals should remain at 0.007 mg/L because of similar mode of action.

*** *PAH = Polyaromatic hydrocarbon*

NOTE: Anthracene and Benzo(g,h,i)perylene—not proposed in Phase V.

NOTE: Changes from the last version are noted in Italic and Bold Face print.

This first page is illustrative of how the drinking water standards and health advisories look when they have been established.

APPENDIX B

Abbreviations and Acronyms

ACO	Administrative Consent Order
ADR	Alternate Dispute Resolution
AEC	Atomic Energy Commission (now NRC)
APA	Administrative Procedures Act
AQCR	Air Quality Control Regions (CAA)
BAT	Best Available Technology or Best Available Technology Economically Achievable
BCT	Best Conventional Control Technology
BDAT	Best Demonstrated Available Technology
BDT	Best Available Demonstrated Control Technology
BLM	Bureau of Land Management
BMP	Best Management Practices
BNA	Bureau of National Affairs
BPT	Best Practicable Control Technology Currently Available
CAA	Clean Air Act
CEQ	Council on Environmental Quality (executive office of the president)
CERCLA	Comprehensive Environmental Response, Compensation, and Liability Act
CFR	Code of Federal Regulations
CWA	Clean Water Act
DNR	Department of Natural Resources
DOA	U.S. Department of Agriculture
DOI	U.S. Department of Interior
DOJ	U.S. Department of Justice
DOT	U.S. Department of Transportation
EA	Environmental Assessment
EC	European Community
ECRA	Environmental Cleanup Responsibility Act
EDF	Environmental Defense Fund
EIS	Environmental Impact Statement
ELR	Environmental Law Reporter
EO	Executive Order
EPA	U.S. Environmental Protection Agency
EPCRA	Emergency Planning and Community Right to Know Act
EPCRTKA	EPCRA—Emergency Planning and Community Right to Know Act
ERC	BNA Environmental Reporter—Cases
ESA	Endangered Species Act
FDA	U.S. Food and Drug Administration
FEPCA	Federal Environmental Pesticide Control Act
FHWA	Federal Highway Administration
FIFRA	Federal Insecticide, Fungicide, Rodenticide Act
FLPMA	Federal Land Policy and Management Act
FOE	Friends of the Earth
FOIA	Freedom of Information Act
FONSI	Finding of No Significant Impact (NEPA)

283

FR	Federal Register
FRCP	Federal Rules of Civil
FWPCA	Federal Water Pollution Control Act (CWA)
FWS	Fish and Wildlife Service
GAO	General Accounting Office (congressional)
HRS	Hazard Ranking System (CERCLA)
HSWA	Hazardous and Solid Waste Amendments (of 1984)
ICJ	International Court of Justice (The Hague)
IGO	Intergovernmental Organization
IJC	International Joint Commission (U.S.-Canada)
ILM	International Legal Materials
IPM	Integrated Pest Management
ISC	Interagency Scientific Committee (ESA)
IWC	International Whaling Commission
LAER	Lowest Achievable Emissions Rate
MACT	Maximum Available Control Technology
MCL	Maximum Contaminant Level (CWA)
MCLG	Maximum Contaminant Level Goals
NAAQS	National Ambient Air Quality Standards
NAM	National Association of Manufacturers
NCP	National Contingency Plan (Superfund)
NEPA	National Environmental Policy Act of 1969
NESHAP	National Emissions Standards for Hazardous Air Pollutants
NFMA	National Forest Management Act
NGO	Non-Governmental Organization
NOAA	National Oceanographic and Atmospheric Administration (Department of Commerce)
NPDES	National Pollutant Discharge Elimination System (CWA)
NPL	National Priority List (Superfund)
NPS	National Park Service
NRC	U.S. Nuclear Regulatory Commission or (state) Natural Resources Commission
NRDC	National Resources Defense Council
NSPS	New Source Performance Standards (Air)
NFW	National Wildlife Foundation
NWQS	National Water Quality Standards (CWA)
OCS	Outer Continental Shelf
OMB	Office of Management and Budget (executive offices of the President)
OSHA	Occupational Safety and Health Act, Occupational Safety and Health Administration
OSWER	Office of Solid Waste and Energy Response
OTA	Office of Technology Assessment (congressional)
PMNs	Pre-marketing Notifications
POTW	Publicly Owned Treatment Works (CWA)
PRP	Potentially Responsible Party (Superfund)
PSD	Prevention of Significant Deterioration
RCRA	Resource Conservation and Recovery Act
SARA	Superfund Amendment and Reauthorization Act
SCS	U.S. Soil Conservation Service
SDWA	Safe Drinking Water Act
SIP	State Implementation Plan (CAA)
SMCRA	Surface Mining Control and Reclamation Act
Superfund	CERCLA
SWDA	Solid Waste Disposal Act
ToSCA or TSCA	Toxic Substance Control Act
TRO	Temporary Restraining Order
TSD	Treatment, Storage, and Disposal (CERCLA)
TVA	Tennessee Valley Authority
USDA	U.S. Department of Agriculture
USFS	United States Forest Service
WQS	Water Quality Standards (CWA)

Index